THE CASE AGAINST FREE TRADE

Ralph Nader

William Greider

Margaret Atwood

Vandana Shiva

Mark Ritchie

Wendell Berry

Jerry Brown

Herman Daly

Lori Wallach

Thea Lee

Martin Khor

David Phillips

Jorge Castañeda

Carlos Heredia

David Morris

Jerry Mander

THE CASE
AGAINST
FREE TRADE

GATT, NAFTA,
and the Globalization
of Corporate Power

EARTH ISLAND PRESS

NORTH ATLANTIC BOOKS

Published by Earth Island Press and North Atlantic Books

Earth Island Press
300 Broadway
San Francisco, CA 94133

North Atlantic Books
P.O. Box 12327
Berkeley, CA 94701

ISBN: 1-5643-169-4

Grateful appreciation is extended to the following publishers for permission to reprint copyrighted materials: Sierra Club Books for "Megatechnology, Trade, and the New World Order," by Jerry Mander, reprinted in revised form from *In the Absence of the Sacred*, © 1991 by Jerry Mander; World Policy Journal for "Another Nafta," by Jorge Castañeda and Carlos Heredia; *The Ottowa Citizen* for "Blind Faith and Free Trade," by Margaret Atwood; The Loyola Law Journal for "From Adjustment to Sustainable Development," by Herman E. Daly; Pantheon Books, a division of Random House, Inc. for "A Bad Big Idea," from *Sex, Economy, Freedom and Community* by Wendell Berry, Copyright © 1993 by Wendell Berry. This essay was originally published in the May 1993 issue of *The Progressive*; Simon & Schuster, Inc. for "The Global Marketplace: A Closet Dictator," Copyright © 1992 by William Greider.

Cover and book design by Amy Evans
Editorial research by Victor Menotti
Production by Susanna Tadlock & Associates
Composition by Wilsted & Taylor

Printed in the United States of America on acid-free paper containing a minimum of 50% recovered waste paper of which at least 10% of the fiber content is post-consumer waste.

10   9   8   7   6   5   4   3   2   1

CONTENTS

THE CASE
AGAINST
FREE TRADE

Ralph Nader

INTRODUCTION: FREE TRADE & THE DECLINE OF DEMOCRACY

Citizens beware. An unprecedented corporate power grab is underway in global negotiations over international trade.

Operating under the deceptive banner of "free" trade, multinational corporations are working hard to expand their control over the international economy and to undo vital health, safety, and environmental protections won by citizen movements across the globe in recent decades.

The megacorporations are not expecting these victories to be gained in town halls, state offices, the U.S. Capitol, or even at the United Nations. They are looking to circumvent the democratic process altogether, in a bold and brazen drive to achieve an autocratic far-reaching agenda through two trade agreements, the U.S.-Mexico-Canada free trade deal (formally known as NAFTA, the North American Free Trade Agreement) and an expansion of the General Agreement on Tariffs and Trade (GATT), called the Uruguay Round.

The Fortune 200's GATT and NAFTA agenda would make the air you breathe dirtier and the water you drink more polluted. It would cost jobs, depress wage levels, and make workplaces less safe. It would destroy family farms and undermine consumer protections such as those ensuring that the food you eat is not compromised by unsanitary conditions or higher levels of pesticides and preservatives.

And that's only for the industrialized countries. The large global companies have an even more ambitious set of goals for the Third World. They hope to use GATT and NAFTA to capitalize on the poverty of Third

World countries and exploit their generally low environmental, safety, and wage standards. At the same time, these corporations plan to displace locally owned businesses and solidify their control over developing countries' economies and natural resources.

It is only recently that corporations developed the notion of using trade agreements to establish autocratic governance over many modestly democratic countries. The world community founded GATT after World War II as an institution to peacefully regulate world trade. At present, more than 100 nations responsible for more than four-fifths of world trade belong to it. In its first 40 years of existence, GATT concerned itself primarily with tariffs and related matters; periodically, the GATT signatories would meet and negotiate lower tariffs on imported goods. In 1986, however, when the current Uruguay Round of GATT negotiations began, things changed. Multinational corporations thrust an expanded set of concerns on GATT that went far beyond traditional trade matters. They demanded that they be free to invest anywhere in the world with no restrictions; that environmental and safety standards be "harmonized" (made the same everywhere)—with the practical result that they would be pulled down toward a lowest common international denominator level; and that monopoly rights governing ownership of intellectual property (patents, copyrights, and trademarks) enforced throughout the world be entrenched. They also asked that food, agriculture, and services (banking, insurance, shipping, etc.) be brought under GATT disciplines. Finally, they crafted a new structure called the Multilateral Trade Organization to enhance GATT's power over each participating country. In short, these companies sought to expand GATT's reach and elevate its importance as a means of undermining the ability of local, state, or national governments to impose any sort of controls on business.

In 1990, George Bush announced his proposal for a U.S.-Mexico-Canada free trade pact. NAFTA is basically a mini-GATT, except that NAFTA offers even greater privileges to business and allows for fewer restrictions on corporate operations in the three countries.

American Express, Cargill, Imperial Chemical and their allies have managed to turn trade talks into a debate over whether nations may retain their sovereign right to protect their citizens from harm. Global commerce without commensurate democratic global law may be the dream of corporate chief executive officers, but it would be a disaster for the rest of the world with its ratcheting downwards of workers, consumer, and environmental standards.

The Uruguay Round expansion of GATT and NAFTA would establish a world economic government dominated by giant corporations, but they do not propose a democratic rule of law to hold this economic government accountable. It is bad enough to have the U.S. Fortune 200 along with European and Japanese corporations effectively ruling the Seven Seas of the marketplace, which affects workers, the environment, and consumers. But it is a level of magnitude worse for this rule to be formally expanded over entire political economies without any democratic accountability to the people.

Thieves in the Night

Secrecy, abstruseness, and unaccountability: these are the watchwords of global trade policy-making. Every element of the negotiation, adoption, and implementation of the trade agreements is designed to foreclose citizen participation or even awareness.

The process by which a policy is developed and enacted often yields insights into who stands to benefit from its enactment. Narrow, private interests inevitably prefer secrecy; in the halls of the U.S. Congress, for example, corporate lobbyists roam the corridors before a budget or tax package is to be voted on, hoping to insert a special tax exemption or subsidy in the dark of night and have it voted on before the public (or even most Congressional representatives) knows it exists. By contrast, citizen-based initiatives generally succeed only if they generate public debate and receive widespread support.

One can be properly suspicious of the intent of these trade agreements given the process by which they have been negotiated.

Negotiations over the Uruguay Round expansion of GATT—different from those over NAFTA only in that they involve more than 100 countries rather than just three—are taking place behind closed doors in Geneva, Switzerland, between unelected and largely unaccountable government agents who are mainly representing business interests. The provisions decided there, if approved by Congress, could undermine existing U.S. domestic laws and limit future action, not only in the direct regulation of commerce, but in areas ranging from food and auto safety to patent laws.

In a virtual self-parody, on the order of the old television show "Get Smart," secrecy predominates even within the GATT negotiating process itself. Small cliques of powerful nations regularly retreat to "green rooms" to cut deals that will then be forced on a take it or tough luck basis on other GATT signatory countries as "consensus" positions. The process would be hilarious were the consequences not so serious.

Corporate lobbyists, cruising in the halls outside the negotiating rooms, have been able to exert tremendous influence over the negotiations. Citizen groups have not been able to play a parallel role; with few exceptions, citizen organizations do not have the resources nor the contacts to post lobbyists in Geneva.

As if the advantage in resources were not enough, the corporate lobbying function has been institutionalized in the United States in a set of official trade advisory committees to the U.S. trade negotiators. Appointed by the President, the advisory committees are composed of over 800 business executives and consultants, with token labor representation, five representatives of environmental groups who were supportive or neutral on Bush's trade policy, and no consumer or health representatives.

On occasion, business groups are even willing to admit their influence over the process. The business coalition calling itself the Intellectual Property Committee (IPC)—its members include IBM, Du Pont, General Electric, Merck and Pfizer—has bragged in its own literature that its "close association with the U.S. Trade Representative and [the Department of] Commerce has permitted the IPC to shape the U.S. proposals and negotiating positions during the course of the [GATT] negotiations."

This sort of candor is atypical, however. The general rule is secrecy and mystification. Proponents of the trade agreements are so afraid of the consequences of public understanding of the pacts' implications that they believe it is not enough merely for the agreements to be negotiated behind closed doors. Once the agreements are completed—or on those rare occasions when the negotiators deign to make drafts of the agreements public—any person who wants to figure out what the agreements say faces a herculean task.

The first step is to obtain a copy of the agreement. This is not always possible. When then-President Bush announced that he had come to a final agreement with Mexico and Canada in August 1992, he gave an optimistic spin to the deal—but he did not make the text of the agreement available to the news media or to the American people so they could judge for themselves how beneficial the agreement might actually be. An unofficial text of the agreement was not available for over a month after its official conclusion. Once the official NAFTA text was finally made available through the Government Printing Office after President Bush left office, the government imposed a new barrier to access: it is charging citizens interested in receiving a copy of the two-volume, 1000+ page document $41.

Suppose a person decides to pay $41. The next obstacle they face is decoding the agreement's meaning. The agreement is very complex. It is written in arcane, almost impenetrable technical jargon that bears only a passing resemblance to the English language. Only those with a passing knowledge of GATTese or NAFTAese can comprehend what the trade jargon means for their jobs, food, or environment.

This difficulty in obtaining and understanding the actual agreements is not an accident; it reflects a purposeful effort by government negotiators to conceal the terms and effect of the agreements from the public, the news media, and even Congress. They would rather have citizens read a sanitized summary suitably interpreted by the agreements' boosters.

In the United States, Congress has limited the effectiveness of its own role in the trade agreement negotiation process by deciding that it will consider the agreements according to a uniquely anti-democratic procedure. Called "fast track", the special rule for Congressional consideration of trade agreements allows Congress to avoid its responsibilities by assuring that the agreements will not be subject to the full scrutiny they deserve. Under fast track, Congress must vote up or down on the agreements—with no amendments permitted—within a brief 60 to 90 days of the President's submission of the agreement, and must limit its debate on the agreements to not more than 20 hours in either the House or Senate! Congress must agree to deal with completed trade agreements in this fashion before the President even begins to negotiate.

With citizens shut out of the process at every turn, it is no surprise that these trade agreements pose such a threat to the procedural gains of citizen movements in numerous countries in recent decades, to their potential to rein in multinational corporations, and to both Third World and industrialized countries' ability to maintain control over their economies through some measure of feasible self-sufficiency. On procedural grounds alone, the authoritarian exclusion of citizen participation condemns the GATT and NAFTA operations. Are people to struggle for such rights as freedom of information, openness, and access in their domestic countries only to lose these rights in closed international negotiations dominated by corporate interests and their bureaucratic allies?

The Modern, Global "Race to the Bottom"

U.S. corporations long ago learned how to pit states against each other in "a race to the bottom"—to profit from the lower wages, pollution standards, and taxes. Now, through their NAFTA and GATT campaigns, multinational corporations are directing their efforts to the international arena, where desperately poor countries are willing and able to offer standards at 19th century American levels and below.

It's an old game: when fifty years ago the textile workers of Massachusetts demanded higher wages and safer working conditions, the industry moved its factories to the Carolinas and Georgia. If California considers enacting environmental standards in order to make it safer for people to breathe, business threatens to shut down and move to another state.

The trade agreements are crafted to enable corporations to play this game at the global level, to pit country against country in a race to see who can set the lowest wage levels, the lowest environmental standards, the lowest consumer safety standards. It is a tragic "incentives" lure that has its winners and losers determined before it even gets underway: workers, consumers, and communities in all countries lose; short-term profits soar and big business "wins."

We have already seen the results of "free" trade. California improves its workplace and pollution standards; the furniture industry migrates from Southern California to Mexico. Reeling from decades of underinvestment in quality and safety, U.S. automakers look to regain their "competitiveness" by moving their plants to Mexico, where the wages are far lower and pollution and workplace safety standards are inferior. The free trade deals are designed to make it even easier for business to play the game by harmonizing matters downwards.

Enactment of the free trade deals virtually ensures that any local, state, or even national effort in the United States to demand that corporations pay their fair share of taxes, provide a decent standard of living to their employees, or limit their pollution of the air, water, and land will be met with the refrain, "You can't burden us like that. If you do, we won't be able to compete. We'll have to close down and move to a country that offers us a more hospitable business climate." This sort of threat is extremely powerful—communities already devastated by plant closures and a declining manufacturing base are desperate not to lose more jobs, and they know all too well from experience that threats of this sort are often carried out.

Want a small-scale preview of the post-GATT and NAFTA free trade world? Check out the U.S.-Mexico border region, where hundreds of U.S. companies have opened up shop during the last two decades in a special free trade zone made up of factories known as *maquiladoras*. When U.S. factories have closed down and moved to Mexico, this is where they have gone. The attraction is simple: a workforce that earns as little as four to five dollars a day and does not have the means to defend itself against employer aggression because it is effectively denied the right to organize, and environmental and workplace standards are either lax or largely unenforced.

Don't make the mistake of thinking the *maquiladora* system is benefitting the Mexican people; they have to live in the polluted areas and accept the low wages and dangerous work. Here are some examples of the conditions that prevail in the U.S.-Mexico border region:

- In Brownsville, Texas, just across the border from Matamoros, a *maquiladora* town, babies are being born without brains in record numbers; public health officials in the area believe there is a link between anencephaly (the name of this horrendous birth defect) and exposure of pregnant women to certain toxic chemicals dumped in streams and on the ground in the *maquiladoras* across the border. Imagine the effect on fetal health in Matamoros itself.
- U.S. companies in Mexico dump xylene, an industrial solvent, at levels up to 50,000 times what is allowed in the United States, and some companies dump methylene chloride at levels up to 215,000 times the U.S. standards, according to test results of a U.S. Environmental Protection Agency–certified laboratory.
- Both U.S. and Mexican-owned factories in the *maquiladora* zone engage in widespread violations of Mexican environmental laws, according to the U.S. General Accounting Office. Moreover, a 1993 random examination of twelve U.S.-owned *maquila* plants showed not one was in compliance with Mexican environmental law. An Arizona-based environmental group, The Border

Ecology Project, found that *maquiladoras* are unable to account for 95 percent of the waste they generated between 1969 and 1989.
- Working conditions inside the *maquiladora* plants are deplorable. The National Safe Workplace Institute reports that "most experts are in agreement that *maquila* workers suffer much higher levels of injuries than U.S. workers," and notes that "an alarming number of mentally retarded infants have been born to mothers who worked in *maquila* plants during pregnancies."

In many instances, large corporations are already forcing U.S. workers and communities to compete against this Dickensian industrialization—but the situation will become much worse with NAFTA and the Uruguay Round expansion of GATT. This is the case because the agreements will lock in rules for countries' treatment of multinational companies and capital that will make it even less risky for U.S. and other foreign companies to open factories in Mexico and other impoverished countries. Further, GATT and NAFTA set out rules limiting countries' ability to exclude imports on the basis of labor, human rights, or environmental conditions in the country of production.

Worst of all, the corporate-induced race to the bottom is a game that no country or community can win. There is always some place in the world that is a little worse off, where the living conditions are a little bit more wretched. Look at the electronics industry, where dozens of assembly and other factories, in search of ever lower production costs, have migrated from California to Korea to Malaysia. Many of those businesses are now contemplating moving on to China, where wages and workplace and environmental standards are still lower. The game of countries bidding against each other causes a downward spiral.

The most important tool countries have to combat this corporate blackmail is to say, "Go abroad. Only you are not going to be able to sell back in this country if you play that game." But the Uruguay Round expansion of GATT and NAFTA would take this power out of the hands of national governments. The trade pacts label such efforts to protect national standards "non-tariff trade barriers," and they outlaw them.

Dirty Milk, Dangerous Cars, and Dying Dolphins

"Non-tariff trade barriers," in fact, has become a code phrase to undermine all sorts of citizen-protection standards and regulations. Literally, the

term means any measure that is not a tariff and that inhibits trade—for instance restrictions on trade in food containing too much pesticide residue
or products that don't meet safety standards. Corporate interests focus on
a safety, health, or environmental regulation that they don't like, develop
an argument about how it violates the rules of a trade agreement, and then
demand that the regulation be revoked. Several examples illustrate how in-
sidious this concept of non-tariff trade barriers can be.

In 1991, Puerto Rico, a U.S. territory, upgraded the quality of its milk
supply by instituting the Pasteurized Milk Ordinance, a tougher system
of regulation than it previously had in place. Ultra-high temperature
(UHT) milk from Canada was unable to meet the island's new, more rig-
orous standard. Puerto Rico subsequently banned the sale of Canadian
UHT milk.

Canada is now challenging Puerto Rico's consumer safety measure as a
non-tariff trade barrier under the existing U.S.-Canada free trade agreement. A panel of five trade bureaucrats—three from Canada, two from the
United States—will hear the case. (The ratio was decided by a coin toss.)
If Canada wins its challenge, Puerto Rico will either have to allow the Canadian milk in or face economic sanctions.

Most Americans probably find this unbelievable; after all, they would
suppose, the United States can surely impose whatever standards it wants
on products made or consumed in this country without being second-
guessed by anonymous trade bureaucrats. But in signing the U.S.-Canada
trade agreement, the United States surrendered such laws to the review of
trade bureaucrats, and the United States will do so on a much larger and
more significant scale if it signs GATT or NAFTA and Congress approves
the agreements.

Consider what would have happened to current auto safety developments if these trade agreements had already been in operation. To push for
airbags in cars, auto safety advocates had to convince the federal government to *mandate* the equivalent of airbag protection in cars.

If the trade agreements had been in place at the time, the auto companies and their political allies in Washington, D.C. would have said, "Oh
no. You can't have airbags because the international standard only provides
for three-point seatbelts. And if we require cars produced or imported into
the United States to have airbags, that is really a disguised way to keep foreign car imports from coming into the United States, and then they won't

let our cars into their markets. That's a non-tariff trade barrier and therefore a violation of the trade agreement."

The milk and airbag examples are only the tip of the iceberg. Already, a Dutch and several U.S. states' recycling programs, the U.S. asbestos ban, the U.S. Delaney clause prohibiting carcinogenic additives to food, a Canadian reforestation program, U.S., Indonesian, and other countries' restrictions on exports of unprocessed logs, CAFE standards, the gas guzzler tax, driftnet fishing and whaling restrictions, U.S. laws designed to protect dolphins, smoking and smokeless tobacco restrictions, and a European ban on beef tainted with growth hormones have either been attacked as non-tariff barriers under existing free trade agreements or threatened with future challenges under the Uruguay Round when it is completed. The most recent version of the European Community's list of alleged U.S. non-tariff trade barriers includes the Consumer Nutrition and Education labeling act, state recycling laws, dolphin protection laws, and fuel efficiency regulations for motor vehicles.

U.S. citizen groups already have enough problems dealing in Washington with corporate lobbyists and indentured politicians without being told that decisions are going to be made in other countries, by other officials, and by other lobbies that have no accountability or disclosure requirements in this country. The problem is exactly the same for citizen organizations in other nations, already struggling against the entrenched monied interests (including foreign subsidiaries) in their own countries.

To compound the autocracy, disputes about non-tariff trade barriers are decided not by elected officials or their appointees, but by secretive panels of foreign trade bureaucrats. Only national government representatives are allowed to participate in the trade agreement dispute resolution; citizen organizations are locked out. The European press reported that the Bush Administration had "thrown" a case brought by Mexico attacking the Marine Mammal Protection Act of 1972 as an illegal trade barrier. The Administration had long opposed the law, yet under GATT they were the law's only defender behind closed doors. The GATT panel ruled in Mexico's favor. Imagine if the Uruguay Round expansion of GATT had been completed, so that Japan had been able to use it to challenge the mandatory air bag rule in 1991. The Bush administration, which, in keeping with the Reagan administration, had long opposed the air bag requirement, would then have been its only theoretical defender—the auto safety advocates who pressed on the Bush administration to adopt it would be locked out. Moreover, under the Uruguay Round expansion of GATT the burden of proof is on the defending country; thus once a challenge is lodged, a law is considered GATT-illegal unless proved innocent.

It is hard enough when people in local communities have to defer to the state government, or when the state government has to defer to the federal government. But it is quite another order of democratic surrender to defer to trade agreement bureaucracies, where the decisions are made by unaccountable members of tribunals in Geneva, Rome, or elsewhere.

GATT and NAFTA: Headed in the Wrong Direction

As the world prepares to enter the twenty-first century, GATT and NAFTA would lead the planet in exactly the wrong direction.

One of the clearest lessons that emerges from a study of industrialized societies is that the centralization of the power of commerce is environmentally and democratically unsound. No one denies the usefulness of international trade and commerce. But societies need to focus their attention on fostering community-oriented production. Such smaller-scale operations are more flexible and adaptable to local needs and environmentally sustainable production methods, and more susceptible to democratic controls. They are less likely to threaten to migrate, and they may perceive their interests as more overlapping with general community interests.

Similarly, allocating power to lower level governmental bodies tends to increase citizen power. Concentrating power in international organizations, as the trade pacts do, tends to remove critical decisions from citizen influence—it's a lot easier to get ahold of your city council representative than international trade bureaucrats.

All over this country—and indeed all over the world—there is a bubbling up of citizen activity dealing with consumer rights, the environment, and public health. People want safe and healthy food, products, and services. They want solar energy instead of fossil fuels; they want recycling; they want to contain soil erosion and to clean up toxic waste dumps; they want safer, environmentally benign materials instead of others that happen to be sold in greater numbers worldwide. And if local or state governments can make decisions to help achieve these goals, then people can really make a difference. But if local and state standards can be jeopardized by a foreign country's mere accusation that the standards are a non-tariff trade barrier, if countries must pay a bribe in trade sanctions to maintain laws ruled to be trade barriers by foreign tribunals, if a company's claim that the burden the standard would impose is so great that they would have to pick up their stakes and move elsewhere, then the evolution of health and safety standards worldwide will be stalled. For it is rare that regulatory breakthroughs occur at the national, let alone international, level. Usually, a smaller jurisdiction—a town, city, or state—experiments with a standard, other cities and states copy it and, eventually, national governments and international governments, lagging behind, follow their lead. This percolating-up process will be squelched by GATT and NAFTA, with top-down mercantile dictates replacing bottom-up democratic impulses.

This book contains essays by leading citizen-oriented trade experts. They dissect the ideological roots of the free trade mantra, discuss the trade negotiations themselves and, most vividly and most importantly, detail the devastating effect that such trade governance has had—and the much more severe effect it will have if the Uruguay Round expansion of GATT and NAFTA are enacted—on real people and real communities around the world. The common interests of the farmer in Kansas and the farmer in India, and the auto worker in Toledo and the auto worker in northern Mexico—all in opposition to the trade pacts—are clearly illustrated. Of course all of humanity has a shared interest in opposing trade agreements that threaten to exacerbate rather than diminish the great global threats to human well-being—reckless exploitation of people and environments.

In two, three, or four decades, when historians look back on this period during which so much of the world's system of self-organization is being reconfigured, they will point to this book and other similar efforts to reveal the defects of GATT and NAFTA as having had one of two effects. Either they will focus on them as a powerful call to arms that helped educate and mobilize a population that resisted the destructive GATT and NAFTA programs designed by business's most powerful forces, or they will view them as prescient, unheeded warnings. It is up to you, and your fellow citizens, to determine which appraisal prevails.

Jerry Mander

MEGATECHNOLOGY, TRADE, AND THE NEW WORLD ORDER

The United States-Iraq war of 1991 was a watershed event for reasons far beyond Middle Eastern power politics. It was the first event to reveal, in a harsh, clarifying light, the new shape of modern economics and its inexorable drive toward the globalization of corporate power.

In explaining why it was necessary to send half a million troops and to mobilize the entire industrial world against Saddam Hussein, George Bush initially suggested that the flow of oil or the rise in its price "threatens our way of life" and the "new world order." This latter phrase—the new world order—was at first greeted with puzzlement and concern, so Bush changed his emphases to "naked aggression," "stopping another Hitler," and "restoring the legitimate government of Kuwait."

But President Bush had already demonstrated in Panama that he was comfortable with aggression. Comparing Saddam to Hitler obviously trivialized Hitler (which angered many Jews). And calling the Kuwait royal family legitimate rulers, when in truth they had been arbitrarily installed by British colonists only a few decades earlier, was simply farcical. No, George Bush had it right in the first place. He was fighting for a new world economic order, the dimensions of which were just beginning to be revealed in Bush's parallel, very energetic, worldwide lobbying campaign for global free trade agreements.

Though I feel sure Saddam's invasion of Kuwait was not primarily intended as a direct threat to corporate free trade or to the new world economic alliance then taking form—surely his goals were more limited and predatory—it was nonetheless exactly the sort of free-lance military and economic expression that could no longer be permitted. It showed that he did not understand the nature of the new deals that were being carved among the world's major economic players or what happens to nonplayers.

Technopolitics

The late 1980s and early 1990s were breakthrough years in the evolution of technology. Brand new compatibilities among global-scale technologies such as satellites, lasers, television, high-speed computation, advanced high-speed travel, instantaneous resource transfer, and others "popped" communications capabilities into a global dimension. This made it possible, and inevitable, for corporate powers to rapidly accelerate their expansion beyond national boundaries. In fact, corporate form and technological form *coevolved* in a symbiotic relationship: the corporations pushed the technologies that, in turn, made it possible for the corporations to become *primary* international players, beyond the control of the sovereign states that had spawned them. The corporations could not have achieved such extra-national status until this new generation of technology was firmly in place. It was the technologies that made it possible for central corporate management in one locale to have instantaneous contact with and control of its hundreds of distant parts throughout the world.

The vast expansion of corporate power had actually been predicted and planned-for three decades earlier at the notorious Bretton Woods meetings (discussed elsewhere in this book) held after the Second World War. Already at that time there was a vision of centralized worldwide economic management including huge new international institutions for banking and trade, with multinational corporations as the glue that held them all together, and guided their activities.

This dream of global economic governance was further boosted during the 1950s and 1960s via the Trilateral Commission, a secretive international body that comprised the industrial world's top corporate, banking, and political leaders. Conceiving of themselves as the world's elite players, taking upon themselves the responsibility to make order out of chaos, the commissioners planned and encouraged an utter restructuring of the world's political and economic agenda with much of its new power arrangements built to favor transnational corporate activity. (See Holly

Sklar's magnificent book, *Trilateralism*, published by South End Press.)
The commissioners were actually liberal in their orientation. They favored
détente between the Soviet bloc and the West. They believed that all
the world's problems could be eventually solved through accelerated,
Western-style economic development, the benefits of which would trickle
down to the world's poorest peoples. And they believed that gigantic corporate enterprise would be the most efficient delivery system for this global
economic strategy.

The Trilateral Commission gave great importance to the powerful supportive institutions like the World Bank, the International Monetary
Fund (IMF), other development banks, and the General Agreement on
Tariffs and Trade (GATT). But no true breakthrough in world economic
control could have been made without the technical infrastructure that
made global communications, commodity movement, and resource control more rapid, logical, efficient, and powerful.

By 1990, the technology was in place to map all the world's land and sea
resources from space. And the new merger of computer, laser, and satellite
technologies combined to produce instantaneous worldwide corporate
communication, capital transfer and resource control. Meanwhile, the
globalization of television transmission via satellite and the ubiquitous-
ness of advertising enabled Western industrial corporations to spread commodity culture and Western material values everywhere, even to nonde-
veloped countries that had no roads. This led in turn to rapid global
homogenization of cultures within a Western economic paradigm. At the
same time, developments in high-speed transportation facilitated the
rapid movement of resources and commodities worldwide and unified all
the world's markets so that Washington apples could be sold in Brazil and
fresh fish could be delivered to any country from the other side of the earth.
The notions of *local economy* and *local control* became anomalous and increasingly impossible. Finally, the enforcement capabilities of high-tech war-
fare—so exquisitely displayed in the U.S.-Iraq war—made clear whose
ultimate interests the economic systems were designed to serve. This military capability gave the largest industrial states awesome ability to police
conformity and to dictate terms on behalf of their corporate sovereigns.

Taken together, these technological advances effectively interlocked
with one another and formed a global technological web, a single interlocked machine, *megatechnology*, which made it counterproductive for any

growing corporation to think of itself in strictly national terms. Neither did it make any sense for governments in the Western industrial world— governments which owed their viability to support from the corporate sector—to resist the breathtaking trend toward economic merger with other Western countries. There was no choice but to unify conceptually and politically into a one-world economy that, calling itself "free market," had been planned at least three decades earlier.

The corporate economies of North America, western Europe, Japan, and recently, Russia and the eastern bloc countries, have become so interdependent that it is really meaningless to speak of these economies as separate from each other. While it still remains true that trade wars can erupt among individual corporate-states, long-term goals are becoming clearer, better understood by all players, and unified. Whether on the transnational-corporate level or the international-bank level, among trade bureaucracies or among government leaders (Bush or Clinton, Mitterand or Chirac, Pinochet or Alwyn, Miyazawa or Deng or Salinas) all agree that a global economy run by central corporate interests, with the eager support of banks, governments, and transnational trade institutions, is the means to greater efficiency, more rapid development, and mutual aid. There is also agreement that the international institutions—banks and bureaucracies—must be given sufficient powers to keep pathways greased, and to suppress an ever more conscious and growing resistance from unions, small farmers, environmentalists, and advocates of democracy, national culture, and sovereignty, who still cling to ideas of political and economic organization that are fed by other values.

Soviet Defection

Despite the inevitabilities brought by the evolution of technology and its formation into a single global *megatechnology* sphere, another critical change was required before the pace of globalization could be accelerated: the failure of communism and the breakup of the oppositional voice of the Soviet Union. As long as Soviet communism existed, the world was rigidly divided into three distinct camps: pro-American, pro-Soviet, and non-aligned. The trilateral model of world organization could never be achieved under such an anarchic political arrangement.

When Soviet communism finally collapsed, its demise was hailed as a victory for both "market economics" and for democracy. In fact the two very different terms quickly became interchangeable in the way politicians—and, alas, the media—used them. Soon, all effective opposition to worldwide economic and cultural homogenization evaporated. The World Bank, the IMF, and the Japanese Overseas Development Bank, only marginally dominant until this moment, seized the chance to turn up the heat on previously nonaligned Third World countries to accept the fact that there were no more alternatives. They would either mold their economies to match the Western model or be isolated. The trilateral model of a unified world economy based on unlimited growth, unlimited commodity consumption, removal of all barriers to economic development, exploitation of nature, and management of the world's resources by corporations in collaboration with like-minded governments, now seemed achievable in the very short run. Renewed emphasis on free trade agreements with added power to enforce conformity (such as the Multi-Lateral Trading Organization in the Uruguay Round of GATT) were clear expressions of an emboldened transnational corporate world moving its guns forward as the enemy retreated in disarray.

George Bush was the ideal leader to guide this process. Born into the economic elite, a multinational oil company president, a member of the Trilateral Commission, a former chief of the Central Intelligence Agency, and, a former international diplomat, Bush came to power just at the moment of Soviet decline. For all his failings, he knew the moment when he could advance the interests of his associates. He also knew how to incorporate military force to ensure that no breaks would develop in the seamless fabric that was being created; industrial economies woven together as one.

Of course, there did still remain a pesky opposition that expressed itself within democratic countries in the form of laws that protected the environment, or consumers, or labor, or wages, or that tried to slow the overuse of resources. Such laws directly impeded the central economic model. Though the laws may have been created by democratic institutions, they were every bit as threatening as Mr. Saddam Hussein and had to be met forthrightly, if not militarily. Trade agreements were the "peaceful" instruments that could overrule and suppress national laws and national will just as efficiently as missiles could suppress individual military excursions. With the great enforcement powers being designated in the Uruguay Round of GATT, all minor discrepancies among member countries should be ironed out, all efforts to protect labor or environment or local economy could be overpowered, all efforts by small countries of the Third World, attempting, for example, to control their own genetic resources, could be disciplined by trade bureaucrats. The goal of a unified world development plan under transnational corporate leadership could be quickly realized.

The European Economic Community was well established by 1950, with a few details still to be worked out. Once the Maastricht Treaty is concluded and ratified, the European economic, political, and cultural homogenization process will be accelerated. The U.S.-Canada agreement and the North American Free Trade Agreement (NAFTA) were designed to create a parallel system on this side of the Atlantic. These will soon be followed by a Western Hemisphere Economic Community, a Pacific Basin Community, an Asian Community, a Central American Community, and so on throughout the world under the unifying control of GATT, which will retain final authority. As these agreements begin to interlock with one another, in the general direction of globalizing trade and massifying markets, any economic threat within one member state, or among states, will be perceived as a direct threat to all members. This became crystal clear when Iraq invaded Kuwait, and the whole world responded.

Unfreedom

The American media tend to encapsulate current economic trends with the term *market economics*, but the term is wildly imprecise. In fact, it is a catchall "pop" phrase that presents a benign, even traditional mask over what is actually a new and very aggressive economic arrangement that is centrally structured, has fixed rules of procedure, makes many exceptions in individual cases, and is not free. The only freedom it provides is the freedom of transnational corporations to circumvent national laws that would otherwise impede their self-interests. "Market economics" can be best seen in action in places like Flint, Michigan, or Houston, Texas, where thousands of workers have lost their jobs because free-enterprise capital has moved to Korea or Thailand or Mexico. Or else it is where a small manufacturer is crushed by a multinational's larger resources; or else where an international energy conglomerate invades some great wilderness to seek oil or logs, and locals do not have the ability to stop them; or else it is in the last great rain forests (no longer protected by Third World governments, who have seen their ability to control development subsumed under international trading rules) where only the bows and arrows of ancient tribal people stand in the way of the Western development assault. "Free trade" and "market economics" are positive-sounding phrases that in reality are public-relations terms designed to conceal what they really stand for: the forced abandonment of local controls on development, ownership, trade, wages, prices, or lifestyle in favor of centrally conceived concepts and interests protected by bureaucracies in Geneva or Brussels and ultimately enforced by the U.S. military.

Mr. Bush's term *new world order* is a far more accurate phrase to describe the fact and the purpose of such a system of organization—one that permits bankers and developers to map and plan the flow of the world's resources according to an overall vision for a world economy that functions the same way everywhere; and which homogenizes lifestyle, culture, values, and the land itself.

Faustian Bargain

The new world order does not exclude smaller countries from the benefits of "free market" economics; on the contrary, it is very important to the overall scheme that all countries participate. It is part of the essentially liberal rationale that the new world order will bring wealth and economic growth to the poorest countries. However, most central development aid projects are only implemented if the countries agree *a priori* to play by a certain set of rules: 1) opening all markets to outside trade and investment without requiring majority local ownership; 2) eliminating all tariff barriers; 3) severely reducing government spending, especially in areas of services to the poor; 4) converting small-scale self-sufficient family farming to high-tech, pesticide-intensive agribusiness that produces one-crop export commodities such as coffee and cattle; and 5) demonstrating an unwavering dedication to clearing the last forests, mining the last minerals, diverting and damming the last rivers, and getting native peoples off their land and resources by any means necessary. All such adjustments are intended to make indigenous economies conform to the multinational corporate drives of the new world order.

The second set of rules, which builds on the first, has to do with submission to the new big trade agreements. Such submission takes certain forms: 1) "harmonizing" local or national economies to standards set by trade bureaucracies; 2) abandoning local laws that serve to protect nature or jobs or local industry; 3) eliminating all nontariff barriers to trade, such as health or environmental or consumer laws; 4) permitting transnational access to all genetic resources (considered to be "intellectual property") and their patenting; 5) permitting entry to "service" industries such as banks and ad agencies even if they destroy *local* banks and ad agencies; 6) submitting to the discipline of the enforcement powers of trade bureaucrats, especially the Multi-Lateral Trading Organization. In effect, the rules demand that smaller countries give up all remnants of sovereign power.

In an unabashedly frank article in 1992, the *International Herald Tribune* analyzed the kind of Faustian bargain that Third World countries were being asked to accept, using Malaysia as an example. The good news for Malaysia's economy, said the *Tribune*, was that its textile industry would benefit enormously if the Uruguay Round of GATT succeeded, since the agreement would require Western countries such as the United States to remove all tariff barriers against the import of low-cost textile products from Asia. This would increase employment in Asian textiles and produce economic growth, which presumably would benefit everyone.

The bad news, however, was that Malaysia would be required to abandon its laws that held foreign investment in local industries under 50 percent ownership and that ensured that businesses would continue to be described as Malaysian rather than being, well, *beyond* nationhood. Also, Malaysia would have to accept the invasion of foreign banks and other capital investment sources.

The net effect was that the Malaysian economy would quickly be overpowered by foreign bankers, who naturally would want to invest and perhaps buy-up Malaysian textile industries whose prospects had suddenly improved and who were growing rapidly. But the banks would only do this if the wages were kept at the *very low level* that gave Malaysian textile manufacturers a comparative advantage in the first place, under "free trade."

So, who actually gains and who loses? International bankers gain because they can move instantly where the action is and overpower local economic interests. Certain local industries gain—that is, the *owners* of the industries gain because they can reap the rewards of economic growth or sell their increasingly valuable companies to foreign banks. The sheer number of jobs increases, but at a wage that must remain at rock bottom or else the entire equation is blown. But the vast numbers of poor people in whose name this is being done are no better off than before, while the rich get richer. What else is new? And all that remains of Malaysian sovereignty, as expressed in its ability to control its own economy, is gone forever. (Meanwhile, wages in the Western importing nations *decline* to match the new competition from Malaysia.)

There is one more set of rules. These concern participant countries' commitment to be team players. If any one country steps out of line, all others join forces to bang the offender back into place. The Multi-Lateral Trading Organization of GATT is the primary instrument envisioned as the enforcer, using very extreme economic sanctions, including economic isolation and perhaps worse. The handwriting was already on the wall in the U.S.-Iraq war, long before the MTO was close to being reality, when the countries that refused to participate in the punishment of Iraq were themselves severely punished economically. Jordan, Yemen, Cuba, Malaysia, and Brazil, among others, suffered extreme hardship for their opposition to the concerted world action against Iraq.

I doubt that Saddam Hussein knew he was offending an elaborate worldwide economic scheme when he undertook his invasion of Kuwait, a country that, with Saudi Arabia, is an eager participant in the new world order. Saddam was apparently enraged that the price of oil was being kept too low by Kuwaiti overdrilling (low energy prices directly serve the interest of the larger industrial countries) and he was afraid of the effects on his own economic expansion dreams. He thought he could do something about it but failed to grasp that that kind of individualism doesn't fly anymore.

Saddam was caught in a kind of time warp. Perhaps he felt he was just being a typical, individualistic, nationalistic, corporate-raider type—a Michael Milken with nerve gas and missiles—following the logic of the early Reagan years: "Look out for number one." He did not appreciate that in the new *megatechnological* age, on a tiny planet, all countries with resources have to be on the same team. There is no room for upstarts or freelancers and, now that the Soviet Union has completed its defection to the West, no protection either. His arrogance cost him several hundred thousand of his citizens, devastation to his infrastructure, several years' worth of severe economic sanctions, and the official designation as international outlaw.

One does not have to sympathize with a man like Saddam Hussein to draw a larger conclusion from the situation. There is a juggernaut underway, a plan for international economic order. It has nothing to do with "free markets" or "free trade" or any other kind of "free" anything, except that it frees the largest economic powers on earth to exercise their orderly process of eating up the last resources of the planet, suppressing whatever resistance exists—whether an oil dictator or an environmental group protecting dolphins—and recasting the world economy and the way we live on Earth into a unified pattern that benefits virtually no one but the transnational institutions themselves.

3

Lori Wallach

HIDDEN DANGERS OF GATT AND NAFTA

Introduction

In the maelstrom of clearly relevant news and events, many people, including citizen activists, have not considered trade an issue directly impacting people's daily lives and thus worth monitoring. In fact, many people have an instant My Eyes Glaze Over reaction to the mention of international trade policy or trade negotiations. While citizens' awareness and activity has busily proceeded, under the surface hidden away from notice a shift has been underway in trade policy that threatens to crack the very foundations of citizens' activism and citizens' achievement of the past decades.

International trade agreements including those in effect and those currently on the negotiating table will have a seismic impact on health, safety, and environmental laws in the United States and around the world. Such laws are the product of decades of successful effort by advocates for environmental and consumer protection and worker health and safety. These trade agreements have equally important implications for the economy, environment, and social systems of other countries throughout the Americas and around the world.

Trade agreements are negotiated in secret by governmental representatives working closely with corporate advisors and are enforced through procedures hidden from public scrutiny. Without reforms to trade policy, the 1990s may become a decade of retrenchment, when hard-won environmental and consumer safeguards are preempted or overruled because citizens around the world are being effectively cut out of the decision-making process.

The United States is one of the current 103 members of the General Agreement on Tariffs and Trade. The global trade pact, started in 1947, is currently under its eighth expansion through the so-called Uruguay Round of negotiations. The Uruguay Round includes greater expansion of GATT's powers and the issues GATT disciplines would cover. For the first time, GATT is being expanded to cover services, investment, intellectual property and trade in food. These changes are greater than those accomplished through all of the past Rounds of negotiations combined. A final text for the Uruguay Round was published in December 1991, but the talks bogged down over agricultural and other issues. President Bush ultimately failed to meet his goal of concluding the talks before President Clinton's inauguration. However, President Clinton has recently announced his commitment to complete the negotiations by the end of 1993. In March, the Administration announced its intention to seek extension until December of a special Congressional rule called "fast track" for approval of a Uruguay Round deal.

In 1988, the United States and Canada entered into a free trade agreement. Although Canadian wages, social policies and environmental standards were only slightly stronger than U.S. policy, the agreement has had devastating effects on Canada's economy and social and environmental protections. The record-breaking lack of popularity that recently forced former Canadian Prime Minister Brian Mulroney out of office is closely linked with the 1988 U.S.-Canada Agreement, which was the core theme of his campaign. In Canada, over 16% of the population believes Elvis is still alive according to polling compared to Mulroney's 14% approval rating. In Canada, NAFTA is widely known as "Not Another Fucking Trade Agreement."

Starting in June 1991, the United States, Mexico and Canada began negotiations to extend this model into a North American Free Trade Agreement (NAFTA) with the goal of creating a free-trade zone from the Aleutians to the equator. Working behind a dense veil of secrecy, the Bush Administration finally published a 1000-page text for the agreement on September 6, 1992, three weeks after announcing its completion. The agreement was officially signed on December 17, 1992 by Presidents

Bush, Salinas and Mulroney, two of whom are now out of power. It was not made available to the public until after President Clinton's inauguration. Then, only 100 copies were printed which cost $42 a piece, although a commercial printer can produce it for about $5.

The NAFTA will only come into effect if approved by legislatures in all three countries. President Clinton announced support for the NAFTA text during his campaign, but demanded additional terms be negotiated to address environmental and labor concerns. These negotiations began March 17, 1993. Despite efforts by environmental, consumer and labor groups to shape the supplemental negotiation to focus on NAFTA's many fundamental flaws and omissions, the initial negotiation sessions have not been encouraging. The Administration hoped to have the negotiation completed by June. The NAFTA is predicted to come before Congress in the fall. Under this schedule, it would come into force on January 1, 1994.

These agreements which are international executive agreements, not treaties, will become part of U.S. federal law once approved by Congress. As such, they will supersede previous federal law and trump state and local law. The Agreements contain complete rules systems that taken as a whole basically prohibit signatory countries from restricting imports or exports quantitatively or qualitatively unless the Agreements specially allow such exceptions; the trade *über alles* rule. Further, the Agreements put into place a dispute-resolution system that allows one country to challenge the laws and practices of another country as violative of the rules of the Agreements. Successfully challenged laws must be eliminated, or the losing country would face trade sanctions or other monetary penalties.

If this description of the potential impacts of trade agreements seems far fetched, unfortunately there are already a string of examples of environmental, health and safety laws that have been threatened with challenge or challenged under the terms of trade agreements. Successfully challenged under GATT as trade barriers have been the U.S. Marine Mammal Protection Act of 1972, several laws conserving fish resources, and Thai cigarette limitations. Currently under challenge at GATT are the U.S. Fuel Economy Standards, the U.S. Gas Guzzler Tax, and the E.C. ban on the use of growth hormones in beef. Challenges have been threatened under GATT against restrictions on drift net fishing by the U.S., export bans on raw logs in Indonesia, the Philippines and the U.S., the U.S. 1990 Consumer Education and Nutrition Food Labelling Act,

California's Proposition 65, which requires labeling of carcinogens, German packaging recycling laws, and the recycling laws of several U.S. states, the U.S. "Pelly Amendment," which enforces the ban on commercial whaling, state procurement laws requiring a certain content of recycled paper and more. As a result of the past pressure of such challenge threats, meat inspection along the U.S.-Canadian border was all but eliminated for a period of years and now remains very limited, a bill banning import of wild-caught birds into the U.S. was delayed and then watered down in Congress as contrary to GATT, Danish bottle recycling requirements were weakened, Canada is now required to accept U.S. food imports that contain 30% more pesticide residues than were allowed under their national laws before the 1988 U.S.-Canada Free Trade Agreement, a Canadian plan for provincial auto insurance was scrapped when attacked by U.S. insurers as a subsidy, as was a British Columbia reforestation program challenged as an unfair subsidy to the timber industry.

Despite the immense potential impacts of the trade pacts, unlike legislation, they cannot be amended simply through Congressional action. Rather, the rules and court system of the Agreements are locked in place until changes are negotiated as between all parties. In effect, approval of the Uruguay Round and NAFTA texts negotiated by the Reagan and Bush Administration would cast in steel the very international trickle down economics and deregulatory policies that were resoundingly rejected in the recent U.S. elections.

Thus, in the next year, the U.S. Congress likely will face votes on the North American Free Trade Agreement, the Uruguay Round expansion of the GATT and the reauthorization of the "fast track" procedure for Congressional consideration of the Uruguay Round. While admittedly it is difficult to predict the precise effect that the rather technical language of the NAFTA and Uruguay Round will have, few contest that the impacts on U.S. environmental and consumer health and safety policy will be great. The NAFTA and Uruguay Round will extend the purview of trade agreement into such intimate issues as food safety, control of natural resources, and consumer product safety. U.S. Congressional decisions to approve the NAFTA and the Uruguay Round will have far-reaching future effects on this country's ability to adopt and enforce strong environmental, consumer, and worker safety measures.

In the past three years, environmental, health, conservation and consumer advocates around the world have been focussing increasing attention on trade policy. The overall aim of many of the groups in the United States has been to subject international trade regimes like the GATT and the NAFTA to the standards of democracy and accountability that the groups have promoted domestically, as a prerequisite and part of shifting the trade-only values of the agreements to encompass other important values such as environmental and consumer health and safety protection.

In summary, the international trade arena is an inappropriate forum for decision-making on environmental, health and safety policy. Further, while it is necessary to have international trade rules to rationalize international commerce, it is vital to recognize that trade rules like any system of rules embody certain values and goals. At present, both the procedural and substantive rules that now characterize international trade policy as established in the General Agreement on Tariffs and Trade, and amplified in sub-agreements such as the NAFTA, conflict with the procedural needs and substantive values of environmental and consumer protection. Policy-making on such issues must remain fully within the jurisdiction of more democratic and accountable bodies situated geographically so as to maximize the opportunity for citizen oversight and participation. However, changes aimed at opening current trade procedures to the public and to neutralize current trade rules' negative impact on environmental and consumer protection are necessary to improve the unacceptable status quo. Such changes to domestic trade law and to international trade agreements are urgently needed.

In this paper, I will translate from GATTese and NAFTAese into English the aspects of current trade policy that are incompatible with the procedural and substantive values of environmental and consumer protection. I will then discuss the changes that could neutralize the currently detrimental impact of trade policy on these other important policy areas, including the vital issues of citizen participation in the international trade policy forum.

The Current Conflict Between Environmental, Health and Safety Policies and Trade Policies

The core principle of international trade policy is to remove impediments to the free flow of goods and services between countries. The core procedural rule of trade policy is secrecy.

First, many environmental, health and safety measures do present impediments to an absolutely free flow of goods. Stopping importation of goods that do not meet U.S. standards, for instance food containing pesticide residues, products that do not meet U.S. safety specifications, products made from endangered species including ivory and whale products, or products containing dangerous chemicals, are fundamental tools in environmental, health and safety policy. Further, Congress has passed laws to accomplish environmental goals by limiting importation of goods on the basis of the process through which they were manufactured or harvested. Thus, current U.S. laws prohibit importation of seafood caught in environmentally detrimental ways, and of wild-caught birds, and the Clean Air Act will put into place in the future bans on the import of goods manufactured using ozone-depleting chemicals. Laws limiting export of certain goods for environmental, conservation or safety reasons, such as raw logs from the Pacific Northwest, have also been passed on the federal and state levels.

These measures could run afoul of current trade policy set forth in the GATT and enumerated in the NAFTA and in the Uruguay Round. First, the NAFTA and the Uruguay Round provide dispute-resolution mechanisms through which one country can challenge the validity of another country's environmental, health and safety measures under the rules of the trade agreements. The agreements allow another country to challenge as infringing upon the trade rules U.S. environmental, health or safety law that inhibits the other country's trade opportunities with the United States. If judged by a trade dispute panel to be in conflict with the trade rules, the United States would be ordered to stop enforcing such U.S. laws against the complaining party, or the United States would face trade sanctions. This could be the fate of U.S. environmental, consumer or health laws passed by Congress or state or local legislative bodies, of regulations derived from such laws and of laws enacted through popular referendum.

Second, the current trade regime more subtly undermines a country's establishing, maintaining and enforcing strong environmental, health or safety measures or raising the level of such protections. Under this regime, products of U.S. companies which are complying with environmental, health and safety laws are put at a competitive disadvantage to products imported by companies not required to meet the same product or process standards. This is the case because the agreements require equal access to the U.S. market of goods that are physically the same regardless of their production or harvesting processes. Thus, when the United States began enforcing the same dolphin protection rules for tuna fishing for imported tuna that U.S. fishermen were already required to meet to sell their tuna in the United States, the Mexican government was able to challenge the U.S. law called the Marine Mammal Protection Act as an unfair trade barrier at GATT. The effect of the law had been to equalize environmental costs as between U.S. and foreign fishers. Under the existing GATT rules, this challenge was successful and in August 1991, a GATT dispute resolution panel declared that longstanding U.S. dolphin protection act an illegal trade barrier that must be eliminated.

When insisting that the United States must maintain the ability to control access to its markets on the basis of "process" restrictions, U.S. environmental and consumer advocates working on trade policy have been criticized for ignoring issues of national sovereignty. Namely, we are asked why the United States should be able to make decisions about environmental and consumer protection levels for other countries. The U.S. environmental and consumer argument is *not* about what other countries should do in reference to their own domestic standards. Rather, the concern is that trade policy should in no way inhibit the effective operation in the United States of U.S. environmental and consumer protections. Thus, to effectively establish U.S. standards, policy makers must have available the tools to enforce our laws. They must also ensure that businesses which comply with U.S. laws are not placed at a competitive disadvantage to those who do not comply. Thus, the U.S. must be able to control access to our market by either banning or in some way equalizing the cost of products that do not meet our standards. From an environmental standpoint, this means making it competitively possible for U.S. industry to internalize the environmental costs that are required of them by U.S. law. From a consumer standpoint this means not giving a price advantage, and thus a market advantage, to producers who fail to bear the burden of the cost of their production—namely costs to the environment, worker safety and health that are externalized in other countries—frequently by U.S.-based multinational corporations that have relocated production to avoid just such costs. As part of this process, trade agreements must be harnessed to provide funding and technical assistance to help developing countries raise environmental and other social standards so that such market access restrictions do not continually and unfairly put these countries at a disadvantage.

Third, openness and public accountability over decision-makers has proved to be a procedural necessity for promoting strong environmental and consumer protection in the United States and around the world. Years of citizen advocacy have resulted in systems of policy formation and decision-making in the United States that provide opportunity for aggregation of disparate public interests through public education and debate to push forward environmental and consumer laws. It is only through the ability of voters to hold decision-makers accountable that such laws have been passed over the objection of business interests. The openness provided by the Freedom of Information Act, the Government in the Sunshine Act, the federal Advisory Committee Act, the Administrative Procedure Act and other federal and state procedural safeguards is sharply contrasted by the secrecy and exclusion that currently permeate trade policy formation and the dispute and standards-setting bodies that the NAFTA and Uruguay Round would establish.

Thus, the combination of procedural impediments to public participation, and trade challenges, trade sanctions, threatened challenges and the competitive disadvantage of U.S. producers who follow current U.S. law established under current trade proposals will inevitably lead to increased pressure on U.S. policy makers to decrease the level of environmental, consumer and health protection. This race to the bottom is absolutely contrary to urgently needed changes towards a more sustainable model of trade and development policies.

GATT Articles Impacting Environmental, Health and Safety Measures

The trade values that conflict with environmental, consumer and health values are the basis of, and are enumerated in, the core Articles of the 1947 GATT. The NAFTA and any other subagreements must be compatible with the terms of the GATT. The Uruguay Round simply amplified and explicitly applies such core principles to different issues and areas. Thus, analysis of the environmental, health and safety implications of the GATT Articles is the starting place for consideration of the substantive environmental, health and safety impacts of the NAFTA and the Uruguay Round.[1]

GATT Article I establishes the rule of "Most Favored Nation" treatment. Under its principles, one GATT country may not discriminate between domestic products and "like products" imported from another GATT country. "Like products" has been defined in GATT jurisprudence and in a 1971 paper prepared by the GATT Secretariat to be limited to consideration of product characteristics, and does not allow consideration of how a product is produced or harvested.[2]

Thus, as enumerated in the now infamous 1991 GATT tuna-dolphin ruling, known to some environmentalists as GATTzilla vs. Flipper, under GATT rules, countries cannot limit importation of products which because of their production or harvest method may have detrimental effects on the environment. Article I additionally forbids use of more subtle instruments such as quotas, differential tariffs or taxes. The notion of "like product" has recently been raised in the food context as relates to a pending ban on ozone-depleting post-harvest fungicide fumigants which leave no residue on foodstuffs, but harm the environment. The process-distinction problem would also be triggered by laws limiting importation of goods produced using child labor. The potential problems with banning products produced using child labor or products from countries such as South Africa against which the United States has taken trade measures for human rights reasons were noted by representatives of the Office of the General Counsel of the USTR's Office in a September 17, 1991 hearing on the tuna-dolphin case held by the House Energy and Commerce Committee Subcommittee on Health and Environment.

GATT Article III sets out the principle of "National Treatment." Under this concept, one GATT country may not use tariffs, taxes or any regulations to provide different treatment to imports than it would provide to domestically produced goods. The goal of this GATT Article was to stop the use of trade restrictions to protect domestic industries. The implications for U.S. environmental and consumer protection are that the U.S. is limited in taking action either through differential tariffs or taxes to improve the competitiveness of U.S. industry required by law to internalize certain environmental costs and comply with worker health and safety laws not required in the countries of competing producers.

GATT Article XI reinforces the notion of national treatment set out in Article III by specifically eliminating the use of bans, quotas or licensing systems on exports or imports. Under this section, measures to restrict the export of raw natural resources, such as the raw log bans established under Washington and Oregon state law and federal law could be held to violate the GATT. In fact, the U.S. raw log bans have been threatened by GATT challenges in the press.[3] The European Community has requested consultations under GATT's dispute-resolution mechanisms about a raw tropical timber export ban in Indonesia. The Philippines has a similar law. Similarly, efforts by certain European nations, most notably the Netherlands, to restrict imports of unsustainable harvested tropical timber may be held invalid under GATT. Unofficial reports indicate that a preliminary evaluation of the measure by the Dutch Ministry of Economic Affairs concluded that the proposed ban, which is to come into effect on January 1, 1995, is incompatible with Article XI of the GATT.[4]

GATT Article XVI defines the limitation on governmental use of subsidies, thus limiting an alternative method for equalizing the competitive effect of compliance by U.S. industry with environmental, health and safety measures. Article XVI states that if a subsidy "operates directly or indirectly to increase exports of any product from, or to reduce imports of any product into, its territory," it must inform all other GATT countries. If any nation objects, then the U.S. would be required to negotiate reduction or elimination of such a subsidy. This Article exposes a country that subsidizes pollution reduction or control measures, for instance through tax credits or other preferential treatment, to challenge by other GATT countries with a competing industry.

Exceptions to these general rules are provided mainly in GATT Article XX, which includes everything from exceptions for national security and slave labor to exceptions for the protection of human, animal and plant life and health. Article XI additionally includes one specific short-term exception to export limitations for critical shortages of food or "other products" essential to the exporting country. The exceptions of Article XX allow for trade measures which would otherwise conflict with the basic GATT rules, so long as these measures do not "discriminate between countries where the same conditions prevail, or are a disguised restriction in international trade."

GATT Article XX(b) allows for "measures necessary to protect human, animal and plant health or life." The clause was originally intended for agriculture quarantine and other sanitary regulations.[5] Although it does not specifically mention the environment, environmentalists had hoped that it could be used to update the GATT's notion of exceptions to include measures taken for environmental protection. Such hopes were largely dashed by the 1991 GATT ruling in the tuna-dolphin case, the first formal case in GATT's history in which Article XX was offered to support an environmental defense. The tuna-dolphin case held that Article XX could not be used in defense of extraterritorial measures, a question that had not been settled before the tuna-dolphin panel ruling. This jeopardizes, under GATT, numerous U.S. environmental and conservation measures, including the Endangered Species Act, whale protection measures, and the ivory ban.

Additionally, the notion of "measures necessary to protect" has been interpreted, both in the tuna-dolphin case and in other GATT panel decisions, to require that a measure taken must be the "least trade restrictive" measure possible to accomplish a GATT-legitimate end. Thus, in the tuna-dolphin case, the panel held that the U.S. failed to prove that some less trade restrictive means to accomplish its dolphin protection goal did not exist. The principles of "necessary" and "least trade restrictive" are specifically incorporated in the Uruguay Round, and to a somewhat more oblique extent in the NAFTA.

GATT Article XX(g) allows for "measures relating to the conservation of exhaustible natural resources if such measures are to be made in conjunction with restriction on domestic production and consumption." The main GATT jurisprudence on this exception prior to the tuna-dolphin case was in relation to a 1987 dispute panel in which the United States challenged a Canadian ban on the export of unprocessed herring and salmon. The United States argued that the goal of the law was to protect the British Columbia fishing industry, in violation of GATT Article VI. The Canadians argued that the ban was a core element of the Canadian West Coast fishery conservation and management plan. The dispute panel ruled that the ban was contrary to Article VI, and that no exception was available under Article XX(g) because conservation was not the primary goal of the law. This ruling brings into question the applicability of Article XX(g) for measures with mixed environmental and commercial goals, including the raw log bans in the Pacific Northwest.

The tuna-dolphin panel further limited the application of Article XX(g) to environmental measures by holding that Article XX(g) did not have extraterritoriality application and that the limitation on consideration of process standards would also apply. Further, the tuna-dolphin panel report concluded that a country may not restrict trade in one product to accomplish a goal pertaining to another product—namely tuna to protect dolphins. Article XX(g) would have been the likely defense if the Packwood-Magnuson Amendments to the Fisherman's Protective Act were challenged under GATT. However, the tuna-dolphin case effectively eliminates the usefulness of that defense.

GATT Article XX(h) allows for waivers "undertaken in pursuance of obligations under any intergovernmental commodity agreement," which is relevant to certain commodity agreements such as the International Tropical Timber Agreement, which includes conservation and sustainable management goals. Environmental advocates have hoped that this exception might be extended to include international environmental agreements and protocols. However, such an extension was not part of the Uruguay Round Draft Final Act Text. To the contrary, a GATT Committee on Trade and Environment is currently discussing the trade conflicts problems raised by three major environmental agreements—the Convention on International Trade in Endangered Species, the Montreal Protocol on the Ozone Layer and the Basel Convention.

When a GATT country fails to follow the rules established in the GATT Articles, GATT provides dispute resolution to challenge such behavior, and allows trade sanctions when a law is found by a GATT dispute panel to be in conflict with the GATT rules unless a country withdraws such a law. Article VI establishes the rules for one GATT country to retaliate against another; and specifies the countervailing duties that can be used. These countervailing measures are based on comparison of product costs which do not take into account the extent to which environmental or worker health or safety costs have been externalized. The failure of the GATT to recognize these differences amounts to what several environmental advocates have called an "environmental subsidy" of "allowing polluters to freely appropriate and/or degrade common resources such as the air and water."[6]

While multilaterally negotiated solutions to such thorny issues as internalization of environmental costs are clearly the best option for the future, in the interim countries must have available the tools to effectively enforce their domestic environmental measures. This includes leveling the anti-competitive effect compliance with environmental, health and safety measures currently has on domestic industry by considering differences in production process as part of "like product" definition and putting in place differential tariffs or taxes or subsidies for affected domestic industry. Additionally, in the absence of multilateral environmental agreements, countries must maintain their ability to promote the protection of extra-territorial resources and the environment by limiting access to their markets of goods that would undermine such protection.

The original 1947 GATT contained less than 60 pages. The Final Draft Act for the Uruguay Round contains over 500 pages and the complete NAFTA text is over 1000 pages. These lengthy documents contain the numerous specific rules applying the general principles laid out in the GATT articles to different issues and circumstances.

Historically, trade negotiations and trade disputes addressed matters, such as tariffs, that seemed purely economic in nature. Now, under the concept of "non-tariff trade barriers," trade agreements have begun to focus more directly on legitimate health, safety and environmental measures that have impacts on trade. Non-tariff barrier is a trade term of art that technically means any measure that restricts trade, such as a quota, that is not a tariff. In recent years, trade officials have begun to view many environmental, health and safety measures such as restrictions on foods containing pesticide residues or hormones that restrict access to a domestic market as non-tariff barriers.

For example, the Tokyo Round of GATT, which concluded in 1979, developed the Agreement on Technical Barriers to Trade to extend GATT disciplines to product standards, testing, labeling, and packaging schemes, including those designed to protect health, safety, or the environment. Similarly, in recent years, many countries have invoked the GATT and the United States-Canada Free Trade Agreement to call into question such health and environmental laws as restrictions on cigarette advertising and promotion, a ban on smokeless tobacco products, a phase-out of asbestos, a ban on hormone-treated beef, and fuel economy standards.[7] Both the NAFTA and the Uruguay Round negotiations continue this trend in the development of provisions under which domestic environmental, health and safety regulations may be challenged in trade agreement dispute resolution as nontariff trade barriers.

Some Environmental and Health Implications of the Uruguay Round Negotiations of GATT

On Dec. 20, 1991, GATT Director-General Arthur Dunkel released a comprehensive Draft Uruguay Round Final Act Text which contained supposedly final negotiated text for every subject in the Uruguay Round. Public Citizen, a Washington, D.C.-based consumer advocacy group, has focussed mainly on three issues in the Uruguay Round text—consumer and environmental standards, the establishment of a new global commerce agency called the Multilateral Trade Organization (MTO), and dispute resolution. A brief discussion of these limited issues shows more clearly the implications of the current trade negotiation on environmental and consumer policy.

There are many other important issues and problems with the Uruguay Round text, including: the environmental implications of its macroeconomic effects and incentives, the detrimental effect on sustainable resource management of its terms, the effect on sustainable agriculture of its inclusion for the first time of agricultural trade, its effect on the principles of sustainable development undermining of UNCED and its principles, the detrimental effects on biodiversity of its Intellectual Property provisions, implications for global forest protection and more.[8]

In two sections on standards called Sanitary and Phytosanitary Standards covering food, and Technical Standards covering all other issues, the Uruguay Round text promotes downwards harmonization of environmental and consumer standards. "Harmonization" is a euphemism for making consistent standards across countries so as to lubricate trade. The mechanisms in the Uruguay Round and the NAFTA designed to promote harmonization ratchet standards only in the downwards direction. Thus, standards that are "too protective" can be challenged as trade restrictions. Standards that are "too low," however, cannot be challenged as unfair trade "subsidies" on the environment. These rules in the Uruguay Round standards sections also apply to state and local law, mandating that the federal government take "affirmative action" to force states and localities to alter non GATT-compliant laws. Further, in the food standards section, environmental goals are not considered legitimate objectives for regulation. Thus, the ban on DDT residues in food, which was based more on DDT's environmental persistence and effects on other species than on direct human health effects, would not be considered to be based on a legitimate objective.

In the Sanitary and Phytosanitary section, which includes pesticide and other contaminant levels, additives, inspection, labeling, and packaging, countries are limited in the level of consumer or environmental protection they may choose. First, countries are only guaranteed the ability to maintain or establish food or environmental standards relating to agriculture or food that have the effect of limiting trade if such standards are not more protective than international standards named in the agreement. For instance, the standards of the Codex Alimentarius Commission are named in the Sanitary and Phytosanitary Standards as the international standards for food and agriculture. Codex Alimentarius Commission is a Rome-based subgroup of the U.N. Food and Agriculture Organization that is heavily influenced by the food and agribusiness industry. A 1992 GAO Report found that Codex's standards for residues of carcinogenic pesticides in food were weaker in over 50% of the instances than current U.S. standards. Currently, Codex standards are merely advisory. However under the Uruguay Round (and NAFTA), they would become the officially acceptable standards for global food and agriculture trade.

Under the Uruguay Round, national, state or local governments could maintain environmental or consumer measures relating to food and agriculture *more* protective than international standards only if such laws meet a series of highly constrictive tests. Those tests, set out in the Uruguay Round text, limit both the level of environmental or consumer protection a country may choose and the means it may apply to attain such a level of protection. These Uruguay Round rules expose to challenge many of the most fundamental environmental and consumer protection laws now in existence on the federal and state levels.

Thus, under the Uruguay Round, a country must be able to show, among several other tests, that in choosing a level of protection, standards:

- are based on a vague amount of science, thus threatening laws which get ahead of scientific certainty, such as preventive measures taken under the precautionary principle;
- are not maintained "against available scientific evidence," meaning that one contrary industry-financed study could set off a battle of the scientists over the continued legitimacy of a standard;
- are based on risk assessment that balances trade effects with health objectives, thus eliminating the right to take measures on the basis of a policy determination (such as the food safety law called the Delaney Clause based on a Congressional decision in the 1970s to allow no carcinogens in the food supply) and on the basis of popular referenda;
- do not cause a different level of risk than chosen in other regulatory circum-

stance, meaning that a difference in the level of risk for carcinogenic pesticide residues and level of risk for salmonella in raw foods could provide a basis for challenge.

In choosing the means to achieve that chosen level of protection, a country is limited to use only a measure that:

- is least trade restrictive, regardless of political or practical consideration for why another means is more appropriate;
- has no extraterritorial implications; and
- is not based on distinction in manufacturing or harvesting procedures.

Second, for the many environmental and consumer laws from recycling and nonfood toxics restriction to product safety rules that would be covered by the Technical Barriers text, countries must use international standards unless there are fundamental climactic or geographic reasons not to. Such standards must also be proved to be the less trade restrictive means to a GATT-legitimate objective.

Third, GATT dispute resolution has been dramatically amended through the Uruguay Round to increase the power GATT has to force compliance by member countries to GATT rules. The Uruguay Round continues the system of empowering a three person panel of trade officials to conduct secret dispute hearings to decide if a challenged law complies with GATT rules. However, under the Uruguay Round, unless an appeal is filed or there is unanimous consensus among all GATT parties to *stop* adoption of a GATT panel ruling within 60 days, panel rulings are automatically adopted.[9] If an appeal is taken, 30 days after the decision is published it is automatically adopted, unless there is unanimous consensus to stop it. This is a major change from current GATT dispute resolution procedure, which although troubling, at least has a built-in "emergency brake" of sorts in that all dispute resolution panels had to be approved by unanimous consensus to be binding. Under current GATT rules and under the Uruguay Round, countries that have lost a panel ruling must either comply with the panel's recommendations by eliminating or changing the GATT-inconsistent law or face trade sanctions.

Finally, in what may be its most disturbing provisions, the Uruguay Round would greatly enhance the power of the global trade rules by establishing a new global commerce agency called the Multilateral Trade Organization (MTO) to enforce them. This new body, which is tucked into the last pages of the 500-page Uruguay Round proposal, would have "legal personality" like the United Nations, and unlike the current GATT. The proposed MTO would have as its rules GATT updated through the Uruguay Round, including the General Agreement on Trade in Services (GATS) and the Agreement on Trade Related Intellectual Property (TRIPs). The MTO proposal requires nations to cede substantial sovereignty, for instance requiring MTO member nations to "take all necessary steps, where changes to domestic laws will be required to implement the provisions . . . to ensure conformity of their law with these Agreements." Despite this great power boost, the MTO proposal contains no provisions to safeguard environmental or consumer protections or to promote sustainable investment or use of natural resources. The MTO provides greatly enhanced enforcement of bad GATT rules. Without fundamental reforms to the procedural and substantive principles and Articles of GATT itself, granting additional power to such a trade body certainly is not merited.

Finally, nothing is done in the Uruguay Round text to "fix" the damage done to GATT Article XX by the tuna-dolphin panel decision, and in fact some of the worst aspects of the decision are incorporated in the Uruguay Round Standards provisions.

In summary, the Uruguay Round Final Act text is not acceptable from an environmental and consumer health and safety standpoint. The text was rejected by 29 national environmental, consumer, conservation and animal welfare groups in January 1992. These groups called for Congress to reject the text if it were brought up for approval. (See Appendix.)

The Clinton Administration has the opportunity to address the many flaws of the Uruguay Round, but must make clear now that they do not intend to accept a Uruguay Round unless the environmental, consumer and democracy flaws are repaired. Unfortunately, the Administration does not seem to be taking this course. Rather, the Administration has asked Congress for a relatively short five month period of fast track extension to complete the Uruguay Round. This timeline suggests that the Administration will proceed on the basis of the fundamentally flawed Dunkel text with minimal changes. This notion has also been confirmed by recent statements of USTR Mickey Kantor. Kantor has been quoted in the press recently admitting that major changes including those on the environment will have to wait until after the Uruguay Round. Unfortunately, adoption of the Dunkel Uruguay Round text would fundamentally undermine environmental and consumer health and safety goals, as well as democratic decision-making and sovereignty. Dealing with these vital issues after adoption of the Uruguay Round text would be like conducting major reconstructive surgery on someone in an irreversible coma.

Some Environmental and Health Implications of the NAFTA

As with the Uruguay Round, Public Citizen mainly has focussed on two issues in the NAFTA negotiations—consumer and environmental standards and dispute resolution. However, the NAFTA also would impact many other vital environmental and consumer issues, some of which are touched upon below.[10]

Unfortunately, both in what it contains and what it omits, the September 6, 1992 text of the North American Free Trade Agreement is not good news for environmental or consumer health and safety protection. The terms of the NAFTA text expose numerous existing U.S. federal, state and local environmental and consumer laws to challenge as nontariff trade barriers under chapters on Sanitary and Phytosanitary Standards and Technical Standards. The standards provisions also create downward pressure on industrial and agricultural worker safety standards in the United States. The exact terms of the NAFTA standards sections are somewhat less draconian than those in the GATT, a situation many attribute to the sharp and continual criticism of the Uruguay Round text by environmental and consumer groups and their allies in Congress. However, the same core principles apply in the NAFTA which, for instance, also lists Codex as the official standard for food trade, and requires that higher standards pass certain tests concerning both the level of protection and means of accomplishing that protection.

Further, NAFTA would promote environmentally unsound commercial activity in the areas of agriculture, energy and in the incentives it creates for manufacturers to relocate to Mexico to avoid strict enforcement of environmental regulation. All of these problems are intensified by the absence in the NAFTA of any enforcement or funding provisions for environmental protection. Moreover, the NAFTA text establishes highly secretive negotiation and dispute resolution processes that deny citizen oversight of NAFTA on vital concerns such as food safety, consumer product standards, and environmental regulations on hazardous substances. NAFTA dispute resolution procedures are like those of the Uruguay Round, except that the panels of trade officials include five members instead of three.

The NAFTA text that President Bush signed on December 18, 1992 simply does not measure up to the consensus position on minimal environmental safeguards signed by 40 U.S., Mexican and Canadian environmental and consumer groups presented to the Bush Administration in May 1992.

The environmental shortcomings of the NAFTA were identified by President Clinton during his campaign in an October 3, 1992 speech on NAFTA. Then-candidate Clinton endorsed the NAFTA, but stated that without several supplemental agreements and other improvements, the NAFTA would not be a good deal for most citizens in the three NAFTA countries. Shortly after taking office, the Clinton Administration set into motion a process to negotiate supplemental agreements.

On March 5, 1993, 25 U.S. national environmental, consumer, conservation, animal protection and sustainable agriculture groups, including Public Citizen, Sierra Club, Greenpeace, Friends of the Earth, and the Humane Society of the U.S., sent a joint letter to U.S. Trade Representative Mickey Kantor laying out in detail both what was missing from the NAFTA from an environmental, conservation, health and safety viewpoint and what fundamental problems were contained in the existing NAFTA text. Following is a summary of that letter.

ENFORCEMENT

The Group of 25 argued that trade should not be based on weak enforcement of established standards. U.S. citizens should not be subjected to economic, health, safety, or environmental injury as a result of weak enforcement of standards elsewhere. Nor should our NAFTA partners be harmed by a failure of U.S. enforcement. The Group of 25 called for the availability of sanctions, including both trade and nontrade measures, to ensure compliance. Recognizing that sovereignty concerns existed, we proposed a trilateral mechanism that had some similarities to the North

American Commission on the Environment (NACE) that the Clinton Administration was exploring. The idea of the commission would be to provide a mechanism for investigation, using subpoena or other similar powers to gather information, of lack of enforcement of domestic environmental laws that have transboundary effects, exist in the global commons, or have competitive effects. As well, the Group of 25 wanted the commission to provide a non-secretive panel of environmental and health experts to consider all NAFTA disputes involving environmental or consumer health or safety issues.

ENVIRONMENTAL REMEDIATION

Despite the fact that the several border agreements between the NAFTA parties have been considered separate from the present NAFTA, the Group of 25 did not believe that NAFTA should go forward until enforceable commitments have been made to clean up the border regions. Estimates for the U.S.-Mexico border clean-up range from $5 to 15 billion. The U.S.-Canada border also suffers from trade induced problems.

FUNDING

The Group of 25 felt that a secure source of funding for proper infrastructure development, environmental enforcement, increased investigation, and clean-up for all NAFTA-related environmental programs was vital. Because national appropriations processes do not provide a secure source of funding, we argued that designated funding sources, based on fairness and the "polluter pays" principle, must be developed as a prerequisite to implementation of NAFTA. Ideas that the Group of 25 felt deserved attention included: a) "snap-back" tariffs applied to sectors with lax enforcement of existing standards; b) a small transaction fee on all goods and services that could be phased out over a specified number of years; c) a directed "green" fee; d) an environmental countervailing duty on economic activity that is environmentally unsustainable or below standard; e) "earmarked" tariffs, which could be phased out during the first 10–15 years of NAFTA; and f) development of a "green investment bank," which could utilize established trust funds to leverage additional money through bond proposals. Regardless of which funding scheme(s) is eventually utilized, we believe it is imperative to channel such funds back into environmental infrastructure improvements, enforcement, border inspection, worker transition programs, certain farmer support programs, and funding of the NACE itself.

PUBLIC PARTICIPATION AND TRANSPARENCY

Public accountability of governing bodies is an essential element of environmental and consumer protection and democratic governance. Accountability includes the rights of notice, comment, the opportunity to participate, the ability to bring complaints, and access to decision-making processes. For the NAFTA package to address these serious concerns, the Group of 25 felt that the process of crafting any supplemental agreement must provide public accountability, and the protocol itself must ensure accountability in the administration and implementation of any NAFTA package.

The current NAFTA dispute panel provisions completely fail to provide citizens from the NAFTA countries with the means to obtain information from, and participate in, resolution of trade disputes concerning environmental, conservation, health, and safety matters. The Group of 25 insisted that any supplemental NAFTA agreement must provide the public with participatory rights in whatever forum ultimately resolves trade/environmental disputes under a NAFTA. Furthermore, any NAFTA package must ensure that the public can participate meaningfully in the remaining negotiations of NAFTA. Prior NAFTA negotiations failed to provide the public with sufficient participatory rights, resulting in the deficiencies outlined in the Group of 25 letter.

INTERNATIONAL AND DOMESTIC
PRODUCTION/PROCESS (PPM) STANDARDS

The Group of 25 argued that trade law must recognize that how a product is produced is as important as the quality of the product itself. Only by recognizing process-based trade restrictions will governments retain their ability to keep high domestic standards without placing domestic producers at a competitive disadvantage. Although Article XX of GATT provides for health and natural resource conservation exceptions, these provisions have been constricted by recent GATT panel decisions. Without explicit clarification, the Group of 25 felt that NAFTA would repeat the mistake of the GATT panels and the Dunkel Uruguay Round text by incorporating unacceptable provisions or interpretations of GATT. For example, laws that would restrict the import of products made with CFCs, timber produced in an unsustainable fashion, or that penalize the inhumane treatment of animals could be subject to challenge under the current NAFTA.

STANDARDS

A formal trading relationship between countries with significantly different environmental standards possesses predictable tensions. On the one hand, a country with high standards does not want its environmental quality or economic competitiveness to suffer as a result of weak (or nonexistent) standards elsewhere. On the other hand, a country with lower standards does not want its sovereignty infringed upon by other countries. The Group of 25 argued that no NAFTA party's environmental, health, or safety standards should be weakened by NAFTA, and the NAFTA package should encourage, rather than inhibit, the ability of any NAFTA party to raise standards. In addition, the full jurisdictional range of each party's domestic standard-setting abilities must be protected, such as proposals to prevent the export of domestically prohibited or restricted products (e.g., pesticides).

The Group of 25 believed that the test for environmental, conservation, health, and safety standards should be the same as for other NAFTA provisions—national treatment and nondiscrimination. NAFTA's standards provisions must not provide a mechanism to challenge another country's chosen level of environmental, conservation, health or safety protection, nor the means chosen to achieve such protection if the means is facially non-discriminatory in intent.

NAFTA's two chapters specifically covering standards, Sanitary and Phytosanitary Standards (SPS) and Technical Barriers to Trade (TBT), contain ambiguous and contradictory language, and may be interpreted to encourage harmonization towards generally lower international norms. The current TBT and SPS texts set up numerous committees with broad policy jurisdiction, and establish detailed procedures for "conformity assessment" and other harmonization mechanisms. The Group of 25 argued that standard-setting is a matter for local, state, and national democratic bodies, and should be subject to trade disciplines only when there exists a discriminatory intent. To the extent that such committees and standard-setting procedures will exist in a NAFTA, the SPS and TBT texts must be supplemented and clarified to ensure openness, mechanisms for public participation and oversight, and participation of environmental, health, and safety experts.

The Group of 25 also argued that NAFTA must be repaired to assure that the role of "science" as a necessary basis for standards-setting is not an absolute prerequisite to the adoption and implementation of standards. Standards based, for instance, on the precautionary principle or on consumer preference must be allowed, so long as their intent is transparent and facially non-discriminatory. Similarly, standards not based on risk assessment, like referendums and "zero-risk" standards, must not be challengeable by NAFTA. We argued that a NAFTA package must also make clear the ability of countries to maintain more than one level of acceptable risk. Further, the role of international standard-setting bodies must be only advisory.

In addition the NAFTA standards sections threaten to expose legitimate environmental, conservation, health, and safety protections to attack as trade barriers on the basis of how a particular level of protection is implemented. The Group of 25 thus argued that the NAFTA text must be clarified so that a non-discriminatory measure will not be held to violate NAFTA because some less NAFTA-inconsistent measure may conceptually exist, a measure has extrajurisdictional implications, or is based on process distinctions.

Finally, the protections afforded by the wide range of standards applicable in the NAFTA countries can only be as strong as the commitment of the NAFTA parties to effectively monitor, inspect, and enforce these standards. For example, with the increased movement of products expected from NAFTA, the Group of 25 argued that the U.S. will need to implement new inspection mechanisms to ensure that meat and livestock imported from Mexico and Canada meet all applicable U.S. standards.

IMPACT ON STATE AND LOCAL LAWS

Because states and localities are not parties to NAFTA, they cannot directly defend their standards. Although the federal government is allowed to set standards it deems "appropriate" in accordance with the terms of NAFTA, states and localities do not explicitly possess this right, and are thus dependent upon the federal government for defense. Furthermore, NAFTA Article 105 states, all parties "shall ensure that all necessary measures are taken in order to give effect to the provisions of this agreement . . . by state and local governments." This situation will have a chilling effect upon progressive sub-federal legislation that often drives effective federal action. Thus, the Group of 25 argued that any NAFTA package must provide sub-federal governments standing and a major role in NAFTA disputes. It must also assure the ability of sub-federal governments to establish initiatives that exceed federal and international standards.

INVESTMENT

Although Article 1114 of the existing NAFTA recognizes "that it is inappropriate to encourage investment by relaxing domestic health, safety or environmental measures," it does nothing to actually prevent such an occurrence. No NAFTA country should become a "pollution haven" for unscrupulous investors, American or otherwise. The United States, for example, frequently applies limitations to investment, domestically and abroad, for important political and national security reasons; that definition must now be broadened to include ecological security. The Group of 25 argued that a NAFTA package must provide a means, including for instance offsetting tariffs to make "polluters pay," so that environmental, health, and safety costs are fully internalized. Moreover, NAFTA's investment provisions should permit access to dispute settlement as a means of preventing environmentally damaging investment.

INTERNATIONAL AGREEMENTS

At present, only three multilateral environmental agreements are given some *limited* measure of protection under NAFTA: CITES, the Montreal Protocol, and the Basel Convention. The Bush Administration's defense to this limitation was that only these three agreements possess direct trade implications. Not only is this assertion false, but the logic behind the argument is also needlessly narrow. The Group of 25 argued that all NAFTA parties must possess the ability to *implement* and *enforce* any international agreement by imposing trade restrictions, if such restrictions are an effective way to secure complete compliance with the agreement in question. Therefore, we argued that *all* present and future international environmental, health, safety, animal welfare or conservation agreements, to which any NAFTA party is a signatory, should be referenced in the protocol and added to Article 104.

AGRICULTURE

NAFTA, as written, threatens the survival of family farmers who have the most experience and potential to be good stewards of the land and provide safe, nutritious food for our country. If agricultural production is to be put on a sustainable footing (e.g., decreased production on marginal land and the use of fewer chemicals), then environmental and social costs must be internalized. This will not happen if family farmers have to compete with cheaper imports produced in less sustainable ways.

The Group of 25 argued that NAFTA must preserve the capacity to employ supply management as a policy tool to promote sustainability. This capacity has been seriously undermined by NAFTA's tariffication of quantitative import controls, including Section 22 of the Agricultural Adjustment Act and the Meat Import Act. We therefore proposed that the tariffication provision be altered through the supplemental agreement to allow for import controls on supply-managed crops and to create the possibility for the future supply management of crops not currently in the program.

CONSERVATION ISSUES

The Group of 25 argued that a NAFTA package must not allow or encourage natural resources such as water, forests, and the diversity of species to be unsustainably consumed or harmed. If countries are to develop and implement sustainable natural resource management programs, they must possess unfettered authority to regulate resource extraction. Of critical importance is the power to determine whether, and under what terms, a NAFTA party's resources may be exploited for export markets. Under NAFTA, particularly Articles 309 and 316, the sovereignty of countries to regulate the export of natural resources is severely curtailed. In fact, Article 316 goes much further than GATT by assuring perpetual access to other party's resources, notwithstanding domestic shortages, for as long as those resources last. A particularly serious problem in this regard is the prospect that NAFTA could be used to compel major interbasin transfers of water despite existing water management regimes. Thus we argued that NAFTA must be supplemented explicitly to provide that all parties possess unfettered authority to embargo natural resource exports for legitimate conservation ends.

A related problem centers upon the impact of NAFTA's intellectual property framework on efforts to protect the biological diversity of this continent's ecosystems. The Group of 25 argued that a NAFTA package must ensure that equal protection be afforded to both the "stewards" or "owners" of biological resources, including indigenous and minority peoples, as well as to patent holders.

To help deal with wildlife habitat conservation in particular, we proposed that the Convention on Nature Protection and Wildlife Preservation in the Western Hemisphere be revitalized and specifically linked to NAFTA so that acceding countries to NAFTA make specific accommodations to habitat protection within their borders.

GOVERNMENT PROCUREMENT

The use of preferential purchasing policies is an important tool that has been used by governments at all levels to create markets for, and encourage the development of, green technology and environmentally sound products. Under Chapter 10 of NAFTA, such green procurement initiatives are vulnerable to challenge. For instance, under the CUSFTA, Canadian paper manufacturers have argued they possess a trade claim on the basis of recycled paper content requirements by U.S. governments. Thus, the Group of 25 argued that a NAFTA package must assure the rights of governments to implement environmental purchasing policies and practices free from the threat of trade sanctions.

THE "NECESSARY" TEST AND OTHER PROBLEMATIC NAFTA LANGUAGE

Like many other NAFTA provisions, Chapter 21's environmental "exceptions" incorporate GATT terminology and jurisprudence. Unfortunately, recent GATT panel decisions have interpreted the term *"necessary* to protect human, animal or plant life or health" as requiring "necessary" measures to be "least-GATT" or "least-trade" restrictive. Under this standard, many present federal and state measures could be found to be NAFTA-inconsistent—from bans on the trade in elephant ivory to state recycling programs. The Group of 25 argued that the environmental exceptions in NAFTA, therefore, need to be clarified and strengthened to ensure that the GATT jurisprudence does not affect the interpretation of NAFTA.

Also potentially problematic is NAFTA Article 903, which could be read to incorporate GATT provisions and jurisprudence in a way that diminishes a NAFTA country's ability to protect environmental resources. Furthermore, Annex 2004's allowance to seek dispute settlement if a party feels "any benefit it could reasonably have expected to accrue it . . . is being nullified or impaired" invites attack upon U.S. standards. Here again, the Group of 25 argued that a clarifying standard should be adopted that protects all U.S. environmental, health, and safety standards, as long as they are not arbitrary, discriminatory, or disguised trade barriers.

SUSTAINABLE DEVELOPMENT

While the Group of 25 lauded the goal of "sustainable development" in NAFTA's preamble, they argued that the goal must be made binding, and appear in Article 102's Objectives. By truly integrating the concept of sustainability into this protocol, the NAFTA parties will establish an environmental benchmark for hemispheric trade and development.

These fourteen points would effectively change the NAFTA from a purely commercial "free trade" agreement, to an environmental, health and safety neutral trade and development agreement. However, as noted above, the scope of the supplemental negotiations that President Clinton has called to "fix" the NAFTA has been very narrow. Eleven of the issues raised in the consensus letter are dead on the floor, two issues are clinging to the negotiation table by their fingernails and only one issue, the establishment of a North American Commission on the Environment, is squarely on the table.

Moreover, even the U.S. NACE proposal is minimal, with the central role of the commission being studies and public disclosure of environmental problems.

President Clinton is in an unenviable position on the NAFTA. He has inherited an agreement that is fundamentally flawed in its text, missing important aspects and reliant on the fast track mechanism for Congressional consideration that was extended on the basis of promises to the Congress that were not kept. He has promised that he will not renegotiate it.

However, unless there are major changes, the NAFTA will find almost the entire citizens movement arrayed against it.

As the following section discusses, current trade policy-making and dispute resolution procedures also conflict with the procedural values and norms of environmental, health and safety policy-making.

Secrecy

Public Citizen is striving to ensure that international trade agreements do not undercut domestic consumer protection and environmental laws. Since its founding in 1971 by Ralph Nader, Public Citizen has worked to strengthen domestic consumer and environmental protections. We have had many successes, but have faced industry groups that have fought against stronger standards and have tried to weaken the protections that are currently in place. International trade agreements are providing industry a more preferential forum in which to challenge those standards. That forum, moreover, does not afford citizens the same rights of access to information and to the decision-making processes that they have domestically.

In contrast to U.S. legislative and rule-making processes, international trade negotiations are cloaked in secrecy. The recent NAFTA negotiations are a case in point. Indeed, some Members of Congress have called the NAFTA negotiations the most secret ever.[11]

Not only do environmental and consumer advocates have no meaningful access to information as negotiations are underway, but when draft trade agreement texts are completed, they are not available to the public. Despite strenuous efforts throughout the course of the NAFTA negotiations, Public Citizen was only able to obtain one draft text and, at a different time, several draft sections when disgruntled negotiators leaked copies. Though it was officially released by GATT in Geneva in December 1991, the Uruguay Round text was not available to U.S. press until two days later. To obtain a copy of the "Dunkel" Uruguay Round Draft Final Act text in a timely manner, Public Citizen had to arrange for a copy obtained by a journalist from the GATT press office to be flown at its expense from Switzerland. Had we not made it available to the press ourselves, the coverage of the December 1991 Uruguay Round text would have been based solely on summaries provided by the Bush Administration.

In order to focus attention on flawed elements of the ongoing negotiations, Public Citizen has made available draft copies of the text whenever it has been able to obtain them. Public Citizen has received continual criticism from trade officials for making public draft texts. However, the impact of having access to such information has been demonstrated by the course of negotiations. For instance, Public Citizen obtained a copy of the NAFTA dispute resolution text which contained many of the problems environmental and consumer advocates had criticized in the Uruguay Round text. It has been suggested by trade officials sympathetic to citizens' concerns that Public Citizen's critique, which received attention in the press and in Congress, was an important reason for changes in the final NAFTA dispute resolution text which make that text, though still deeply flawed, an improvement over that of the Uruguay Round. Had environmental and consumer advocates had regular access to draft texts, it is not unreasonable to conclude that there would have been improvements during the negotiations in many of the other sections we now assert must be altered.

Trade Advisory Committees: Special Industry Access, Limited Public Interest Access

Industry has much greater access to information about trade negotiations and input into the negotiation process than environmental and consumer advocates through membership on numerous governmental advisory committees. The Advisory Committee for Trade Policy and Negotiations, as well as more than 30 other industry policy, sectoral, and functional committees that advise USTR on trade negotiations, have access to inside government information about the overall negotiating objectives and positions of the United States, and their effects, even where such information is classified, contains trade secrets, or is otherwise confidential.[12] Until recently, none of these advisory committees had any representation of public health, consumer, or environmental interests. Rather, they had been comprised entirely of industry representatives, with the exception of an occasional representative of a labor organization and one free-standing labor advisory committee.

Public Citizen conducted a study in 1991 to analyze the environmental records and political positions on environmental issues of the industry representatives to three of the trade advisory groups with jurisdiction most directly relating to environmental, health and safety issues.[13] The study used computer data bases available from the Environmental Protection Agency on industry violations and government enforcement actions, reports of other nongovernmental groups on pollution emissions, and federal and state legislative histories to cross a list of environmental "bad actors" with the memberships on the selected committees. Public Citizen learned that the members of the advisory groups with greatest influence on environmental and consumer health and safety issues in trade negotiations had among the worst environmental records within U.S. industry. For instance, five members of the advisory committees are listed in EPA's 1989 Toxic Release Inventory database as ranking among the 10 biggest dischargers of hazardous waste in America: Du Pont, the biggest polluter in America; Monsanto, the second biggest; 3M, the sixth biggest; General Motors, the eighth biggest; and Eastman Kodak, the ninth biggest.[14] Similarly, as of January 1, 1990, 50 companies (or their affiliates) represented in the advisory committees, nearly half of all trade advisors in the study, were listed as Potentially Responsible Parties for hazardous waste dumps on the EPA's Superfund List. Although more than one company may share responsibility for polluting a Superfund site, each of these 50 offenders is at least partially responsible for an average of more than 11 different Superfund sites.[15]

In response to public and congressional objections at this skewed representation expressed during the 1991 debate over extending fast-track authority, the Bush Administration appointed representatives of environmental organizations to five trade advisory committees. The five organizations appointed had been neutral towards or supportive of Bush Administration trade policy; groups such as the Sierra Club, Friends of the Earth, and Greenpeace who had been involved in the issue but more critical of Bush trade policy were excluded. No representatives of consumer or health organizations were named. The remaining twenty-plus committees still lack any environmental, consumer, or public health representation. Moreover, the five individuals who serve on the trade advisory committees are prevented by secrecy rules from sharing any of the information that they gain through their service on the committees, even with their own staffs.

Given that more than 800 industry representatives serve on these com-

mittees, while only five environmental representatives do, industry interests have obtained more information about the NAFTA and Uruguay
Round negotiations, and have obviously had far greater opportunities to
provide input into those negotiations than the few environmental representatives. Moreover, it should be noted that John Adams, Executive
Director of the Natural Resources Defense Council, the environmental representative to one advisory group, the Services Policy Advisory
Committee, issued a dissenting opinion from that committee's endorsement of the NAFTA, based on his opinion that the NAFTA did not adequately address key environmental concerns.

Public Citizen has formally requested the United States Trade Representative's Office to make additional appointments of consumer, health
and environmental representatives to the trade advisory committees.[16] But
the Office took the position that no such representation is legally required,
and it has thus refused to make any additional appointments. Virtually all
of the meetings of the trade advisory committees are held in closed session,
and the Office routinely withholds their records from the public. The secrecy that pervades the trade advisory process cuts the public out of the establishment of standards that may dictate the future viability of U.S. environmental, health and safety standards.

Fast Track Limits Congress's Role

The fast-track approval process limits Congress's ability to scrutinize and
modify trade agreements. Thus, under fast-track procedures, no amendments to the implementing legislation or the trade agreement are permitted,[17] debate in either House is limited to not more than 20 hours,[18] and a
floor vote must be taken within 60 to 90 legislative days of the submission
of the agreement to Congress.[19] In other words, the implementing legislation must be adopted by a "yes" or "no" vote within 60 to 90 legislative
days of its submission by the President.

The current five year fast-track authority established in the 1988 Om-
nibus Trade and Competitiveness Act expires on June 1, 1993. The Clinton Administration announced its intent to request new fast-track authority from Congress almost immediately after the inauguration. A formal
request for a fast-track extension for the Uruguay Round through December 1993 was transmitted to Congress in April 1993. That request was

tucked into the massive Budget Reconciliation Bill in the House Ways and Means Committee and was passed out of committee and thrown onto the House floor as part of the 100-plus-page budget bill. As of May 1993, the Senate has not yet passed the Uruguay Round fast track. The Administration is expected to ask for additional fast-track authority to begin extending NAFTA throughout South America if the NAFTA is successfully completed.

Public Citizen is opposed to fast track on principle because of its anti-democratic nature.[20] The fundamental democracy deficit of fast track is made most relevant by the expansion of trade negotiations into the very policy areas—environmental and consumer protection—in which wide public participation and involvement have been most beneficial.

USTR Refuses to Prepare Environmental Impact Statements

The Office of the U.S. Trade Representative has refused to prepare environmental impact statements for trade agreements, even though such statements have been prepared for many domestic matters that will be undermined by the agreements, and for other international agreements, such as the Panama Canal Treaty and the Montreal Protocol on Depletion of the Ozone Layer. The Clinton Administration has not shown that it will reverse the policy of arguing that NEPA does not apply to international trade.

Public Citizen, on behalf of itself, the Sierra Club, and Friends of the Earth initiated a suit to compel compliance of USTR with the National Environmental Policy Act (NEPA), which requires Environmental Impact Statements for all major federal action affecting the environment or health.[21] Our initial NEPA suit was held not to be ripe because trade negotiations had not been completed for the NAFTA and Uruguay Round.[22] We refiled our case limited to NAFTA immediately after the NAFTA negotiations were completed.[23] That case awaits argument in the District Court for the District of Columbia.

USTR's refusal to prepare an environmental impact statement on the NAFTA has deprived the public and the Congress of an objective analysis of NAFTA's environmental effects. What the negotiators have conveyed has been one-sided, political endorsement of the Agreement designed to conceal any of its adverse environmental or health consequences. A super-ficial analysis of environmental effects of the NAFTA prepared by the Bush Administration in response to Congressional pressure failed to meet the requirements of NEPA.[24] Additionally, the Bush Administration's "Review of U.S.-Mexico Environmental Issues" was premised on the as-sumption that there would be little relocation of U.S. companies to Mex-ico because of the NAFTA. Thus, the conclusion of the report predictably was that environmental impacts of NAFTA would not be great.

While many nongovernmental organizations have done detailed analy-sis of the possible environmental, health and safety effects of both NAFTA and the Uruguay Round Draft Final Act Text, the government has avail-able the information and analytical resources to study such impacts most comprehensively. Without such full analysis, Congress will be asked to vote to approve these agreements without benefit of basic, vital informa-tion on their environmental, health and safety impacts.

NAFTA and GATT Disputed Resolution Weighted Against Environmental and Consumer Interests[25]

Trade challenges will be resolved in a dispute settlement system that con-trasts sharply with the open administrative and judicial systems for resolv-ing challenges to food safety measures domestically. Both the NAFTA and the proposed Uruguay Round dispute settlement processes can give rise to automatic trade sanctions, if the parties do not agree on how to resolve the dispute in light of the panel's decision.[26] In contrast to the current dispute resolution provisions of GATT, no separate authorization for trade sanc-tions is required to permit a party to impose such sanctions under the NAFTA and Uruguay Round proposals. These trade sanctions may con-tinue until an agreement is reached on a resolution of the dispute, which will, in all likelihood, place pressure on the losing party to change the of-fending measure.

Both the Uruguay Round and NAFTA mandate that the dispute set-tlement process be conducted in secret. Thus, NAFTA provides that the "panel's hearings, deliberations and initial report, and all written submis-sions to and communications with the panel shall be confidential."[27] The Uruguay Round Final Act Text states, "written memorandum . . . shall be considered confidential . . . Panel deliberations shall be secret . . ."[28] Moreover, in NAFTA, the panel is prohibited from disclosing which panelists are associated with majority and minority opinions.[29]

This secrecy prevents domestic proponents of health and environmental measures that are being challenged from obtaining sufficient information about the proceeding to provide input into it. Such individuals are not permitted to participate in the proceeding as parties or *amici*. As a result, the only way that they can provide input is by giving it to the country defending the measure. However, if they are kept uninformed as to the arguments being made, the timing of the submissions, and possibly even the fact of the dispute, they cannot provide that input to their government. Moreover, such individuals cannot determine whether their government is mounting a strong legal defense of the measure, nor can they put pressure on their government to make a stronger showing, without access to its submissions.

When Public Citizen has sought access to the United States' submissions to GATT dispute panels under the Freedom of Information Act, the Office refused to release them until after the proceeding had concluded. In Public Citizen's challenge to the Office's refusal to make such submissions immediately available to the public, the district court held that the Office's practice was illegal because it was not mandated by the GATT itself.[30] The NAFTA would likely preclude the United States from making its own submissions available to the public under existing domestic access laws.

International trade dispute bodies have traditionally been composed of trade specialists who view domestic environmental and health measures with suspicion. The NAFTA charges Parties with establishing a roster by consensus of individuals who "have expertise or experience in law, international trade, other matters covered by this Agreement, or the resolution of disputes arising under international trade agreements."[31] The Uruguay Round lists the qualifications of panelists as, "persons who have served on or presented a case to a GATT panel, served as a representative to the GATT or in the GATT Secretariat, taught or published in international trade law . . ."[32] It is theoretically possible for an environmental lawyer with expertise in the Montreal Protocol or a consumer advocate with expertise in food safety law to be placed on one of these rosters. However, that is unlikely since the roster is drawn up for trade disputes generally and the countries would be more likely to select trade experts, in the tradition of the past GATT and U.S.-Canada Free Trade Agreement panels. Moreover, since under NAFTA panelists selected from outside the roster may be vetoed by the other Party to the dispute, an environmental or food safety advocate would be unlikely to be selected to serve on a panel dealing with their areas of expertise.[33] In addition, although NAFTA panelists are required to comply with a code of conduct to be established in the future by the North American Free Trade Commission,[34] there are no requirements in the NAFTA that the code of conduct limit or require disclosure of panelists' conflicts of interest or other significant biases.

Trade tribunals have historically lacked the ability to obtain the expertise necessary to address complex scientific determinations relating to health and environmental measures. The NAFTA specifically allows with the permission of all Parties, but does not require, panels to seek information and technical advice from outside individuals and bodies.[35] Because this is optional, rather than mandatory, it does not ensure that the panels can obtain the needed expertise through this device. The Uruguay Round similarly allows, but does not require, such consultation.[36]

The NAFTA also permits a panel to request a report of a science board on factual issues concerning environmental, health, safety or other scientific matters raised in a trade dispute.[37] Again, the panel *may*, but is not required to seek such a report, even if one of the disputing parties requests it. Moreover, the disputing parties may disapprove such a request, in which case the panel may not seek such a report. The ability of a panel to seek such a report is further limited by the requirement that it address factual issues only. This may limit a panel's ability to seek a report on the effectiveness of various means of regulating a particular matter. Moreover, NAFTA Article 2015(2) requires that the science review board be composed of independent experts, but it contains no guarantees that the board will be balanced in terms of the viewpoints or backgrounds of the members. Finally, it is unclear what is meant by the requirement that the panel shall take the board's report, along with the parties' comments on it, into account in preparing its own decision.[38] The Uruguay Round Draft Final Text does not contain any related provision.

The NAFTA dispute settlement provisions provide that a country whose measures are challenged may elect to have certain disputes that arise under both NAFTA and GATT resolved under NAFTA.[39] This right exists with respect to actions subject to international environmental agreements incorporated into NAFTA Article 104, which is essential to give NAFTA Article 104 meaning, since the GATT does not protect trade measures taken under such agreements. This right also extends to food safety and technical measures adopted to protect health or the environment, where the dispute raises factual issues concerning the environment, health, safety, or conservation. It is not clear the extent to which this reference to factual issues will limit the range of food safety and technical disputes that must be resolved under NAFTA, and the effect such a limitation will have. However, for non-factual issues arising under the named provisions, as well as for trade challenges involving environmental and consumer protections that are not covered by the noted chapters, the challenger has the right to decide whether the dispute will be resolved under the GATT or the NAFTA, and presumably in most cases, the challenger will opt for the GATT, because it has fewer safeguards than the NAFTA for such measures and no mechanism for obtaining scientific input.

As this discussion shows, the international trade system is poorly suited to address environmental health and safety policy. Its secrecy deprives the public of meaningful input into the process, while at the same time, industry has secret, inside influence. This imbalance is amplified by the limited role given Congress under the fast-track procedure. The negotiators and dispute settlement bodies have an inherent bias against environmental, health and safety measures, which are viewed as restraints of trade. For these reasons, the United States must not allow the international trade system to restrict its authority to establish environmental, health and safety protections that respond to current needs and whatever problems arise in the future.

Recommendations for Neutralizing the Detrimental Impacts of Current Trade Policy on Environmental, Health and Safety Protections

An NGO consensus is building about the best strategy for dealing with the intersection of environmental and consumer policy and trade policy. Most simply, the idea is to neutralize trade policy's detrimental effects, rather than trying to shape international trade agreements to directly accomplish environmental or consumer protection goals. Thus, below are listed some of the recommendations provided to the Clinton Administration by a variety of citizens groups. If these changes were put into place in both the NAFTA and the Uruguay Round, countries would be free to establish, maintain, and effectively enforce environmental and consumer laws on the local, state, federal and international level that would be out of the grasp of contradicting trade disciplines. Similar citizens' amendments are also desperately needed to deal with the fundamental labor, agricultural and other problems in the Uruguay Round and the NAFTA.

A. GENERAL RECOMMENDATIONS

1. *Procedural Safeguards*

- Conduct Environmental Impact Statements for all trade agreements, as required by the National Environmental Policy Act.
- Develop a Code of Ethics for U.S. trade negotiators which would pertain to U.S.T.R. and any other government officials involved in trade policy.
- Open trade negotiations and dispute processes to the sunshine of public oversight by creating processes through which citizens can access information.
- Allow increased participation of citizen representatives throughout the trade policy-making and dispute settlement processes.
- Provide mechanisms for citizen enforcement of environmental, health and other social laws against U.S. corporations doing business in other countries by establishing citizen standing in trade dispute mechanisms. Enact a Foreign Environmental Practices Act compelling U.S.-based corporate operations in other nations to follow U.S. environmental standards.
- Step up border food inspection of produce, meats, dairy and poultry.

2. *Make Dispute Resolution More Open, More Fair, and More Sensitive to Consumers and the Environment*

- Ensure the burden of proof in trade challenges is on the challenging party.
- Limit the role of science to informing the political decisions of risk management.
- Establish a separate dispute resolution mechanism outside of GATT for environmental and consumer cases which would provide procedural and substantive rules favorable to environmental and health goals.

B. NAFTA RECOMMENDATIONS

See summary of the Group of 25 letter on NAFTA above.

C. GATT RECOMMENDATIONS

Following are some of our GATT recommendations. We strongly believe that the Uruguay Round should not go forward until its threats to environmental and consumer protection are neutralized.

1. *Improve Environmental, Health, and Safety Protection*

Establish the ability for countries to establish, maintain, enforce or raise their environmental or consumer protections by:

- Changing the general exception clauses in GATT Article XX and the definition of "like product" in the context of Article I Most Favored National treatment specifically to allow consideration of how a product is processed in determining the legitimacy of import restrictions. The Uruguay Round Sanitary Phytosanitary Standards and Technical Standards texts must also be modified to allow distinctions based on non–product-related processes.

- Changing the general exception clauses of Article XX, Article VI, and the Uruguay Round Sanitary Phytosanitary Standards and Technical Standards texts to specifically allow long term export and import limitations for environmental, health and safety purposes.

- Changing the general exception clauses of Article XX and the Uruguay Round Sanitary Phytosanitary Standards and Technical Standards texts specifically to allow extraterritorial application of environmental, health and safety measures as long as they are facially nondiscriminatory in intent.

- Bringing the general test for environmental, health and safety laws that limit trade into line with general trade theories of nondiscrimination and national treatment so that the applicable test is simply whether such measures are facially nondiscriminatory in intent.

- Making clear the limitations in the role of science merely to informing the political decisions of risk management. The Uruguay Round must specifically allow environmental and consumer health and safety standards based on referendum or consumer preference in accord with the precautionary principle.

- Ensuring that trade agreements meet the objective of sustainable development, including allowance for limitations on natural resource trade and biodiversity protections.

2. *Procedural Safeguards*

- De-link the MTO proposal from the Uruguay Round.

- Renegotiate a new multilateral trading system through procedures that

guarantee openness and a role, as members of country delegations, for the non-governmental organizations representing citizens around the world.
• Begin national political debate to approve membership in any new global trading organization. For the United States, the decision to join such a new organization should be given treaty treatment, including two-thirds majority vote in the Senate.
• Place jurisdiction over issues of trade and the environment and trade's conflicts with other social and health measures with the existing U.N. agencies which encompass values beyond trade liberalization, such as UNCED and UNEP.

3. *Make Dispute Resolution More Open, More Fair, and More Sensitive to Consumers and the Environment*
• Modify the Uruguay Round Sanitary and Phytosanitary and Technical Standards sections to make clear that the burden of proof in trade challenges is on the challenging party. This should also be made clear in the Uruguay Round dispute resolution provisions.
• Establish a separate dispute resolution mechanism outside of GATT for environmental and consumer cases which would provide procedural and substantive rules favorable to environmental and health goals.

Conclusion

The problems and issues presented in this paper are complex. While environmental and consumer advocates have made great steps in identifying problems with current trade policy, it is now the task of the Clinton Administration to propose specific alternatives and remedies. The Clinton Administration should be more hospitable to such changes than was the Bush Administration. While environmental and consumer groups hope that the new Administration will address these vital concerns, current indications in Congressional testimony and press statements are not encouraging. With negotiations nearing conclusion on two trade agreements that will lock in U.S. and global trade policy for decades, time is of the essence.

NOTES

1. The WWF-World Wide Fund for Nature (formerly the World Wildlife Fund) discussion paper by Charlie Arden-Clarke is the best source for a more detailed

discussion of GATT and environmental protection and sustainable development. (Arden-Clarke, WWF International, Discussion Paper: The General Agreement on Tariffs and Trade, Environmental Protection and Sustainable Development, Revised November 1991, ISBN 2-88085-086-X.)

2. Report of the Panel, United States—Restriction on Imports of Tuna, GATT Doc. No. DS21/R (September 3, 1991.) Panel Decision Concerning U.S.; Note by the GATT Secretariat, GATT, Industrial Pollution Control and International Trade, 1971.

3. Journal of Commerce, "Japan Threatens U.S. Raw Log Bans."

4. Arden-Clarke, p. 15.

5. GATT, Export of Domestically Prohibited Goods and other Hazardous Substances, DPG/W/6, 1990.

6. Arden-Clarke, p. 13.

7. Mintz, "Tobacco Roads: Delivering Death to the Third World," *The Progressive* 24 (May 1991); Council on Scientific Affairs, "The Worldwide Smoking Epidemic: Tobacco Trade, Use & Control," 263 *JAMA* 3312 (June 27, 1990); GATT Panel Report, *Thailand Restrictions on Importation of & Internal Taxes on Cigarettes*, BISD, 37th Supp. (adopted Nov. 7, 1990); Letters from U.S. Ambassador Re: U.K. Moist Snuff Ban (1990 & 1991); U.K.-U.S. Tobacco Co. Agreement Re: Moist Snuff (1991); Brief of *Amicus Curiae* Gov't of Canada, in *Corrosion Proof Fittings v. EPA*, 947 F.2d 1201 (5th Cir. 1991); *The U.S.-E.C. Hormone Treated Beef Conflict*, 30 Harv. Int'l L.J. 549 (1989); *The U.S.-E.C. Hormone Beef Controversy & the Standards Code: Implications for the Application of Health Regs. to Agric. Trade*, 14 N.C.J. Int'l L. & Com. Reg. 135 (1989); Services of the Commission of the European Communities, *Report on U.S. Trade Barriers & Unfair Trade Practices* at 34–37 (1991).

8. Other important issues exist in reference to the Uruguay Round. The following authors have fully analyzed these issues: the environmental implications of the Uruguay Round's macroeconomic effects and incentives—John Audley, Sierra Club, Washington, D.C.; the effect on sustainable agriculture of the Uruguay Round's inclusion for the first time of agricultural trade—Mark Ritchie, Institute for Agriculture and Trade Policy, Minneapolis, Minnesota and Tim Lang, Parents for Safe Food, London, England; the effect of the Uruguay Round on the principles of sustainable development—Alex Hittle, Friends of the Earth, Washington, D.C. and Charlie Arden-Clarke, WWF International, Gland, Switzerland; the undermining of UNCED principles by the Uruguay Round—Greenpeace International, "UNCED Undermined" available through Greenpeace, USA, Washington, D.C.; the detrimental effects on biodiversity of the Uruguay Round's Intellectual Property provisions—Vandana Shiva, Third World Network, Penang, Malaysia; Uruguay Round implications for global forest protection—Rain Forest Action Network, San Francisco, CA.

9. Under the current GATT dispute resolution rules, panel decisions must be adopted by unanimous support of the GATT nations. Thus, each country has

the option of exercising an "emergency brake" in blocking the consensus and stopping full approval of the panel's decision.

10. Many other issues of equally vital importance to the NAFTA have been discussed by the following authors: environmental impacts of the macroeconomic effects of NAFTA—John Audley, The Sierra Club, Washington, D.C.; NAFTA's undermining of environmentally sound energy policy—Ken Stump, Greenpeace USA, Washington, D.C.; NAFTA's impact on sustainable agriculture—Karen Lehman, Institute for Agriculture and Trade Policy, Minneapolis, MN; NAFTA's detriment to biodiversity—Beth Burrows, Washington Biodiversity Action Committee; NAFTA's undermining of natural resource and conservation policy—Steven Shrybman, Canadian Environmental Law Association, Toronto, Canada; NAFTA and Wildlife Trade—World Wildlife, Washington, D.C. (two volumes).

11. See, e.g., Remarks of Congressman Richard A. Gephardt, Address Before the 21st Century Conference (Sept. 9, 1992).

12. 19 U.S.C. § 2155.

13. Hilliard, Public Citizen's Congress Watch, Trade Advisory Committee: Privileged Access for Polluters, December 1991.

14. Toxics in the Community: National and Local Perspectives. The 1989 Toxics Release Inventory National Report. Report, Economics and Technology Division, Office of Toxic Substances, U.S. Environmental Protection Agency. September 1991. p. 66. January 1, 1990.

15. Site Enforcement Tracking System database of U.S. Environmental Protection Agency. January 1, 1990.

16. See Letter to the Office of the U.S. Trade Representative from Patti Goldman, Public Citizen (Dec. 16, 1991); Letter to Public Citizen from Joshua Bolton, General Counsel, Office of the U.S. Trade Representative (February 3, 1992).

17. 19 U.S.C. § 2191(d).

18. 19 U.S.C. § 2191(f)(2) & (g)(2).

19. Normally, Congressional committees to which the implementing bill is referred have 45 legislative days to review the matter, at which time it is automatically referred to the full House, and a floor vote must then be taken within 15 legislative days. (19 U.S.C. § 2191(e).) However, where the implementing legislation contains revenue measures, the approval period may be extended from 60 to 90 legislative days because revenue measures must originate in the House of Representatives, and additional time may be added to permit Senate committee consideration after referral of the matter from the House. (Id. § 2191(e)(2).)

20. Hilliard and Wallach, Public Citizen's Congress Watch, The Consumer and Environmental Case Against Fast Track, March 1991.

21. Civil Action No. 92-5010.

22. 970 F. 2d 916 C.D.C. Air 1992.

23. Civil Action No. 92-2102.

24. U.S.T.R., Review of U.S.-Mexico Environmental Issues, January 1992.

25. For more details on NAFTA and Uruguay Round proposals on dispute resolution, see Annexes 1 and 2.

26. NAFTA Articles 2018–2019, Uruguay Round Draft Final Act, Chapter "S" para. 20.1.

27. NAFTA Article 2012(1), at 20-10.

28. Uruguay Round Draft Final Act, Chapter "S", para. 12.1–12.2.

29. NAFTA Article 2017(2), at 20-12.

30. *Public Citizen v. Office of the U.S. Trade Representative*, No. 92-659-GAG (D.D.C. Nov. 1992), appeal dismissed (Jan. 1993).

31. NAFTA Article 2009(1) & (2).

32. Uruguay Round Draft Final Text Act, Chapter "S", para. 6.1.

33. NAFTA Article 2011(3).

34. NAFTA Article 2009(c).

35. NAFTA Article 2014.

36. Uruguay Round Draft Final Text, Chapter S, para. 11.

37. NAFTA Article 2015(1).

38. NAFTA Article 2015(4).

39. NAFTA Article 2005(3) & (4).

4

Edmund G. Brown, Jr.

FREE TRADE IS NOT FREE

The new rules for trade across international boundaries should not be designed to please the captains of industry and their economist allies who almost always view such matters through a self-serving prism of corporate efficiency. Virtually all leaders of labor unions and environmental organizations, together with hundreds of religious and community activists across the country, condemn the proposed North American Free Trade Agreement (NAFTA) and recent versions of the General Agreement on Tariffs and Trade (GATT) for one simple reason: they believe that these proposed trading regimes will impose horrible consequences on defenseless communities which they represent.

Listening to free trade cheerleaders, one would never guess that the doctrine of free trade was invented back in the late 18th and early 19th centuries when conditions were totally different from our own. Then, companies were grounded in a specific country and not footloose to open and close factories whenever they found lower wages and taxes or weaker health and safety laws. In those days, business capital was not mobile in the way it is today and was normally guided by national interests and loyalty to the country of its origin. Today, the transnational corporation has virtually no allegiance except to its own global expansion and profit. What brings financial value to the shareholders is the only criterion even if jobs are destroyed and whole communities devastated.

Perhaps the most famous exponent of free trade was David Ricardo, the 19th century political economist who formulated the theory of comparative advantage. Under his doctrine, trade between two different countries always made sense even when one country was totally different and considerably richer than the other. Completely forgotten, however, is his parallel doctrine: the infamous Iron Law of Wages, under which the natural price of labor was deemed to be that amount which permitted bare subsistence plus enough to reproduce. Tragically, that sums up the inhuman condition millions of English workers were forced to endure during the heyday of 19th century free trade.

Today, the modern ideologues of free trade don't publicly assert that working people should live at bare subsistence levels. Generally they ignore altogether the issue of wages and working conditions and instead focus on algebraic modeling of economic efficiencies. Miraculously the print-outs which they produce always show everyone benefitting from a "free market" expanding relentlessly across all borders. Utterly absent, however, from their complex equations are any moral ideas about social justice or environmental stewardship. That is why, in evaluating the seven-inch thick NAFTA trade agreement, one must do more than consider conflicting econometric models.

The crucial matter is to understand how enmeshing the divergent economies of the United States and Mexico, as NAFTA requires, actually affects people in their daily lives. As a starting point, recognize that NAFTA, drawn up behind closed doors under the watchful eyes of President Bush and industry lobbyists, places primary emphasis on lowering costs, not on responsibly protecting people, the environment or community well-being.

Washington insiders talk as though "free trade" were some kind of magic bullet that naturally raises wages and generates jobs. Yet, look at the facts. Since 1973, American trade with other nations has doubled while the value of American weekly paychecks has fallen 18%. In the last decade alone, the number of young men working full time who earn only a poverty wage has increased 100%. Whole communities, like South Central Los Angeles, Camden, New Jersey, Flint, Michigan, and Toledo, Ohio, to name only a few, have suffered continuing economic and social decline. The economy got bigger—our national income per capita grew 28%— but the benefits were channeled to those with the highest incomes. Inequality grew, not so much because of the Reagan tax cuts as many assume, but because the structure of the American economy was significantly deregulated and internationalized and thereby tilted to favor corporate executives, investors and business lawyers to the detriment of almost everyone else. What was lacking here—and it still is—was not expanding foreign trade, but government policies that ranked community well-being as our most important national priority.

Under the banner of free trade and corporate restructuring, American employers continue the hemorrhaging of U.S. jobs to more "efficient" foreign production sites. For example, Smith Corona, the last American typewriter company, recently announced that it was discharging 875 of 1300 employees and moving its production plant to Mexico. The reason given was typical: equally skilled Mexican workers would do the same work for a lot less pay. This case illustrates the painful reality behind President Clinton's boast that NAFTA will create high paying jobs. The truth is more like a race to the bottom in terms of wage levels and environmental standards. Such a result is inevitable if we link ourselves to the profoundly different conditions prevailing in Mexico, where average wage levels are one-tenth our own, environmental laws are unenforced, unions are the captive of the state, and the political system is weighed down by corruption and electoral fraud.

One would think that such a mixed marriage of political and economic difference would inspire deep foreboding and widespread debate. Instead, Congress allowed NAFTA to be negotiated in secret and written in such abstruse language that debate about its provisions invariably falls prey to arcane economic assumptions. Any non-experts who then refuse to think in terms of the econometric models marshalled in NAFTA's defense are chastised as Neanderthals and narrow special interests out to protect their obsolete jobs at the expense of progress.

Compounding all this is the grossly undemocratic "fast track" process for congressional consideration of NAFTA. Here we have nothing less than a perversion of parliamentary procedure that undermines the authority of Congress by abrogating its power to amend—only a yes or no vote is allowed—and by imposing strict time limits on debate. As a consequence, the active participation of those who represent labor, environmental, consumer and human rights concerns is drastically limited.

Watch as the national media, the business elites and the Clinton administration all gang up to steamroll Congress into a yes vote by minimizing serious labor and environmental issues. The real world consequences to millions of ordinary people are sytematically obscured by the constant appeal to economic science and the dogmatically assumed virtue of expanding markets.

Politically connected industries, however, are spared the rigors of unconstrained free trade; they are given instead special and favored treatment. For example, NAFTA creates a "Yarn Forward Clause" to protect American textile manufacturers from foreign competitors. This exception to free trade doctrine, like dozens of others in NAFTA, demonstrates that trade restrictions are widely used, with the only question being: whose financial interests are to be protected and for what reason?

The short answer is that global companies and their shareholders must be protected because of their enormous political power. Those without powerful lobbyists or financial clout are left to fend for themselves. For example, NAFTA removes protections on Mexican corn and other food stuffs. As a result, U.C.L.A. economists estimate that 800,000 Mexican farming families will be driven off their communal lands because of competition from lower cost American agriculture. According to the same economists, approximately 700,000 additional migrants will then cross into America illegally in search of work. The outcome will be untold suffering and depressed wages on both sides of the border as the number of desperate and available workers rapidly increases.

Another more subtle danger of NAFTA was exposed in a series of recent legal challenges brought under the 103-nation General Agreement on Tariffs and Trade (GATT), on which NAFTA is based. Both trade agreements use similar dispute resolution procedures that allow unelected officials to declare national and local environmental, health and safety standards non-tariff barriers to trade and therefore subject to financial sanction.

For example, in August 1991, a three-person, secret GATT dispute panel in Geneva ruled that the U.S. Marine Mammal Protection Act of 1972 was an illegal barrier to trade because it restricts importing tuna into the United States that are caught using techniques that kill large numbers of dolphins. The case was brought by Mexico. In February 1992, a GATT panel ruled that numerous U.S. states' alcohol taxes and regulations were inconsistent with GATT, and that as a matter of international law GATT was superior to U.S. state and local law. Under this kind of reasoning neither Congress, nor individual states could demand refillable bottles or impose restrictions on the export of raw logs to protect local jobs or the environment.

These cases clearly underline the sharp conflict between intrusive international trade regulations and American democracy. Our constitutional system rests on democratic accountability with significant legal and regulatory authority reserved to the states and localities. NAFTA, in the name of breaking down non-tariff trade barriers, would restrict citizens from setting their own community standards. Instead of democratic decisions made at the state and local level—a major source of innovation in America—we would all be subjected to a super-government of distant and unelected trade bureaucrats. These experts would inevitably bring to their jobs the narrow frame of reference of economic utility and not the dynamics and diversity of democratic participation.

Instead of going along on the "fast track," Congress should forthrightly reject NAFTA as contrary to democratic traditions and inconsistent with our growing understanding that political and economic power have become too centralized.

What is needed in place of NAFTA is a trading relationship among Canada, Mexico and the United States which emphasizes social justice, the enrichment of local communities and respect for the environment. Such a relationship is possible but only after the reigning fallacies behind free trade are thoroughly debated and refuted. Until this is accomplished, the shocking growth of American and world-wide inequality and the accelerating assault on the environment will continue.

Before new trade agreements are drawn up, principles must be developed for the imposition of sanctions for products that fail to meet the highest health, safety, and environmental standards and just wage and working conditions. Neighborhoods and local communities must take back their rightful power, which has been relentlessly siphoned off by transnational companies and the political structures that protect them. The automatism of corporate growth must be recognized and challenged.

This will not happen overnight. It is too radical a departure from conventional thinking. Yet, it is precisely this type of change which the principles of social justice and a sustainable environment insistently demand.

5

Thea Lee

HAPPILY NEVER NAFTA

There's No Such Thing as a Free Trade

After deliberating in secret for 14 months, negotiators for the United States, Mexico, and Canada finally unveiled a North American Free Trade Agreement (NAFTA) last September. One thing was immediately apparent to both critics and proponents of the pact: it does not represent classic free trade. Rather, the 2,000-page document orchestrates imports and exports with remarkable attention to detail, and it has as much to do with investment as with trade.

NAFTA is a guide to political and economic clout in North America. The agreement favors multinational corporations and big investors at the expense of workers, farmers, small businesses, and the environment. If ratified by the legislatures of all three countries, NAFTA would hasten the movement of U.S. and Canadian firms to Mexico to profit from cheap labor and lax environmental and workplace regulations.

A fair, humane trade pact would set in motion a process of raising labor and environmental standards for the entire continent. It would not limit the power of domestic governments to regulate trade and investment in the interest of their own countries. If NAFTA meets defeat, the three countries will have a chance to start over, with a more democratic process of negotiation. At the very least, the current agreement could be much improved if citizen groups apply enough pressure. While President Bill Clinton hedged on NAFTA during his campaign, he has indicated willingness to seek substantial reforms.

THEA LEE   71

More Jobs

Much of the debate over NAFTA concerns employment. "Jobs, jobs, jobs," promised Carla Hills, the U.S. Trade Representative, at the Republican Convention. Proponents of free trade argue that it fosters growth by removing artificial barriers, thus rewarding efficient firms. All nations benefit. Without tariffs and subsidies, countries specialize in goods they make relatively cheaply. Higher efficiency means lower prices, so workers see their purchasing power grow. While some people lose their jobs in the shakeup that follows newly liberalized trade, other jobs open in expanding industries. In the case of North America, by further opening Mexico's consumer market to imports, NAFTA will supposedly create hundreds of thousands of export-related jobs in the United States and Canada.

So the theory goes. In the real world, however, the touted benefits won't necessarily come to pass. In the absence of full employment, for example, displaced workers don't automatically find new jobs at comparable wages. Unemployment currently runs at about 20% in Mexico, 11% in Canada, and 7.5% in the United States.

According to the U.S. Bureau of Labor Statistics, displaced American manufacturing workers who find new jobs take an average 10% pay cut, after accounting for inflation.

Second, lower costs don't necessarily translate into lower prices. NAFTA would allow already huge U.S. corporations to expand their share of the Mexican market. As they drive small Mexican firms out of business, multinationals would face dwindling competition. Therefore, they will not necessarily face pressure to pass cost savings to consumers dollar for dollar.

And as for efficiency, it's not much to get excited about when the savings come from cheap labor rather than better technology or easier access to resources. In fact, as firms shift production to Mexico, lured by wages of $1 or $2 an hour, they lose some incentive to invest in cutting-edge techniques that improve productivity. For years, U.S. firms have been setting up "maquiladora" factories just over the Mexican border, and NAFTA would simply speed the trend.

Given such contradictory visions of free trade, it's no surprise that competing studies of NAFTA predict contrasting results. Proponents forecast job and wage gains in all three countries, while critics predict wage erosion and job losses for Canada and the United States, with small gains for a minority of Mexicans.

Some difference of opinion over NAFTA's impact is legitimate. Reasonable people might disagree about how many U.S. and Canadian companies would shift production to Mexico, for instance. But for the most part, the debate in political circles hasn't been reasonable at all. Virtually all of the models predicting job gains for the United States are disingenuous. They focus solely on lower trade barriers, ignoring the shift in investment from north to south. The Bush administration has consistently cited studies that are even less realistic, including one by the Peat-Marwick accounting firm and another done jointly by researchers at the University of Michigan and Tufts University. These studies acknowledge that investment will increase in Mexico, but they assume no corresponding loss in the United States. That's equivalent to assuming that Mexicans will wake up one morning to find an extra $25 billion in the middle of Main Street.

When the likely shift in investment is correctly taken into account, most models do show a net job loss for the United States. For example, research by the Economic Policy Institute, a Washington think tank, and a study by economists at Skidmore College and the University of Massachusetts at Amherst suggest NAFTA would cost the United States at least half a million jobs over the next decade. That's less than 0.5% of the total U.S. workforce, but the decline would likely be sharp in several industries, including apparel, autos and auto parts, consumer electronics, and food processing. The loss, or even the threat of it, would be enough to reduce wages across much of the labor force. U.S. wages and benefits are seven times higher than Mexico's on average, and the gap is much wider in some occupations. Professor Ed Leamer of the University of California at Los Angeles predicts a loss of about $1,000 a year per person for approximately 70% of the U.S. work force—everyone but managers, scientists, and technicians.

If Canada's experience with free trade offers any lessons, the prospects for the United States look grim. Canada has lost almost a quarter of its manufacturing jobs since it entered into a free trade agreement with the United States in 1989. And Canadian wages are only slightly higher than in the United States. While the agreement is only partly to blame, proponents of that pact, too, promised job gains for Canada. As it turned out, hundreds of plants left Canada for the United States in pursuit of labor savings, lower taxes, and cheaper real estate. A depreciated U.S. dollar also fueled the flight.

A recent *Wall Street Journal* poll of U.S. corporate executives found that 40% have plans to move some production to Mexico in the near future. Twenty-five percent admitted that they plan to use the threat of moving as a bargaining chip to cut wages and benefits.

Dubious Gains for Mexico

NAFTA locks Mexico into a dead-end development strategy: attracting foreign investment with low wages, weak unions, and toothless regulations. While U.S. multinationals would bring new manufacturing jobs to Mexico, these gains will not be large enough to employ all the new entrants into the labor force. The country's labor force is growing rapidly, due to a burgeoning population and a massive number of youth who are coming of age. Thus, continuing high unemployment and underemployment will likely maintain downward pressure on wages. Mexico's minimum wage has already fallen by almost 50% since the early 1980s, after accounting for inflation. The country is already suffering from growing unemployment, massive debt, and an anti-labor government.

In addition, losses in farming and small business would offset some of the new factory jobs, as huge corporations and agribusiness consolidate power and find ways to save on labor. Domestic production of U.S. and Canadian transnationals would drive some small entrepreneurs out of business. So would cheap imports. Despite low labor costs, some protected Mexican industries are ill-prepared to meet new competition from abroad because they don't have up-to-date facilities. Lifting subsidies and tariffs on agriculture would likely give Mexico an advantage over the United States in fruits and vegetables. But the United States stands to gain in corn, grain, and beans. NAFTA could spur improvements in agricultural productivity, but farmers shouldn't have to bear the entire burden of adjustment.

Labor and Environmental Standards

NAFTA is silent on the disparate labor laws, wages, and working conditions among the three signatory countries. The agreement stands in sad contrast to the integration plan of the European Community, which is trying to set minimum job standards and benefits, so that countries can't compete by pummeling workers. The EC's more just plan reflects the way it was negotiated: publicly, with more democratic participation and an explicit concern for workers' rights. NAFTA negotiators, on the other hand, have virtually guaranteed that competition will debase the standards of countries that now offer the best protection.

Mexico has lenient child labor laws, and they aren't well enforced. 14- and 15-year-olds are allowed to work up to 36 hours a week, while the U. S. limit is 18 hours during school season. Children make up almost one-third of Mexico's work force, according to the Mexican Center for Children's Rights.

Mexican labor laws are better than the United States' in many areas, such as maternity leave. But they are poorly enforced. The Mexican constitution protects the right to bargain collectively and to strike. In practice, however, the largest Mexican unions are allied with the ruling political party, the Independent Revolutionary Party (PRI). The government may declare a strike illegal, allowing the company to fire strikers.

NAFTA should require all countries to meet the highest labor standards now in place in any of the three nations. To enforce those standards, workers and unions should have the right to challenge the import of goods produced in a way that violates standards of their own country.

NAFTA would be a big step backward from current U.S. trade law, which at least nominally protects worker rights. Under certain trade agreements, such as the Caribbean Basin Initiative, the United States must allow workers to bargain collectively and must set certain minimum standards for pay, hours, and workplace health and safety. These trade agreements also prohibit forced labor and limit child labor. While enforcement often falls short, these laws provide leverage in putting a stop to some of the worst abuses.

NAFTA offers a bit more protection to the environment than to workers, but not much. William Reilly of the U.S. Environmental Protection Agency has called NAFTA the "greenest trade agreement ever negotiated," referring to a clause that supposedly prevents countries from relaxing their health, safety, or environmental standards to attract foreign investment. But the text does not actually prohibit such a move, only deems it "inappropriate." The penalty for violation? The injured party could "request consultations" but could impose no legal sanctions. Ouch. In addition, NAFTA states that technical standards imposed by the pact refer only to the end product, not the way products are made. So an electrical appliance maker that dumped toxic waste into a Mexican stream could freely export "safe" products to the United States or Canada.

Investment

While NAFTA all but ignores labor standards, it devotes five out of 22 chapters to investment. The text is designed to foster corporate mobility, to make it as easy for a U.S. company to operate in Matamoros, Mexico as in Milwaukee. In the process, the pact invades territory traditionally reserved for domestic policy, in order to promote and protect the interests of investors. All three countries would sign away important tools of economic policy.

For example, given Mexico's history of nationalizing private businesses, a potential investor might worry about a government takeover. Article 1110 would put that fear to rest, restricting expropriation to certain circumstances and specifying the compensation, currency, and interest rate that would apply in the event of nationalization.

The cautious investor might also fret about limits on exchanging pesos for dollars, or a requirement to reinvest some profits locally. Not to worry. Article 1109 would mandate that all transfers of business income shall "be made freely and without delay" and would prohibit any of the three countries from requiring domestic reinvestment of profits.

Under Article 1106, none of the three countries could require a company's exports to match or exceed its imports, as Mexico currently does for autos. The article rules out other national policies that would foster domestic development, like requiring foreign-based firms to buy domestic supplies, hire local scientists and managers, or make technology available to domestic firms. Such requirments have to date been routine in Europe, Mexico, and Canada.

This article even goes so far as to apply to countries outside the pact. This provision says that the United States, for instance, couldn't require Japanese auto plants producing in the United States to buy a certain number of parts from domestic suppliers or to transfer technology. Those are policies the United States has so far failed to pursue, but should have the option to at least consider.

NAFTA would also thwart domestic policy in the area of intellectual property rights, that is, copyrights and patents on printed material, sound or video recordings, pharmaceuticals, and computer software. Developing nations often show little regard for intellectual property rights, since exclusive authority to make a product generally means steep prices. By ignoring drug patents, for example, Mexico has provided relatively cheap pharmaceuticals.

No longer. The U.S. trade representative boasts that "NAFTA provides a higher standard of protection for patents, copyrights, trademarks, and trade secrets than has been established in any other bilateral or international agreement." For pharmaceutical and agricultural chemical companies, NAFTA offers an opportunity to exert long-sought control over other countries. The Mexican government is willing to make this sacrifice in exchange for access to the markets of industrialized countries. But the tradeoff enhances corporate profits while imposing higher costs on consumers in poor countries. Even Canadians would pay more for pharmaceuticals under NAFTA, since Canada limits patent rights more than the United States does. NAFTA would cost Canada an extra $400 million a year in higher drug prices.

Disputes

NAFTA includes elaborate provisions for resolving disputes, calling for arbitration by a panel of international trade lawyers and financial "experts" appointed by the executive branch. Like NAFTA in general, the proposed penalties for violations put property before people. Madonna's record company could seek lost profits and legal fees from anyone who made unauthorized copies of her cassettes. The offending tapes and the factory used to make them could be confiscated. Yet, since NAFTA imposes almost no labor standards, it offers no way to block U.S. imports of clothing made by a Mexican company that exploits child labor.

What to Do

With enough pressure on political leaders in all three countries, NAFTA could be rejected, or at least reformed substantially. While the pact will probably sail through the Mexican Senate with little debate, it faces strong opposition in Canada and the United States. Canada's recent free trade pact with the U.S. is unpopular, and Canadians don't consider NAFTA much better. Prime Minister Brian Mulroney faces serious political risk in pushing the agreement through Parliament before the next election.

Before he was elected, Bill Clinton criticized NAFTA for omitting labor and environmental standards. Yet he said he favored free trade with Mexico in principle and thought the pact could be fixed without renegotiating the basic agreement.

He faces a skeptical public. Bush's resounding defeat at the polls was a pretty clear indicator that, with unemployment stuck at 7.5%, most people are looking for a more plausible jobs bill than this one. A CBS–New York Times poll in July 1992 found that Americans thought NAFTA was a "bad idea" by a 2-to-1 margin. Another poll cited by the Los Angeles Times in September found only 16% of the population believed NAFTA would create jobs in the United States.

Citizen groups are pressing for a pact that provides for labor and environmental standards no weaker than the strongest now in force in North America. The standards should be enforceable through trade sanctions, not simply encouraged by an advisory commission. The agreement should provide for money to clean up pollution and aid displaced workers. That's a costly proposition, and the companies that benefit from transnational trade and investment should pay. U.S. Rep. Richard Gephardt (D-Missouri) has suggested a tax along these lines, which he calls a "cross-border transaction fee."

A renegotiation of NAFTA should be open to democratic participation by labor, environmental, farming, and consumer groups. It's possible to manage trade in the interest of working people and the environment.

RESOURCES

Jeff Faux and Thea Lee, "The Effect of George Bush's NAFTA on American Workers: Ladder Up or Ladder Down?" Washington, D.C., Economic Policy Institute (EPI), July 1992, 800 537-9359. Robert Blecker and William Spriggs, "Manufacturing Employment in North America: Where the Jobs Have Gone," EPI, October 1992. Tim Koschlin and Mehrena Larudee, "The High Cost of NAFTA," Challenge, September/October 1992. Labor Advisory Committee on the NAFTA, "Preliminary Report," September 16, 1992.

6

Jorge G. Castañeda and Carlos Heredia

ANOTHER NAFTA:
WHAT A GOOD AGREEMENT
SHOULD OFFER

Most Mexicans, and probably many Americans and Canadians, believe
that a North American free-trade agreement is inevitable and that the
agreement now before the three governments will benefit all. But they are
wrong. There is no reason to believe that the almost century-long process
of economic integration between Mexico and the United States (leaving
aside Canada for now) would halt without some kind of formal trade agreement. Nor is it at all certain that this particular agreement is good for all
involved. The agreement is advertised as a commercial accord suitable for
two individualistic and deregulated market economies. But the question
is: Do we Mexicans really want a market economy like the one the United
States has? No one has asked us. Neither President Carlos Salinas de Gor-
tari nor President George Bush even suggested that their agreement sur-
reptitiously chooses between two different market economies and types of
economic integration: Anglo-Saxon neo-liberalism and a European
Community-style social market economy.

In the same way that Bill Clinton's election opens the possibility for a
free-trade agreement that is quite different from the current Bush-Quayle,
trickle-down, conservative agreement, the debate in Mexico is shifting toward the formulation of a viable alternative. And indeed, the entire

NAFTA process involves considerably more complex and substantive nuances than Republican conservatives—in Mexico and the United States—have acknowledged.

False Choices

There is a process of economic integration under way between Mexico and the United States, and if anything is inevitable in today's world, that process probably is. But it is a process that did not just begin with President Salinas or former president Miguel de la Madrid, or on the basis of the economic reforms set in motion in 1983. Economic integration began toward the end of the last century, when the United States became Mexico's major trading partner. Since then between 60 percent and 90 percent of Mexico's trade (depending on the period of time and method of reckoning) has been with the country north of us, as have comparable shares of foreign investment, tourism, and credit.

In principle, we could sufficiently diversify trade, investment, financing, and tourism to bring about a real shift in our ties with the United States. If we were to withdraw from the General Agreement on Trade and Tariffs (GATT) and adopt tariffs of 100 percent on U.S. products and 0 percent on Japanese or European products, if we were to maintain that policy for 20 years, and if we could close the border, perhaps we could manage to diversify our external trade. If the cost of an American product were twice that of its Japanese or German equivalent, diversification would surely become feasible.

But the cost to Mexico of making that attempt would be extremely high, both politically and economically. And Mexican society is not prepared to pay that cost. This, and this alone, is why the process of economic integration is inevitable.

While trade is inevitable in this sense, is a formal free-trade agreement? Do we need to regulate, administer, and codify economic integration? Probably not. The informal process has been going on for half a century without being governed by any agreement at all and would doubtless continue.

Finally, is there anything indicating that this agreement is the only possible one? Even if the abstract process of economic integration is inevitable, and even if some kind of agreement is also inevitable, there is no reason to suppose that *this* agreement, as negotiated, must be the one. In fact, the agreement signed by Salinas, Bush, and Canadian Prime Minister Brian Mulroney differs significantly from the one they began with. It now includes many issues and regulations that were not on the original agenda and rules out others. Similarly, the agreement that will ultimately be ratified by the U.S. Congress and the Canadian parliament (the Mexican Congress has no voice in the matter) will undoubtedly be different from the text agreed upon in August 1992.

The government of Mexico, and the Bush administration to a lesser extent, have set up a false choice that many have fallen for: either this agreement or autarchy. It is simply untrue that the only alternative to the Bush-Salinas agreement is autarchy, protectionism, or a return to the status quo ante. There is a wide range of agreements concluded around the world in the last 30 years that provide many options for formalized integration. In reality, the choice is between the agreement already negotiated, a right-wing agreement of a neo-liberal Republican cast, and an agreement of some other kind, more like a social-democratic agreement, with a strong dose of regulation and planning, inspired by an emerging progressive social compact for a new North America. The choice is between what is called an exclusively commercial agreement, proper to the Anglo-Saxon world's individualistic and deregulated capitalism, and an accord that would go beyond the strictly commercial, also encompassing social issues and the relation between the state and the market. The contrast between those two agreements, the "bad" one we have and the "good" one we want, reflects the difference between the kinds of market economies that exist in the world today.

What We Got from NAFTA

What is the bad agreement all about? Its conceptual premise is to leave free trade exclusively to the free market. In Mexico, leaving everything to the market means giving free rein to those who command it: the most powerful, the richest. Second, the agreement supposedly covers only economic issues. In reality, NAFTA is an agreement that encompasses not only financial matters, investment, intellectual property, and of course commerce, but also dispute-resolution, banking, transport, and services. Clearly, the agreement is not solely commercial.

But it *is* a strictly economic agreement, one that does not include other possible issues: social, political, environmental, cultural. What we have here is an accord that is fundamentally opposed to the idea of planning, to choosing what each country will produce, to defining how established goals will be met, and to clarifying how certain sectors will be protected or exposed in order to reach long-term objectives.

Just as deregulation was a major feature of the economic policy of both the Bush administration and the Salinas government, so, too, NAFTA lacks a strict regulatory framework. To the greatest extent possible, it seeks to eliminate all social, economic, consumer-protection, and environmental regulations. True, that is no easy task, since the United States and Canada have legislative bodies, courts, and citizens' organizations that have struggled for years to pass the present regulatory framework.

Here, the Salinas government stands to the right even of the Bush administration. It was the Mexicans who insisted on dismantling the various regulations in force in the United States, alleging that they constituted disguised forms of protection (in some cases true). Ironically, Mexico, completely lacking in effective regulation of anything, lacking a minimum regulatory framework in any area, now opposes the preservation of the U.S. regulatory framework, arguing that it is contrary to the market and free trade.

Finally, the bad agreement is an agreement without asymmetries, without real recognition of the enormous disparities between Mexico and the United States. From the beginning, the Mexican government sold the United States and the Mexican public on the idea that Mexico did not need longer time-spans for removal of restrictions and deregulation or greater protection for its producers because the country was becoming part of the First World, competitive and modern. However, Mexican negotiators, realizing that the country might need some special treatment, stressed asymmetry. But they were never really able to carry forward this argument to its ultimate conclusion—except perhaps as regards energy—because it was contrary to the spirit of the agreement and the negotiation itself. Salinas, in effect, was saying: The only thing we need is open markets. Just take your foot off the brake, you don't even have to put it on the accelerator.

What We Want from a Free-Trade Agreement

It is easy enough to criticize a bad agreement. But what is the alternative? The alternative is an agreement that includes compensatory financing, encourages industrial planning and a common regulatory framework, confronts the issue of worker mobility, harmonizes upward labor standards and rights, creates an environmental and consumer protection charter, and institutes a broad multi-purpose dispute-resolution mechanism.

The premise underlying a good agreement is that there is no single model of formal economic integration, just as there is no single model of a market economy. In the past, the diametrical clash between capitalism and real socialism tended to obscure the contrasts between the various market economies in the industrial world. But today the differences between individualistic, predatory Anglo-Saxon capitalism and the social-democratic market capitalism of Germany (or of the Rhineland, as some European observers have put it) or the public-private capitalism of Japan are striking. The U.S. model, presently under severe strain, is highly dynamic but antisocial, short-term oriented, anti-interventionist, and tends to exacerbate inequalities. The European and Japanese models—looking beyond their differences—are less dynamic but more socially oriented and regulated with a more active and dominant role for the state, and tend to forge more egalitarian and homogeneous societies.

There are also various models of formal economic integration, from the U. S.-Canada model of 1988, which leaves almost everything to the will of the market, to the European plan of Jean Monnet and the Treaty of Rome, which emphasizes the state's role in planning, regulation, and social policy-making.

The free-trade agreement proposed and imposed by Salinas and Bush is not the only possible scheme for Mexico. Actually the conservative agreement is probably the worst program.

PAYING THE COSTS OF ADJUSTMENT

A good agreement would call for compensatory financing or the creation of regional funds. As markets are integrated, painful adjustments often occur: as the factors of production are redistributed with greater efficiency, some industries are weakened, others lost altogether. In theory, the costs of such adjustment are equitably shared. In practice, however, Mexico will bear a heavier burden than the United States. Our per capita income is eight to 10 times less than that of the United States, the distribution of income is much more skewed, levels of wages, productivity, efficiency, and technology are clearly inferior.

Although parts of the United States and Canada will also suffer disproportionately great adjustment costs, even larger than those borne by some parts of Mexico, in general Mexico's situation will be worse because we are starting from a weaker economic position. Other trade agreements have redressed such disparities among partners by creating compensatory financing facilities.

The European Community established structural adjustment funds to mitigate economic and social differences and strengthen economic and social cohesion. EC members seek to stimulate productivity and enhance development in depressed areas by strengthening infrastructure, training workers, and introducing appropriate technology. This is a policy specifically designed to redistribute wealth to the poor: the funds are given to the *most impoverished* areas, not necessarily those *most affected* by the integration process.

In Europe, the amount of money involved has been large. Ireland, perhaps the European country that has benefited most from regional funds, receives 8 percent of its annual GDP from community aid. It is as if Mexico were to receive $20 to $25 billion a year from the governments of the United States and Canada. In the Maastricht Treaty, the Spanish and Portuguese persuaded other members that they should continue receiving help, even with a per capita GDP above 75 percent of the European average. The per capita GDP of Mexico is about 15 percent of the U.S.-Canada average. This injection of resources is in no way a disguised form of charity: in fact, out of every 100 ecus the EC invests in Portugal, 46 return to the other member states by way of increased exports to Portugal.

In North America, the transfer of resources would have three aims: to improve infrastructure, harmonize standards, and subsidize excessive adjustment costs. It is clear how additional funds could be used to achieve the first two goals. Some explanation is needed, however, of how regional aid could be used to lessen local burdens. Certainly factories, farms, and firms in Mexico (and in the United States and Canada) will be forced to close as a result of the new North American competition. This will mean layoffs, which will indirectly affect suppliers and cities that depend on one or two companies, and a drop in the tax base for certain entities. Regional funds could be used to establish a temporary unemployment insurance scheme for those laid off by companies forced to close due to the free-trade agreement, or to finance programs of conversion or vocational training, or to alleviate drops in income.

The central problem of compensatory financing is finding the resources. The European approach ranges from adoption of a general value-added tax to direct governmental transfer payments. This has not been accomplished without controversy, particularly by the more conservative governments. And, given the prevailing ideological climate in the United States, the idea of transferring resources from U.S. taxpayers to build Mexican roads seems a bit far fetched.

There are, however, several ways of financing the transfer of resources from rich areas to poorer ones without passing on the bill to every U.S. taxpayer. The first is a tax on cross-border transactions, such as the one proposed by the Democratic leader of the House of Representatives, Richard Gephardt, to finance an environmental clean-up program along the border.[1] Another mechanism is to tax the windfall profits that some companies would make upon moving to Mexico (by reducing their labor costs and continuing to sell their products at the same price in the United States and Canada).

Still another way to raise funds would be to create a North American Development Bank and an adjustment fund to provide compensatory financing to Mexico.[2] For U.S. taxpayers and Mexican citizens to accept such a program the bank and/or fund would have to finance poor areas or groups of people *in all three countries*. Also, negotiators would have to decide whether only governments can apply for loans or subsidies, or whether private parties would have access to the resources. Finally, the three governments must ensure stable and sustained sources of funding. For NAFTA, there might be a combination of public and private resources, channeled both in the form of loans (development bank) and subsidies (support fund for depressed areas). Ideally the bank would finance projects submitted directly by organized groups of citizens—rural or urban community organizations.

Finally, the Mexican external debt could be renegotiated to free up funds. Resources earmarked for debt servicing could be recycled by using debt-for-investment swaps to finance social development funds in agreement with the creditors.

Compensatory financing facilities, of course, face serious challenges. This is a policy whose results become apparent only over the medium term, and which may lead to the most depressed areas becoming dependent on external transfers. In Europe, however, the gap between rich and poor areas has been narrowing.

STRATEGIC ALLIANCES

A good agreement includes the idea of a trilateral industrial policy—a strategic alliance between the private sector and states to capture markets, develop technologies, achieve dynamic competitive advantages, and reach new levels of competitiveness.

What is needed is active and effective coordination among the three countries. The idea is explicit involvement by government. But success depends on the *meaning* and *purpose* of government intervention. It is not enough to expand physical infrastructure and make things easier for the transnational corporations whose investments are being courted. Each country must invest in social infrastructure to improve wages and standards of living.

A REGULATORY FRAMEWORK

To complement a North American industrial policy, the three countries should create an economic commission to plan which industries should be developed and where, how each stage will be reached, where the money will come from to reach that stage, and what regulations will be established. In Mexico we do not have excessive regulation, on the contrary, we suffer from a notoriously sparse regulatory environment.

WORKER MOBILITY

If NAFTA is to improve access to the United States market for our exports, then two major exports have been left out of the agreement: drugs and people. Call it what you will, but Mexico has been exporting Mexicans for over a century now. Yet those who negotiated NAFTA almost completely ignored this situation.

It is not true that it is impossible to legalize migration from a poor to a

rich country. On the contrary, the great discovery of the Europeans was le-
galizing the previously existing movements of undocumented people.
When the Treaty of Rome entered into force there was already a very large
number off workers from southern Italy working in Germany, Belgium,
Holland, and France. Most were undocumented. The only solution was to
give them papers, granting them entitlements, rights, and power. Indeed, in the United States, the process of legalization in recent years has
been impressive: nearly three million Mexicans have benefited from it.
Many Americans understand that it is not possible to have an enormous
undocumented population concentrated in 10 or 15 cities. The result will
be more disturbances such as the one in Los Angeles in May 1992. The
problems began in the Afro-American community, but Mexicans and Sal-
vadorans did much of the looting. A population flow that cannot be
stopped or controlled has to be legalized.

The negotiation of the free-trade agreement was a good opportunity to
move in that direction. Obviously, complete legalization of all the undocumented Mexicans in the United States, or free entry for all those still in
Mexico, would not have been possible. But including the topic of migration was possible, just as the United States succeeded in including oil on
the negotiating agenda. Mexico should have insisted on the gradual and se-
lective liberalization of migration, offering in exchange much of what
Mexico's immigration authorities are unfortunately already granting unilaterally.

The free-trade agreement says little about the free movement of unskilled labor. Only some provisions concerning temporary and limited entry for professionals have been included. The Mexican authorities have
been unable to explain why the negotiations resulted in free entry for officials, bankers, or consultants, but not for everybody else. Worse, entry for
professionals from the United States and Canada into Mexico was significantly liberalized. The governments are opening borders to goods and capital flows, while labor, Mexico's main export, is barred from entry.

A SOCIAL CHARTER

A good agreement will provide for upward harmonization of labor standards and rights—not just labor legislation but also implementation of
standards. Harmonizing standards would sometimes mean improvements by the United States, since its legislation occasionally falls short of

Mexican legislation (although the enforcement of the Mexican laws is often lax).

Including a social charter is the best way of starting to minimize differences between productivity and wages. It does not guarantee it, but it is a start. The case of the auto industry, especially the Ford-Mazda plant in Hermosillo, Mexico, illustrates a well-known paradox. The plant manufactures vehicles at a productivity rate and quality comparable or higher than the Ford plants in Dearborn or Rouge, and slightly below those of Mazda in Hiroshima. Nevertheless, the wage of the Mexican worker with equal productivity is between 20 and 25 times less than that of the U.S. worker. The Mexican government argues that the wage differential between the two countries is justified because productivity is not comparable: workers cannot expect equal pay for unequal productivity. But what about when the productivity *is* the same?

One reason why workers at factories belonging to the same company, producing the same cars with the same quality and productivity, earn 20 times less, is that the right to strike in Mexico is more a metaphor than anything else. Because of the union-exclusion clause and the unions' subordination to the state and its party, the workers' ability to use the strike as a weapon is negligible. Although it is difficult to legislate equal pay (though not guidelines for gradual equalization), it is possible to harmonize standards for collective bargaining, labor tribunals, the right to strike, and wider union freedom. With such power the workers themselves can achieve, over time, those levels of wages and benefits, as well as dignity in the workplace.

Beyond harmonization of labor standards, a free-trade agreement should promote workers' rights.[3] One way to do this is to allow workers to organize and negotiate collectively at a continental level. NAFTA allows General Motors to decide what to produce in North America and where, but does not create conditions so that workers in Michigan and Coahuila can act jointly to influence industrial policy and wages in their areas. A good agreement will also require the United States and Mexico to adopt the Canadian system of recognition of unions as a de facto matter, so that collective bargaining begins when the majority of the workers at a company decide to form a union or join an existing one. Finally, a social charter should include the adoption of workers' councils, establishing the right of workers' representatives to participate in decisions regarding contracts or layoffs, assignment of workers to a particular place of work, matters of health and safety in the workplace, and access to training. The idea is that all of these rights go hand in hand with the commitment to increase productivity.

Other elements of the social charter might include: no favorable tariff treatment for goods whose production fails to comply with given conditions; prohibiting child labor (under age 16); and requiring employers to provide a healthy workplace, without exposure to toxic substances.

AN ENVIRONMENTAL AND CONSUMER PROTECTION CHARTER

One of the biggest incentives for U.S. companies to move to Mexico is to evade environmental protection laws. In Mexico, the environment is not protected, nor is society itself very comfortable with the idea. Harmonizing consumer protection and environmental standards, which tend to be similar, is intended to prevent Mexico from becoming like the border—a toxic waste-dump for the United States.

The *Coalición para la Justicia en las Maquiladoras* (Coalition for Justice in the Maquiladoras), a bi-national body made up of workers and social groups in the United States and Mexico, has proposed a code of conduct for labor and the environment for those enterprises. Unfortunately, not only Matamoros and Ciudad Juárez are disaster areas, vast areas of Mexico's territory are deteriorating. In order for any environmental program to succeed it must encourage citizen participation. It is possible to include in a good agreement a bill of rights for the defense of the environment and the consumer and to establish a common regulatory framework, on the condition that the costs of these measures are equitably financed. And that means that the polluters pay for what they have polluted.

DISPUTE-RESOLUTION MECHANISMS

If there is no mechanism available to all sectors, not just governments and corporations, then many of the features outlined above will not get beyond the drawingboard. And if the machinery created lacks its own resources and full competence to cover all aspects of the issues, the best free-trade agreement will remain a dead letter.

There is no point in harmonizing standards for environmental, labor, and consumer protection without providing sanctions for those who violate them. It is impossible to determine who is complying and who is not if the matter is left entirely in the hands of governments. In this respect, it is indispensable to have a mechanism for dispute resolution that is supranational, autonomous, with resources, and open to all.

If the dispute-resolution mechanism decides that a standard has indeed been violated, the manufacturers would lose the free-trade privilege, the only sanction that a mechanism of this kind can impose, but one which would prove to be highly effective. It implies a real cost for the violating party. Anyone should be able to use the dispute-resolution mechanism to report violations and demand inspection, monitoring, control, and, if necessary, a ruling and the determination of a sanction. The costs of using the mechanism by all the parties concerned is less than that of indiscriminate violation of harmonized standards. Again, citizen participation is a key element. The mechanism should be open to organized citizens and to governmental bodies from each country.

A Progressive Social Compact

The agreement suggested here implies greater transfers of sovereignty to supranational entities than that of Salinas and Bush; it may even imply a more substantive abdication of sovereignty. Not that the regime's conservative agreement preserves sovereignty as well as it pretends to. But it would be illusory and dishonest to pretend that the accord proposed here does not involve curtailments in several areas.

At the same time, this kind of agreement seeks to enable Mexico to more vigorously and effectively defend what sovereignty remains to it; it proposes achievements and changes so that the defense of the Mexican nation as a whole will be a more plausible undertaking than it is today. A good agreement involves going further toward integration, building more supranational forums, dovetailing our society and institutions more fully with those of the United States and Canada.

The elements of a good agreement do not amount to a list of protectionist measures or suggest that workers should be a privileged group. The idea is simply to put into practice the principle that governments often repeat, but seldom live up to, that a country's most valuable asset is its work force, the majority of the population who are systematically left out of decision making circles but are affected by what the elites decide. The idea is also to go beyond the myopic vision that seeks to divorce the free-trade agreement from labor, emigration, environmental, or human rights provisions on the ground that it is only a commercial agreement. This narrow view overlooks an incontrovertible truth: flows of trade, capital, and investment bring with them social implications that cannot be divorced from their causes and have to be addressed. The only way of guaranteeing compliance with social, labor, or environmental standards is to link them to the granting or denial of tariff relief. Otherwise, there are a thousand ways of getting around them, as the Mexican experience proves.

This agreement is not a socialist or statist or populist agreement; nor is it a nationalist agreement. It is an accord based on the operation of a particular type of market economy. It is an accord that is typically reformist: hence its virtues and its shortcomings—it is viable but filled with costs. The agreement between Salinas and Reagan-Bush-Quayle is a classically conservative agreement, whose premise is the traditional functioning of the U.S. market economy, while the agreement proposed here is based on a European-style or Japanese-style capitalism. It is neither left-oriented or right-oriented. Instead, the proposed agreement takes as its premise a different market economy. Some believe that it is preferable, others believe it is worse: these are political-ethical choices. Either way it is outlandish to suggest that the only agreement and the only type of market economy that is possible is the declining and obsolete model of the most uncouth hardline conservatives in the United States, just booted out of office by more than 60 percent of the electorate.

There remains the problem of the viability of a scheme such as that suggested here. Many may argue that such a plan is desirable but neither viable nor acceptable to Americans under the present conditions: we will never get the money out of them, or the worker mobility, or even the type of regulatory and environmental protection machinery described here. But who is it that will never accept these things, the Republicans or the Democrats, in 1992 or in 1994?

A new, progressive North American social compact could become an example for the rest of Latin America; a bad agreement is merely a Trojan horse for the most reactionary sectors in the United States and the rest of the hemisphere. A conservative covenant can never become a step toward a progressive program; on the contrary, it makes such an agreement all the more difficult and remote a prospect. NAFTA should not become a legacy of the Reagan-Bush era, but a precedent for a different North America.

NOTES

1. "Remarks of Congressman Richard A. Gephardt—Address on the Status of the North American Free Trade Agreement before the Institute for International Economics," July 27, 1992.

2. Raul Hinojosa, Sherman Robinson, and Albert Fishlow, "Proposal for a North American Regional Development Bank and Adjustment Fund," in "North American Free Trade: Proceedings of a Conference," sponsored by the Federal Reserve Bank of Dallas, Texas, June 14, 1991.

3. For further discussion of the possible elements of a social charter see George E. Brown, Jr., William Goold, and John Cavanagh, "Making Trade Fair," *World Policy Journal*, Spring 1992, pp. 309–327.

7

Margaret Atwood

BLIND FAITH AND FREE TRADE

I believe the free-trade issue has the potential to fragment and destroy the country in a way that nothing else has succeeded in doing.

I would dearly like to hope that this agreement is going to be in some way "good for the country." Why? Partly because it's Canadian to take that attitude: as a nation, we do tend to have this touching and naive belief that those in authority know what they're doing. But also because if someone comes along and puts a hand over your eyes and shoves an unknown, dubious substance down your throat, all you've got to fall back on is hope. You just hope like heck it's going to turn out to be good for you in the end. But hope is no substitute for reality.

So I'm sitting around reading the rhetoric in the newspapers, with my ears aflap for news, open to being convinced. But so far I'm not, and I'd like to share with you some of the reasons why not and put to you some of the questions that trouble my waking hours, and even my sleeping ones, during which Dief the Chief appears to me in dreams, jowls quivering in outrage, and asks me what's going on and why the prime minister began by saying that free trade would threaten Canada's sovereignty but changed his mind after the election, while Sir John A. Macdonald revolves rapidly in his grave.

"Don't ask me, ask them," I say. But ghosts have a way of visiting only those who remember them.

My first worry is that there are no hard facts.

Why not? For the simple reason that nobody can predict the future. No matter how many graphs you draw up, as long as they are graphs about the future they don't necessarily hold any more water than a leaky boot.

The future is like life after death. You can say anything you like about it, because nobody can actually go there and come back and tell us about it.

We know more or less what we're giving up—though we won't know the whole of it till after the small print has been passed through the mental digestive systems of the lawyers—but we can't know what we're getting in return.

In short, I don't understand the full scope and implications of this agreement and I don't believe anyone else really does either. Maybe I'm just stupid, but if so there's a lot more stupid people like me running around loose.

But there are two things in particular, having to do with the cultural community, that appear to have been sacrificed so far. These things do not affect me financially in any large way but I must say what I think their effects will be.

One is the film distribution policy, which will soon appear, we are given to understand, in a very watered-down form, because the original would have displeased the great star-spangled Them and interfered with this agreement.

There goes the Canadian film industry in any major form.

I would love to stand corrected on this.

The other is the abolition of special postal rates for Canadian magazines. There go our national magazines, not to mention our literary magazines—which, as any writer who has come up through the ranks will tell you, are the only entry to the larger literary marketplace for most young writers.

Unless steps are taken to counterbalance the effects of this, we're going to be way worse off on the magazine front than we were even in 1960. This deal also severely limits our power to introduce any new initiatives on the cultural front. It gives us, not more freedom of movement, but much less.

Second point: We're told that polls show a 49-percent in-favor response, but I distrust polls. Why? Because I have a background in market research, and I know that the answers you get depend a lot on how you ask the questions.

I expect that if the poll question is simply "Are you in favor of free trade?" you're going to get a certain amount of Yes because "free" is a positive word, as in free gift, free lunch, free world, and free speech.

But if you asked: "Are you in favor of this particular trade deal if it means you have to give up your health insurance, unemployment benefits, and regional development aid—which remain vulnerable to challenge as unfair subsidies under U.S. trade law—and if you also have to give up Canada's foreign affairs autonomy and our visibility in arts and entertainment—and if it means the loss of a million jobs, with only vague notions of how they'll be replaced—and if it also means we're committed to playing only by the other guy's rules?" I expect you'd get a different response.

And what if you asked: "Are you in favor of this deal if it means the disintegration of Canada?" Maybe that's something we should ask. In other words do we really want a country?

A level playing field, after all, is one from which all distinguished features have been removed.

One category of jobs that's not on the table is that of federal member of Parliament. But if that august body is divesting itself of its powers, the ordinary taxpayer is going to start asking, sooner or later, what's Ottawa for? What powers remain? I mean, why pay extra? If it's Washington making the decisions anyway, why deal with the middleman? Why don't we just join them?

Canada as a separate but dominated country has done about as well under the U.S. as women worldwide have done under men; about the only position they've ever adopted toward us, country to country, has been the missionary position, and we were not on top.

I guess that's why the national wisdom vis-à-vis Them has so often taken the form of lying still, keeping your mouth shut, and pretending you like it. But as part of Them, at least we'd get to vote, eh? We'd sure as heck fit in; we already know more about them than we know about one another, or so you'd think.

Short form: Can Canada? If Canada can't, can it.

Third point: It's no use ridiculing scenarios like this, or calling people who talk about them cowards or idiots or Nazis or self-interested, all of which terms have been bandied about recently, just as it's no good calling pro–free traders cowards or idiots or Nazis or self-interested.

It's no good accusing people of wrapping themselves in the flag, and I might point out in passing that it seems to be okay in the States to do this flag-wrapping act—they have this thing called patriotism, it's thought of as standing up for yourself—but in Canada it's seen as bad taste or even subversive. I wonder why.

May I suggest that instead of name-calling, each side should try to find out what will really be "good" for the country.

This throws us back to Philosophy 101: how do you define "good"? Is it only money we're talking about here? I don't think so.

Canadian people, like people everywhere, have values other than money that are important to them. Their fears of losing these values are real fears, by which I mean that they are truly held and must be addressed.

It's no use claiming that there is some mysterious gene of Canadianness, welded into us at conception, that will guarantee the retention of these values even if all the social structures, educational underpinnings, and cultural manifestations of them disappear.

What will be done, if anything, to give these values a fighting chance of surviving?

As George Bernard Shaw commented when a beautiful actress wanted to have a child with him so it would have her looks and his brains, "But madam—what if it has my looks and your brains?"

We'd like to think we're about to get the best of both worlds—Canadian stability and a more caring society, plus American markets—but what if instead we get their crime rate, health programs and gun laws, and they get our markets, or what's left of them?

It's no use saying that this is mere anti-Yank paranoia: a lot of us get on just fine in the country of superlatives, and as for myself it's the land of my ancestors and the haunt of my youth.

It's not about liking the great Them, it's about wanting to be who you are. Anyone from Quebec understands the connections among culture, society, and politics, although others sometimes have to have it spelled out. Short form: just because you like women doesn't mean you want to be one.

And it's no use saying that these are emotional arguments, as if that disqualifies them. Almost all of the arguments heard so far in this debate have been emotional arguments. Fear is an emotion, yes, and love of country is an emotion, but greed is an emotion too.

Some questions us voters would like answered:

1. Has the government signed away its flexibility? The world is in for a rocky ride over the next few years, and shifts in economic ground will demand well-honed and very quick responses. Right now, Wall Street has turned tail and is demanding interventionist fiscal policies it would have spat on even a few months ago. How much room for manoeuvering are we leaving ourselves?

2. Along those lines—if you're going to hitch your wagon to a star, if you're going to merge your economy totally with another one—why not a rising star instead of one that's hovering so close to burnout? How about those U.S. budget and trade deficits? (You're looking at someone who agrees with the Wilsonian goal of reducing the deficit.)

Why not a free-trade deal with Japan, which once it connects with the huge markets in India and China and Southeast Asia, is going to eclipse the U.S.? Do we really want to risk going down with the *Titanic*?

Have we explored viable alternatives? Have we even removed barriers to trade among the provinces?

Biologically speaking, the animals that survive in tough times are generalists, not specialists. They keep their range of options wide. Are we doing that?

3. A related question: Do we have a fall-back position? What if we do this and it turns into a mess? Can we get out of it?

4. The U.S. is already our major trading partner, and vice versa. Why are we sacrificing our options as a society over a "comprehensive" trade deal that is really about the small percentage left?

5. Fifth and most important point: Why are we doing this so fast?

This is a major structural change, and nobody's being given a chance to really look at it. Nor is the U.S. timetable forcing the bulldoze act, apparently; it's our side that's in such an all-fired rush.

As one businessman said to me privately: "It's not a very good deal, but it's the only deal around so we should grab it."

This is an old snake-oil salesman technique—get some now because there's only one left. Is this last-day sale mentality the right approach to deciding the future of a people? Is it even democratic?

We need more time to see a lot more exactly who may be affected and in what ways. We need an informed, truthful national debate. We need an election.

Our national animal is the beaver, noted for its industry and its co-operative spirit. In medieval bestiaries it is also noted for its habit, when frightened, of biting off its own testicles and offering them to its pursuer. I hope we are not succumbing to some form of that impulse.

8

Martin Khor

FREE TRADE AND
THE THIRD WORLD

International economic negotiations taking place in Geneva could lead to the creation of a new body called the 'Multilateral Trade Organisation' (MTO), which might eventually lead Third World countries to further economic dislocation and greater loss of national sovereignty.

The talks, known as the Uruguay Round, are conducted under the umbrella of the General Agreement on Tariffs and Trade (GATT). Some Northern countries (principally the EC) want to vastly expand GATT's powers and institutionalise them in the proposed new MTO.

Whilst the present GATT only deals with issues relating to trade in non-agricultural goods, the proposed MTO would also have powers over agricultural goods, trade and investments in the services sectors, foreign investments, and rights over technology ('intellectual property rights').

There is a possibility that the long drawn out Uruguay Round will be completed this year, perhaps even within a few months. Many Third World–oriented analysts believe the final set of agreements will be weighted against the South's interest. Whilst Northern countries may squabble among themselves in certain issues (agriculture in particular), as a group they stand to gain by the expansion of GATT's powers into new areas.

The EC wants a Multilateral Trade Organisation (MTO) to cement and follow up on the various parts of the Uruguay Round. The US has proposed a 'GATT-2' instead. But whatever new institution or arrangement eventually emerges, an expanded GATT in charge of new areas such as investments, services and intellectual property will not generally be in the South's interests.

GATT's principles of liberalisation (opening up one's national economy to outside market forces) would then be applied not only to trade, but also to investments and services. On the other hand, the South's access to technology would be curbed by new intellectual property rules, thus perpetuating the Northern countries' technological domination.

And the rules the MTO is planning to operate are wide-ranging, with very serious implications for shaping the economic and political models and policies of all countries. Incorporating the various results and agreements of the Uruguay Round, the MTO will be the institution to monitor and implement a wide range of economic (and not just trade) rules. Among them:

- An agreement on services, which is likely to open up the services sectors (such as banking, insurance, tourism, professions, culture) of Third World countries to foreign companies and operators. It will be difficult for local companies and professionals to compete successfully in many areas.
- An agreement on intellectual property rights, in which Third World countries will have to introduce patent and copyright laws that protect the interests of transnational companies, and hinder the local development of technology.
- An agreement on 'investment measures' that would prohibit countries from disallowing the entry of foreign investors. Once established in a country, the foreign firm should be accorded 'national treatment' (treated no differently from a local company). Thus, policies favouring local companies would be prohibited. Moreover, conditions now imposed by many Third World countries on foreign companies (for example, some of their equity should be owned by locals, specified portions of their materials used should be locally supplied, and a ratio of their output should be expanded) would be disallowed.
- An agreement on agriculture that would force countries to stop restricting the import of foreign food and other agricultural products, and to reduce import duties as well. Farmers in countries where agriculture is protected will be adversely affected.

Third World official resistance to an Uruguay Round conclusion that is, on balance, harmful to developing countries' interests is now very low or minimal. The initial fights put up by countries like India have considerably softened, as most of them face pressures caused by external debt and dependence on World Bank loans.

In mid-December, United States representatives at the GATT talks also rejected the idea of establishing the EC-inspired MTO. Instead, they proposed that the present GATT be expanded into a 'GATT-2', which would also deal with monitoring and implementing all the agreements of the Uruguay Round (including intellectual property, investment, services and agriculture). There are some significant differences between the MTO and GATT-2 proposals. The effect of an expanded GATT would however be essentially the same for South countries, and indeed the US proposal may have even more harmful potential.

The following are nine arguments why the MTO and the Uruguay Round package (as it now stands) are against Third World interests. Although the arguments are framed against the proposed MTO, they could also generally apply in substance to other similar institutional arrangements (such as GATT-2 or a Super-GATT) that will implement the Uruguay Round accords.

1. A Strengthened GATT Will Extend the Liberal Model

The MTO institutionalises and expands GATT's powers and greatly extends the neo-liberal model into the area of services and investments. This will result in an economic 'monoculture' with only one (i.e. laissez-faire) model dominating the world. This strengthens the strong and big (the North, big companies, the rich) whilst marginalising and damaging the weak & small (the South, small farms and firms, the poor). At the same time, the MTO would also introduce intellectual property rights regimes that protect the technological monopoly of transnational corporations and deny South countries the opportunity to develop their own technical capacity.

2. The South Will Have to Bear Two Crosses: Retaliation & Conditionality

The South countries will bear the burden of two 'crosses' that bind and lock them into specific economic policies and positions from which there is no future escape. There is a colonial-type imposition of 'free market–free enterprise' policies that open the doors to TNCs to penetrate South markets, enter Southern countries to locate their business and industries, and export Southern natural resources to the world market.

The two 'crosses' are:

(a) Cross retaliation: Since the MTO will expand the GATT-style mechanisms to new areas (services, investments, intellectual property, agriculture) besides the trade in goods, and given the integrated dispute settlement mechanism, Northern countries can threaten Southern countries with cross-sectoral retaliation.

The MTO's power will rest not only on the broad range of economic areas it will command, but also on its enforcement capability. It will have an 'integrated dispute settlement procedure' that enables 'cross-sectoral retaliation'. This means that a country that is found not to comply in one area (say, it does not enact intellectual property laws in conformity with MTO standards) can be retaliated against in another area where it can really cause hurt (for example, restrictions are placed on importing its main export goods). The potential damage for non-compliance is so huge that Third World countries could be pressured to follow the rules. ('If you don't allow my US bank into your country and if you don't introduce patent laws to protect my companies, I will forbid your rubber, copper, textiles, etc., from entering my country.') The Super 301 unilateral (illegal) retaliatory actions of the US could be legitimised and universalised through using the MTO vehicle. Weak countries have no choice but to comply.

(b) Cross conditionalities: The MTO draft specifies that: 'With a view to achieving greater coherence in global economic policy-making, the MTO shall cooperate, as appropriate, with the IMF and with the IBRD (World Bank) and its affiliated agencies'. It is likely that in the future the MTO, IMF and World Bank will synchronise their policies towards the Third World and institute 'cross-conditionalities' to pressure countries to accept the policies of all three institutions.

The MTO, which would become a Super-GATT, would have international regulatory teeth over almost all economic activities generated internationally as well as nationally. It would become as powerful as the World Bank and International Monetary Fund (which deal with finance) and even surpass their influence. This trio of global institutions acting in concert, dovetailing and coordinating their policies, will have overpowering sway over the national policies and structures of weaker countries, namely those in the Third World. For example, a World Bank loan would be given only if the country is given a clean bill of health from the MTO in following its rules. Or the MTO, in determining whether a country is adopting adequate policies to correct balance of payments problems may refer to the IMF and depend on its judgment. Thus, a single set of policies, instituting an economic monoculture, will be put in place, driven by the three global institutions.

3. Erosion of National Sovereignty

The MTO would erode national sovereignty (national control over domestic policies) as member governments have to alter a wide range of laws and policies to conform to the agreements overseen by the MTO. Particularly affected are policies relating to external trade, domestic self-sufficiency (for example, in food or basic manufactured products), foreign investment, intellectual property, technology. But there will be ramifications also for health, safety, environmental, labour and cultural policies. Weak nations (the South) will find their economies placed even more at the service of Northern interests, and their space for independent policies will be very limited.

Once the government of a country signs on to the proposed MTO as part of the Uruguay Round package, it would be very difficult for that government, or any successor government, to amend or get out of the deal. Each country would have to amend its national laws and policies to conform to the Uruguay Round agreement. Whichever government or Parliament comes to power in the future would have severely limited capacity to chart independent policies or laws relating to the major economic aspects such as trade, foreign investments, services and technological development.

4. Erosion of People's Rights

Besides national sovereignty, the MTO would also erode the powers of civil society, including Parliaments, interest groups and local communities. Parliaments have little choice but to enact laws to conform to the Uruguay Round agreements, even though these Parliaments have no prior knowledge and have not given their consent to what the governments might sign.

Whichever party may come to power in the future would also have to follow the same policies dictated by MTO rules which existing governments have signed on to. Small local firms and farms will be seriously affected by each country's agreement to open up trade and investments to the foreign market and companies, but they would have had little say or knowledge of the accords. These small firms and farms are likely to be further marginalised.

5. The MTO Would Cause the Further Loss of Influence of the Global Civil Society and Erode International Democracy

Like GATT, the MTO would not be located within the United Nations system, and thus not answerable to the UN's General Assembly. Since the MTO will have such vast powers, and enforcement capability, it will erode and usurp the already limited powers of UN agencies such as UNCTAD, ECOSOC, the recently formed Commission on Sustainable Development, and the General Assembly itself. The MTO's processes are likely to be untransparent, like GATT's and the major powers can be expected to make their own deals and ask Third World countries to accept them. The MTO will coordinate policies with the IMF and World Bank (which have policies and principles similar to the MTO's) and thus this trio of global institutions will be able to impose a single, consistent laissez-faire model on the South. The 'balancing' force of UN agencies would be much weakened.

6. MTO Decontextualises Commerce from Broader Social and Development Concerns

The MTO decontextualises trade, investment, services, and intellectual property from broader social and development issues. These issues would be treated in the MTO through the narrow perspective of laissez-faire commerce and the overriding imperative for 'liberalisation' and thus side-step and avoid the broader development perspective that stresses employment and income generation, social equity, strengthening of the domestic economy and domestic producers and fulfilment of human needs. The MTO's bias towards commerce will replace the broader social and development perspective that was behind the concept of the International Trade Organisation (ITO) proposed under the UN in the late 1940s.

7. The Aim of Creating a Broader Trade Organisation Will Be Jettisoned

Indeed, the establishment of the MTO would imply the abandonment of the efforts to establish a more universal, democratic ITO with broader development objectives within the UN family, that had been envisaged in the Havana Charter. The MTO, to be run along GATT lines, would become a pretender as successor organisation to the ITO. The old model of a comprehensive trade organisation serving the development needs of all member countries (the ITO) would give way to a new model stressing the survival of the fittest in a liberalised commercial world, with no pity for those left behind. This replacement of models may not even be widely noticed or noted; the vision of a world economic system serving human needs would be reduced to the merciless competition of the world market to which almost all countries are pressed to join.

8. The MTO Is Also Likely to Accelerate the Process of Environmental Deterioration

The liberalising of investment movements through the agreements on trade-related investment measures (TRIMs) and on services would open Third World countries up to faster exploitation of their natural resources by TNCs, as well as to more rapid transfer of environmentally harmful investments, projects and products. The patenting of life-forms through the trade-related intellectual property rights (TRIPs) agreement will have environmentally harmful effects. Governments will also lose some of their autonomy to set their own safety and environmental standards, as these would have to be 'harmonised' (and thus in some cases actually lowered) to norms determined by the MTO or affiliated bodies.

9. Erosion of Cultural Identity & Diversity

The Uruguay Round agreements are also likely to accelerate the evolution of a monoculture in cultural areas such as media, films, TV news and feature programmes, and also educational and health services. This will be through the liberalisation of services that would pressurise Third World countries to accept and receive the cultural and professional services of foreign companies and individuals. Governments will find it increasingly difficult to regulate or prevent such cultural and service imports. Since the largest and most powerful cultural enterprises belong to the North, the already rapid spread of modern Western-originating culture will be accelerated even more. Cultural diversity would thus be rapidly eroded.

The MTO proposal has been mooted by the EC countries as part of the Uruguay Round package that negotiators from Europe and the US are trying desperately to complete within a few months. If these two major powers resolve their differences, mainly over agricultural issues, they will try to get Third World countries to accept the whole package on a 'take it or leave it' basis. Almost all countries would find it difficult to resist the pressure to sign on, because no state wants to be left out in the cold, with prospects that its exports will be hit.

Several citizen groups and non-governmental organisations have launched a campaign against the setting up of an MTO along the proposed lines. At a recent meeting in Hamburg, 25 groups from North and South issued the following statement urging governments to exclude the MTO from the Uruguay Round final document:

As representatives of NGOs from both South and North countries, we are concerned that the substantive issues of the UR have not been adequately explained to the public.

In particular we are very concerned about the proposal in the UR to establish a new body named the MTO (Multilateral Trade Organisation). It would have massive powers that would overcome other multilateral, regional and national rules.

Whilst there are good reasons for a multilateral rule-based trade and economic regime, neither GATT nor the MTO should be the seat of such a body. The MTO would not be open or transparent nor accountable to those who would live under its rules. It would not give an equal voice to developing countries and its narrow commercial approach would render it unable to take account of development needs or environmental concerns.

We appeal to all governments involved in the UR negotiations to review this proposal of the MTO. The creation of the MTO or any implementation body was not part of the Punta del Este declaration of the UR and has to be removed from any UR agreement.

The reasons for concern are as follows:

1. The MTO proposal has very serious consequences that would affect

the social, economic and cultural policies, and the environment and life of all countries. These consequences have not been adequately publicised, discussed or debated by the public in our countries.

2. The MTO would be based on GATT and greatly expand its powers to deal not only with trade in goods but also with investments, services and intellectual property rights. The MTO would thus become the most powerful economic body in the world with powers that override national policies and possibly other international agreements.

3. The MTO would become a powerful new instrument to impose policies on weaker countries. The MTO for the first time would introduce and legitimise an international system of 'cross-sectoral retaliation' to enforce regimes or rules that compulsorily liberalise trade and investments in goods and services and that force all countries to have intellectual property laws that hamper technology transfer. Countries that do not follow these rules could have high duties or bans imposed on their goods. Developing countries would be forced to adopt national economic and social policies that weaken their domestic economic sectors and restrict their local technological development, under the excuse that total liberalisation would benefit developing countries.

4. The binding enforcement powers of the MTO would damage environmental, safety and consumer interests; its emphasis on trade liberalisation is not balanced by national and international commitments to respect sustainable development.

For example:

a. Nations would lose control over their natural resources, e.g. inequitable liberalisation of agricultural trade would preclude sustainable agricultural systems and damage fragile environments around the world;

b. In some cases, nations would be obliged to harmonise environmental and social standards downwards, e.g. the proposals under the Technical Barriers to Trade would prevent the application of adequate environmental standards at the national level;

c. The patenting of life-forms through Trade-Related Intellectual Property Rights (TRIPs) would harm the environment;

d. The liberalising of investment flows through Trade-Related Investment Measures (TRIMs) would severely reduce governments' capacity to impose conditions on foreign companies.

5. Being based at GATT with GATT-style rules, the MTO would be

outside the UN system and would deplete the influence of the UN over economic affairs. The MTO would thus contribute to a loss of international-level democracy, and render global economic decision-making even less transparent and accountable.

6. The MTO would reduce multilateral or national controls over big companies, and counter present efforts in other fora to regulate the restrictive business practices of transnational corporations (TNCs). Thus big corporations would increase their monopoly of markets without responsibility to meet national or international obligations, at the expense of small producers, consumers and the environment.

We do not believe that the MTO would be the answer to the need for multilateral trading rules, as it would increase tensions between strong and weak nations and even among strong nations themselves. It would disrupt the livelihoods of communities, small farmers, small firms, and traders. It would be at the expense of consumers and the environment.

We therefore propose the following:

1. The establishment of the MTO should be excluded from all proposals being negotiated in the Uruguay Round.

2. The issue of the MTO should be publicised and openly discussed by Parliaments, interest groups and the public in every country.

3. Instead of a GATT-based MTO we propose the setting up of an international trade body to be set up under the jurisdiction of the United Nations General Assembly (UNGA)—taking into account that the UN system must also be accountable to the principles of equity, transparency, and democracy.

The negotiations to create any international trade regime and its subsequent deliberations must be conducted in an open and democratic manner, bearing in mind that trade is not an end in itself and should be simply a means to the goal of sustainable development. Any trade body must therefore respect countries' obligations under other UN agreements, and defer to the authority of other UN institutions with social, economic and environmental results. Any trade body must be subjected to a full review by the UNGA after 5 years, upon which its continued functioning would depend.

Northern governments and institutions have tended to highlight, in exaggerated ways, the benefits that a Uruguay Round conclusion would bring. The Western media has in recent months often cited $200 billion as the additional boost the Round would give the world economy. But the supposed source of that figure, the powerful OECD Secretariat, has now distanced itself from this estimate which it says was the result of a 'pretty theoretical study' and the figure was taken out of context (*Third World Economics*, 16–31 December 1992).

In the Punta del Este meeting Declaration that launched the Uruguay Round in the early 1980s, it was agreed that a review be made of the impact of the final agreement on developing countries, prior to its conclusion. So far, no official review has been carried out.

It would appear that the Third World is once again at the mercy of the major Northern powers. If the Uruguay Round is concluded in the next few months, and either an MTO or a GATT-2 is established, this new institution would be an additional powerful vehicle to shape and re-shape the economies and societies of the South to serve Northern interests even more efficiently. The world would then be ruled economically by the G7 and OECD nations, using the trio of World Bank and IMF (for finance, development projects and macro-economic policies via structural adjustment loans) and the MTO or GATT-2 (for trade, investments and technology).

9

Vandana Shiva

BIODIVERSITY AND INTELLECTUAL PROPERTY RIGHTS

The Seed Satyagraha

On 3 March 1993, more than 200,000 farmers from all over India gathered at Delhi's historic Red Fort to protest against the Dunkel Draft Text (DDT) of the Uruguay Round of GATT negotiations. In particular they were protesting against the intellectual property rights clauses of the draft agreement, which threaten to rob Third World farmers, who are the original donors of biodiversity, of their freedom to use, reproduce and modify their seeds and plant material.

Earlier, on 29 December 1992, farmers of the Karnataka Rajya Ryota Sangha (Karnataka State Farmers' Association) had served notice to Cargill Seeds (India) at their head office in Bangalore, calling it the "Second Quit India Movement." The first "Quit India" movement was started by Mahatma Gandhi in 1942, when he had served notice to the British Empire to quit India.

India's freedom movement was based on a series of Satyagrahas (the fight for truth). The Champaran Satyagraha was against the forced cultivation of indigo by British planters in Bihar, which had deprived the peasants of food. The Salt Satyagraha was against imposition of salt laws, which taxed the making of salt to raise revenues for the British army. On 5 April 1930 Mahatma Gandhi launched the national non-cooperation movement with the campaign for the production and distribution of salt at Dandi beach in Gujarat, violating the Salt Law of the British that had guaranteed their monopoly in the production and distribution of salt. Salt is a vital resource for the survival of both human and animal life, especially in tropical countries like India. It remained a common resource till the British monopolised its production and distribution to transform it into a source of revenue. The growth imperative compelled the expansion of the salt industry, as monopolised by the British, at the cost of diversion of resources from essential economic activities like food production. Further, in order to increase revenue the British government raised the salt tax in 1923 through the Indian Finance Bill of the Viceroy. This triggered off strong protests all over the country since a basic resource like salt was being denied to the people in order to increase revenue. The anguish of Gandhi on the appropriation of a common resource was clear when he said,

> They even tax our salt—a necessity of life, only less necessary than air and water. It ought to be free as they are. . . . Nature bestows it on us and we may not use it. There is salt beside the sea and they forbid us to gather it.

The seed too is essential to life, and has been gifted by nature, improved over centuries by farmers and freely exchanged between farmers and between countries. The "Seed Satyagraha" which started with the action against Cargill has been called the second Salt Satyagraha. It is against the attempt by Transnational Corporations (TNCs) to gain monopoly on seed which has so far been a local common resource. The Trade Related Intellectual Property Rights (TRIPs) agreement of the DDT is the equivalent of the salt laws of the British in the area of biodiversity and agriculture. Since seeds and biodiversity are the very basis of food production, monopoly control on seed implies the slavery of all farmers to the TNCs. Farmers of India are fighting against this new threat of slavery and bondage in a new form. When they had a Satyagraha at the Cargill office, this is what they stated in their literature.

Dear Farmers,
The second Salt Satyagraha has started today. This "Seed Satyagraha" is to protect the right of farmers to produce, modify and sell seeds. Seed freedom is freedom of the Nation.
• Our genetic resources are our national property.

- We oppose patents or any form of intellectual property protection on Plants and genes.
- To produce, modify and sell seeds is the right of the farmers.
- We want the preservation of the Indian Patent Act 1970, which excludes patents on all life forms.
- We want a ban on the entry of Multi-National Corporations in the Seed sector.
- We oppose total control of global trade by Multi-National Corporations.

Whose Freedom Do IPRs Protect?

Free trade of TNCs does not translate into freedom for farmers of the Third World. TNC freedom depends on protectionist and monopoly measures like intellectual property rights (IPRs), which must rob farmers of their freedom to produce, reproduce, modify and sell seeds.

However, Third World farmers are not the only community affected by IPRs in the area of biodiversity. Herbalists, forest dwellers, fishing communities, pastoralists who depend on biodiversity for their survival, whose resources and knowledge are freely used by the TNCs which then demand IPR protection, will also be severely affected by IPRs in so called free trade agreements.

Most discussions around Trade Related Intellectual Property Rights (TRIPs) in GATT have focussed on the assumption that only the intellectual contributions of corporate sponsored scientists need intellectual property protection and compensation. The only North-South debate then is on how IPRs will restrict transfer of technology from the industrialised North to the industrialising South.

However, no attention has been paid to how IPRs will encourage the uncompensated free flow of resources and knowledge from the South to North. A very significant issue that has been missing in these debates is how the very construction of IPRs in GATT counts as knowledge and innovation only that which can generate profits. Knowledge and innovation for social ends such as health care and sustainable agriculture is discounted as knowledge and intellectual contribution. The intellectual contribution of societies and communities which have not been motivated by the objective of profits is thus exploited, but not recognised. For example, ethnobotanists transfer knowledge from traditional healers to pharmaceutical firms. The intellectual property rights therefore raise multiple questions of Whose intellect? What property? Whose rights? What rights?

In this wider framework, traditional farmers who have selected, improved and conserved biodiversity, or traditional healers who have used plant diversity for medicine also have prior intellectual property rights which need protection. When this knowledge and biodiversity is exploited for commercial ends, these contributors need to have a role in determining whether such exploitation should take place, and what the terms of compensation should be. IPRs in the area of biodiversity are no longer a mere matter of transfer of technology but become the ground for intercultural dialogue.

It is crucial to recognise that for many communities, knowledge and biological resources are inalienable. No price is high enough to justify their appropriation.

In the hill regions of Garhwal, for example, people have valued their seeds more than their lives. In the *Himalayan Gazetteer*, Atkinson records that during a devastating famine thousands died. Later, it was found that the seeds of rice, wheat, mandua, jhangora were safe in all the homes next to the dead. People preferred to starve to death rather than finish the seed.

Negotiations related to biodiversity and biological innovations are complicated because different groups and actors involved give different meanings to basic concepts. For traditional societies, biodiversity is common property, and knowledge related to it is in the intellectual commons. For biotechnology corporations biodiversity becomes private property through their investments, and IPRs are the means for such privatisation.

Throughout history, biodiversity has been the common property of local communities—with both resources and knowledge being exchanged freely. The absence of a price has however not meant a lack of value. Biodiversity has, in fact, been highly valued in traditional societies through cultural and social mechanisms which have allowed its simultaneous conservation and utilisation.

The emergence of genetic engineering as the new biotechnology has encouraged the emergence of patents and intellectual property rights in products derived from biodiversity. However, the new regime of patent rights to biotechnology products is also rewriting the traditional rights to biodiversity. Instead of being treated as common property of local communities or as national property of sovereign states the Third World's biodiversity has in recent years been treated as the common heritage of mankind. In contrast, the modified biodiversity is sold back to the Third World as priced and patented seeds and drugs. As Jack Kloppenberg has observed, "whereas germplasm flows out of the South as the common heritage of mankind," it returns as a commodity.

From the perspective of the Third World farmers, herbalists and tribals, IPRs in the area of biodiversity are the ultimate threat to the ecological, ethical and economic fabric of life and livelihoods. They do not create freedom for nature or people, they destroy it. They do create unfettered freedom for TNCs to manipulate and monopolise living diversity for the sole end of limitless profits.

Harmonisation of IPR Regimes

The India patent law does not recognise any form of intellectual property in the area of biodiversity. Article 3(h) of the Indian Patent Act 1970 says that "patents cannot be given for a method of agriculture or horticulture" and Article 3(i) says that "they cannot be given for any process for the medicinal, surgical, curative, prophylactic or other treatment of human beings or any process for a similar treatment of animals or plants to render them free of disease or to increase their economic value or of their products." These exclusions of the Indian Patent Act that have kept agriculture out of the monopoly control of the corporate sector are now threatened.

The Dunkel Draft does not allow any exclusion of biodiversity from IPR control. Article 27 of the TRIPs proposals states "that patents shall be available for any invention, whether products or processes." Article 27 also states that "exclusions are allowed for other than microorganisms and essentially biological processes for the production of plants or animals other than non-biological and micro-biological processes. However, parties shall provide for the protection of plant varieties either by patents or any effective sui generis system or any combination thereof. This provision shall be reviewed four years after the entry into force of this agreement."

Article 27 therefore makes it imperative that some form of IPR system be introduced in plants. Patents themselves are not obligatory, but either patents or an "effective *sui generis* system" are compulsory. *Sui generis* means a form of intellectual property rights which is derived from itself. This has allowed the false impression that each country is free to have its own IPR system. However, the key term in Article 27 is "effective". This term was also introduced by the US in Article 16.2 of the Biodiversity Convention. The final draft of the Convention dealt with this issue in Article 16 and introduced a clause in 16.2 which states that

> In the case of technology subject to patents and other intellectual property rights, such access and transfer shall be provided on terms which recognise and are consistent with the adequate and effective protection of intellectual property rights.

As Gareth Porter has pointed out in his study of the United States and the Biodiversity Convention, the phrase "adequate and effective protection", which was introduced by the US in the Convention, was also introduced by it in the TRIPs agreement of the Dunkel Draft of the Uruguay Round multilateral trade agreement. The first sentence of that text refers to the need to "promote effective and adequate protection of intellectual property rights." The same phrase is in Section 301 of the Trade and Competitiveness Act of 1988, which has been used to retaliate against countries whose IPR laws do not conform to US standards. The term was defined by the office of the US trade representative and its introduction in Article 16.2 of the Convention has been used to signify a demand that other countries' IPR laws be made to conform to the US laws. The US did not finally sign the Biodiversity Convention at the Earth Summit in Rio de Janeiro, in spite of having introduced its IPR language in Article 16 and in spite of having succeeded in excluding ex-situ collections of biodiversity in international gene banks from the regulatory framework of the Convention because the US administration would have liked to achieve even more concessions for TNCs, especially the biotechnology industry.

The use of the term "effective" in all global negotiations related to IPRs and biodiversity is a result of a US attempt to globalise US IPR regimes which allow patenting of all life, including plants and animals. In the Dunkel text, the phrase "effective *sui generis* system" implies that such a system will not be determined by individual countries but by GATT. Further, given the trend of the developments in international negotiations the only system recognised as "effective" at the international level is the system of plant breeders' rights as codified in the International Convention for the Protection of New Varieties of Plants (UPOV). Plant breeders' rights as recognised in UPOV give monopoly markets to breeders of new varieties.

The amendments of UPOV in 1991 have increased the monopoly role of breeders' rights. The farmers' exemption which gave farmers the right to save their own seeds has also been removed from the amended version of the UPOV Convention. Farmers now have to pay royalties for saving seed on their own farms even under breeders' rights regimes. Thus, whether it is patents or "effective *sui generis* systems," either system threatens farmers' rights. Under the pressure of farmers' movements against TRIPs, the Government of India has asked for a footnote to be added to Article 27.3 (b) in the context of the sui generis system for the protection of plant varieties.

The amendment proposed states:

> It is understood that the effectiveness of a *sui generis* system for the protection of plant varieties cannot be challenged on the ground that farmers' exemption and/or researchers' exemption is available in a national legislation for this purpose.

This amendment would not have been proposed if the Government of India did not anticipate that the Dunkel text, as it is, threatens the erosion of farmers' rights. In any case, if the Dunkel text of GATT is signed, TNCs will have the power to enforce even stricter IPR regimes after four years of the TRIPs agreement coming into force. Short term safeguards for farmers which might be achieved through minor amendments like footnotes to Article 27 will not be guaranteed beyond four years even if they are accepted.

For the TNCs, the objective is simple—to expand their markets and monopolise seed supply by forcing farmers to buy seed from them every year, through the implementation of IPRs, either in the form of patents or breeders' rights. It is this monopolisation of the first link in the food production system that the Indian farmers, who constitute a quarter of the world farming community, are resisting.

The corporate demand to change a common heritage into a commodity and to treat monopoly profits generated through this transformation as a property right will lead to erosion not just at the ethical and cultural level, but also at the economic level for the Third World farmers. The Third World farmer has a three-level relationship with the corporations demanding a monopoly of life forms and life processes. Firstly, the farmer is a supplier of germplasm to transnational corporations. Secondly, the farmer is a competitor in terms of innovation and rights to genetic resources. Finally, the Third World farmer is a consumer of the technological and industrial products of TNCs. Patent protection displaces the farmer as a competitor, transforms him into a supplier of free raw material, and makes him totally dependent on industrial supplies for vital imputs like seed. Above all is the frantic cry for patent protection *from* farmers, who are the original breeders and developers of biological resources in agriculture. It is argued that patent protection is essential for innovation—however, it is essential only for innovation that brings profits to corporate business. Farmers have carried out innovations over decades without any property rights or patent protection.

Intellectual property rights and patents in the area of life forms and living processes are an enclosure of the intellectual commons. Unlike mechanical artifacts, innovation and knowledge related to utilisation of living resources has been a highly evolved tradition in all cultures. Innovation for which patents are being given often only build on prior knowledge and use of biological systems for food and medicine. Instead of stimulating research and knowledge generation, patents stifle creativity and communication. In the Third World, where privatisation is not the norm, most knowledge generation takes place in the public domain, either in the formal or the informal sector. The formal sector includes all public sector research institutions, the informal sector includes all communities which maintain and generate knowledge related to biodiversity. IPRs as formulated in GATT will undermine knowledge generation and creativity in both these sectors.

IPRs particularly as being imposed worldwide through GATT are a restricting category at 3 levels:

The first restriction is the shift from common rights to private rights. As the preamble of the TRIPs agreement states, intellectual property rights are recognised only as private rights. This excludes all kinds of knowledge, ideas, and innovations that take place in the "intellectual commons"—in villages among farmers, in forests among tribals and even in universities among scientists. TRIPs is, therefore, a mechanism for the privatisation of the intellectual commons, and a de-intellectualisation of civil society, so that the mind becomes a corporate monopoly.

The second restriction of intellectual property rights is that they are recognised only when knowledge and innovation generate profits, not when they meet social needs. Article 27.1 of TRIPs refers to the condition that to be recognised as an IPR, innovation has to be capable of industrial application. This immediately excludes all sectors that produce and innovate outside the industrial mode of organisation of production. Profits and capital accumulation through industrialisation are recognised as the only ends to which creativity should be put. The social good is no longer recognised. TRIPs therefore becomes a mechanism for industrialisation of all aspects of life under corporate control, and a "deindustrialisation" of production in the small scale and in the informal sectors of society.

The most significant reduction of IPRs is achieved by the prefix "trade related". Since most innovation in the public domain is for domestic, local, and public use, not for international trade, and only multinational corporations (MNCs) innovate for the sole purpose of increasing their share in global markets and international trade, TRIPs in MTO will only be an enforcement of the rights of MNCs to monopolise all production—all distribution and all profits at the cost of all citizens, and small producers worldwide, and Third World countries.

Both the informal as well as the formal sectors are affected negatively through the intellectual enclosures engendered by patents. The informal sector innovation is destroyed by non-recognition. For example when ethno-botanists transfer knowledge from traditional healers to pharmaceutical firms and genetic resource conservationists transfer knowledge from farmers to seed corporations, the intellectual property rights go to the corporations, not to the farmers and healers. Over time this appropriation of knowledge kills the original socio-cultural context of knowledge generation.

The formal sector of innovation and knowledge is destroyed by restricting free access to scientific knowledge due to patent restrictions. The broad patents on scientific processes and on life forms block free exchange of ideas and materials, which have in the first place been taken freely from the informal sector in the biodiversity rich Third World. Patents thus block a free flow of knowledge from the formal sector of the North to the formal sector of the South while maintaining a free flow from the informal sector of the South to the formal sector of the North. Patents also block a free flow of knowledge between the formal and informal sectors of the South once research is systematically privatised and transnationalised, breaking the vital umbilical cord of links between science and society, which is the only sustainable source for the nurturance of creativity.

Biodiversity and knowledge about its utilisation, therefore, gets steadily eroded in the public domain, causing both ecological and economic im-
poverishment in the Third World.

TNCs see both nature and Third World farmers as a block to their market expansion. John Hamilton of Cargill India has stated that Cargill's
technology for making hybrid sunflowers prevents "bees from usurping
the pollen." From the TNC perspective even nature's freedom to reproduce
life through its complex ecological webs is seen as usurpation. Similarly,
small peasants freely reproducing seed are viewed as "pirates" by those who
have robbed the Third World of its biodiversity and its biological knowledge.

The TNC demand for IPRs to biodiversity is based on the false assumption that TNCs have made investments and therefore need to be re-
warded with monopoly control and that their investments alone lead to innovation. These assumptions become mechanisms for robbing Third
World farmers of their inalienable rights to control and reproduce seed as
a means of food production. Firstly, by treating capital investment as the
only investment that must have rewards in the form of monopoly control,
the centuries of investment of time and creativity by Third World farmers
in domesticating, breeding and conserving biodiversity is negated.

Secondly, by only recognising corporate manipulation of life as "improvement", improvements made by millions of Third World farmers
over centuries are denied and their seed is reduced to "raw material" to be
saved in international gene banks for corporate breeding programmes.

Farmers' seeds are rendered incomplete and valueless by the process that
makes corporate seeds the basis of wealth creation. The indigenous varieties or land races, evolved through both natural and human selection, and
produced and used by Third World farmers world-wide are called "primitive cultivals." Those varieties created by modern plant breeders in international research centres or by transnational seed corporations are called
"advanced" or "elite". The tacit hierarchy in words like "primitive" and
"elite" becomes an explicit one in the process of conflict. Thus, the North
has always used Third World germplasm as a freely available resource and
treated it as valueless. The advanced capitalist nations wish to retain free
access to the developing world's storehouse of genetic diversity, while the
South likes to have the proprietary varieties of the North's industry declared a similarly "public" good. The North, however, resists this democracy, based on the logic of the market. Williams, Executive Secretary of

International Bureau of Plant and Genetic Resources (IBPGR) has argued that "it is not the original material which cash returns". A 1983 forum on Plant breeding, sponsored by Pioneer Hi-Bred stated that:

> Some insist that since germplasm is a resource belonging to the public, such improved varieties would be supplied to farmers in the source country at either zero or low cost. This overlooks the fact that "raw" germplasm only becomes valuable after considerable investment of time and money, both in adapting exotic germplasm for use by applied plant breeders and in incorporating the germplasm into varieties useful to farmers.

The corporate perspective views as value only that which serves the market. However, all material processes also serve ecological needs and social needs, and these needs are undermined by the monopolising tendency of corporations.

The issue of patent protection for modified life forms raises a number of unresolved political questions about ownership and control of genetic resources. The problem is that in manipulating life forms you do not start from nothing, but from other life forms which belong to others—maybe through customary law. Secondly, genetic engineering biotechnology does not create new genes, it merely relocates genes already existing in organisms. In making genes the object of value through the patent systems, a dangerous shift is placed in the approach to genetic resources.

Putting value on the gene through patents makes biology stand on its head. Complex organisms which have evolved over millennia in nature, and through the contributions of Third World peasants, tribals and healers, are reduced to their parts, and treated as mere inputs into genetic engineering. Patenting of genes thus leads to a devaluation of life forms by reducing them to their constituents and allowing them to be repeatedly owned as private property. This reductionism and fragmentation might be convenient for commercial concerns but it violates the integrity of life as well as the common property rights of Third World people. On these false notions of genetic resources and their ownership through intellectual property rights are based the trade wars at GATT. Countries like the US are using trade as a means of enforcing their patent laws and intellectual property rights on the sovereign nations of the Third World. The US has accused countries of the Third World of engaging in "unfair trading practice" if they fail to adopt US patent laws which allow monopoly rights in life forms. Yet it is the US which has engaged in unfair practices related to the use of Third World genetic resources. It has freely taken the biological diversity of the Third World genetic resources. It has freely taken the biological diversity of the Third World to spin millions of dollars of profits, none of which have been shared with Third World countries, the original owners of the germplasm. A wild tomato variety (Lycopersicon chomrelewskii) taken from Peru in 1962 has contributed $8 million a year to the American tomato processing industry by increasing the content of soluble solids. Yet, none of these profits or benefits have been shared with Peru, the original source of the genetic material.

According to Prescott-Allen, wild varieties contributed US$340 million per year between 1976 and 1980 to the US farm economy. The total contribution of wild germplasm to the American economy has been US $66 billion, which is more than the total international debt of Mexico and Philippines combined. This wild material is "owned" by sovereign states and by local people.

The losses to the Third World due to this unequal and asymmetric biological exchange are illustrated by just a few examples below:

- Of the 127 base collections of genetic resources, 81 are in industrialised countries in the International Agricultural Research Centres, and 17 in national collections of developing countries.
- The value of Third World contribution to US wheat farmers in any year is not less than $500 million. It is $120 million for rice, and $60 million for beans. In sum, American farmers receive for these three crops alone the value of $680 million from Third World farmers.
- A Turkish barley land race resistant to barley yellow dwarf virus was donated freely and saves US farmers $150 million a year.
- The Indian selection that provided American sorghums with resistance to greenbug has resulted in $12 million in yearly benefits to American agriculture.
- An Ethiopian gene protects the American barley crop from yellow dwarf disease to the amount of $150 million per annum.

These illustrative figures merely hint at the losses being suffered by the Third World in an unfair exchange of genetic resources. If to this uncompensated flow are added royalty payments, the Third World debt burden will increase tenfold.

The "Columbian exchange," which started with Europe's colonisation of the Americas (mistakingly called the discovery of America), carries on. IPRs are the new "doctrine of discovery". Instead of land, it is biodiversity which is being colonised. Patents have replaced land titles. GATT has replaced the Church and Dunkel plays the role of the Pope in conferring regimes of rights to resources without consulting with the original custodians and owners.

IPRs are the central instrument of recolonisation 500 years after Columbus. Third World people who struggled for freedom from colonisation within living memory will not give up that freedom without resistance.

The seed has very rapidly become a symbol of this new struggle for freedom. The "Seed Satyagraha" is a "fight for truth" which attempts to tell the truth about "free trade," using the non-violent, democratic methods of Gandhi. Whose freedom will govern the future will be shaped by these struggles between the corporate interest and the citizen interest.

−10−

Herman E. Daly

FROM ADJUSTMENT TO
SUSTAINABLE DEVELOPMENT
The Obstacle of Free Trade

I.

One coming to the development literature for the first time in the early or mid eighties would encounter the word "adjustment" with a frequency several standard deviations above its average in normal English prose. Syntactically the word cries out for two prepositions, with two objects—adjustment *of* what *to* what? These prepositions are usually suppressed for economy of expression, and sometimes for economy of thought as well. But what serious writers generally have in mind is adjustment of the real economy of a country to the theoretical model of an efficient economy as developed by mainstream neoclassical economics. Concretely this involves three main policies:

1. Adjustment of prices to make them better measures of full social marginal opportunity costs (internalization of social and environmental costs into prices) which frequently requires politically unpopular removal of subsidies and addition of taxes.

2. Adjustment of macroeconomic conditions to achieve monetary stability so that correct prices can be properly expressed in reliable monetary units of constant value over time. This means controlling inflation by

The views presented here are those of the author and should in no way be attributed to the World Bank, where he works in the Environment Department.

eliminating fiscal deficits and restraining the money supply. Both inflation and prices that do not measure full social marginal opportunity costs induce "distortions"—that is, situations in which private gain works against public welfare. The object of "adjustment" is then to remove "distortions".

3. Adjustment of national markets and prices to world markets and prices so as to integrate the nation into the world trading system in order to increase productivity by specialization according to comparative advantage, and to reap the further advantages of specialization made possible by expanding the extent of the market beyond national boundaries. Tariffs and quotas and any other restriction on international trade are considered "distortions".

There may be other criteria of adjustment but certainly these three seem to cover most instances of so called "adjustment lending", which invariably are for the purpose of financing a policy change aimed at rationalizing prices, dealing with macroeconomic problems of debt and deficit, and liberalizing international trade. Why a country should find it either necessary or desirable to borrow money at interest in order to adopt more reasonable national policies is not always obvious. Some tend to think of adjustment lending as bribery, although in a good cause. In any case the faith is that the policy change, like any other investment, will add more to national welfare than payment of interest on the loan will subtract from it.

II.

The first two goals of adjustment have a great deal of merit, and, with modifications to be discussed below, should remain as key parts of sustainable development policy. The third (free trade) is highly problematic in that it partially undercuts the first two, and has other serious problems as well. Elaborating this point is the main task of what follows. The problems with adjustment, and the consequent need for a transition to sustainable development as the guiding paradigm stem from the inadequacies of the object of the implicit preposition "to"—i.e. the mainstream model to which the real economy is being adjusted. What has been left out of adjustment is what has been left out of the mainstream neoclassical model— namely any serious concern for distribution, and any recognition whatsoever of biophysical constraints on economic growth, either from the side of finite environmental sources of raw material and energy, or from the side of finite environmental sinks for waste matter and energy. The neoclassical view does recognize externalities, but these are considered to be correctable by substitution or technology, and do not constitute a limit to the growth of the economic subsystem.

To put the matter in other terms, we have three economic problems to consider: allocation, distribution and scale. *Allocation* refers to the apportioning of resources among alternative product uses—food, bicycles, cars, medical care. An allocation is efficient if it corresponds to effective demand, i.e., the relative preferences of the citizens as weighted by their relative incomes, both taken as given. An inefficient allocation would use resources to produce a number of things that people will not buy, and will fail to produce other things that people would buy if only they could find them. It would be characterized by shortages of the latter and surpluses of the former. *Distribution* refers to the apportioning of the goods produced (and the resources they embody) among different people (as opposed to different commodities). Distributions are just or unjust; allocations are efficient or inefficient. There is an efficient allocation for each distribution of income. *Scale* refers to the physical size of the economy relative to the ecosystem. The economy is viewed, in its physical dimensions, as a subsystem of the larger ecosystem. Scale is measured as population times per capita resource use—in other words total resource use—the volume of the matter-energy throughput (metabolic flow) by which the ecosystem sustains the economic subsystem. Scale may be sustainable or unsustainable. An efficient allocation does not imply a just distribution. Neither an efficient allocation nor a just distribution, nor both, implies a sustainable scale. The three concepts are quite distinct, although relations among them exist, as noted above.

Adjustment has been seen overwhelmingly in the context of allocation—adjustment to an allocatively efficient economy. Distribution has not been totally ignored, but has certainly been a poor second in adjustment policy. Scale has been completely outside the field of vision of adjustment. Common sense sometimes compels many economists at least to recognize the importance of population limits (one factor of scale). But within the mainstream model economists become quite agnostic on population since it falls outside the domain of allocative efficiency. In any case neither population control, nor land reform, nor any other form of wealth or income redistribution, are customary objectives of adjustment lending.

Transition to a sustainable development vision will put scale and distribution on center stage along with allocation. The first two features of adjustment (getting relative prices right and controlling inflation) are key to solving the allocation problem and remain fundamental in the sustainable development vision. As mentioned earlier, the third common feature of adjustment, free trade, must be rejected as policy for sustainable development. It is time to consider the reasons why this is so, and the intense controversy surrounding this issue.

III.

International free trade conflicts sharply with the national policies of:

    A. getting prices right,
    B. moving toward a more just distribution,
    C. fostering community,
    D. controlling the macroeconomy, and
    E. keeping scale within ecological limits.

Each conflict will be discussed in turn.

A. If one nation internalizes environmental and social costs to a high degree, following the dictates of adjustment, and then enters into free trade with a country that does not force its producers to internalize those costs, then the result will be that the firms in the second country will have lower prices and will drive the competing firms in the first country out of business.

If the trading entities were nations rather than individual firms trading across national boundaries, then the cost-internalizing nation could limit its volume and composition of trade to an amount that did not ruin its domestic producers, and thereby actually take advantage of the opportunity to acquire goods at prices that were below full costs. The country that sells at less than full-cost prices only hurts itself as long as other countries restrict their trade with that country to a volume that does not ruin their own producers. That of course would not be free trade. There is clearly a conflict between free trade and a national policy of internalization of external costs.

External costs are now so important that the latter goal should take precedence. In this case there is a clear argument for tariffs to protect, not an inefficient industry, but an efficient national policy of internalizing external costs into prices.

Of course if all trading nations agreed to common rules for defining, evaluating, and internalizing external costs, then this objection would disappear and the standard arguments for free trade could again be made in the new context. But how likely is such agreement? Even the small expert technical fraternity of national income accountants cannot agree on how to measure environmental costs in the system of national accounts, let alone on rules for internalizing these costs into prices at the firm level. Politicians are not likely to do better. Some economists will argue against uniform cost internalization on the grounds that different countries have different tastes for environmental services and amenities, and that these differences should be reflected in prices as legitimate reasons for profitable trade. Certainly agreement on uniform principles, and proper extent of departure from uniformity in their application, will not be easy. Nevertheless, suppose that this difficulty is overcome so that all countries internalize external costs by the same rules applied in each case to the appropriate degree in the light of differing tastes and levels of income. There are two further problems arising from capital mobility and wage differentials.

B. Wage levels vary enormously between countries and are largely determined by the supply of labor, which in turn depends on population size and growth rates. Overpopulated countries are naturally low-wage countries, and if population growth is rapid they will remain low-wage countries. This is especially so because the demographic rate of increase of the lower class (labor) is frequently twice or more that of the upper class (capital). For most traded goods labor is still the largest item of cost and consequently the major determinant of price. Cheap labor means low prices and a competitive advantage in trade. (The theoretical possibility that low wages reflect a taste for poverty and therefore a legitimate reason for cost differences is not here taken seriously.) But adjustment economists do not worry about that because economists have proved that free trade between high-wage and low-wage countries can be mutually advantageous thanks to comparative advantage.

The doctrine of comparative advantage is quite correct given the assumptions on which it rests, but unfortunately one of those assumptions is that capital is immobile internationally. The theory is supposed to work as follows. When in international competition the relatively inefficient activities lose out and jobs are eliminated, at the same time the relatively efficient activities (those with the comparative advantage) expand, absorbing both the labor and capital that were disemployed in activities with a comparative disadvantage. Capital and labor are reallocated within the country, specializing according to that country's comparative advantage. However, when both capital and goods are mobile internationally then capital will follow absolute advantage to the low-wage country rather than reallocate itself according to comparative advantage within its home country. It will follow the highest absolute profit which is usually determined by the lowest absolute wage.

Of course further inducements to absolute profits such as low social insurance charges or a low degree of internalization of environmental costs also attract capital, usually toward the very same low-wage countries. But we have assumed that all countries have internalized costs to the same degree in order to focus on the wage issue. Once capital is mobile then the entire doctrine of comparative advantage and all its comforting demonstrations become irrelevant. The consequence of capital mobility would be similar to that of international labor mobility—a strong tendency to equalize wages throughout the world.

Given the existing overpopulation and high demographic growth of the Third World it is clear that the equalization will be downward, as it has indeed been during the last decade in the U.S. Of course, returns to capital will also be equalized by free trade and capital mobility, but the level at which equalization will occur will be higher than at present. U.S. capital will benefit from cheap labor abroad followed by cheap labor at home, at least until checked by a crisis of insufficient demand due to a lack of worker purchasing power resulting from low wages. But that can be forestalled by efficient reallocation to serve the new pattern of effective demand resulting from the greater concentration of income. More luxury goods will be produced and fewer basic wage goods. Efficiency is attained, but distributive equity is sacrificed.

The standard neoclassical adjustment view argues that wages will eventually be equalized worldwide at high levels, thanks to the enormous increase in production made possible by free trade. This increase in production presumably will trigger the automatic demographic transition to lower birth rates—a doctrine that might be considered a part of the adjustment package in so far as any attention at all is paid to population. Such a thought can only be entertained by those who ignore the issue of scale, as of course neoclassicals traditionally do. For all 5.4 billion people presently alive to consume resources and absorptive capacities at the same per capita rate as Americans or Europeans is ecologically impossible. Much less is it possible to extend that level of consumption to future generations. Development, as it currently is understood on the U.S. model, is only possible for a minority of the world's poopulation over a few generations—i.e., it is neither just nor sustainable. The goal of sustainable development is, by changes in allocation, distribution and scale, to move the world toward a state in which "development", whatever it concretely comes to mean, will be for all people in all generations. This is certainly not achievable by a more finely tuned "adjustment" to the standard growth model which is largely responsible for having created the present impasse in the first place.

Of course if somehow all countries decided to control their populations and adopt distributive and scale limiting measures such that wages could be equalized world wide at an acceptably high level, then this problem would disappear and the standard arguments for free trade could again be evoked in the new context. Although the likelihood of that context seems infinitesimal, we might for purposes of *a fortiori* argument consider a major problem with free trade that would still remain.

c. Even with uniformly high wages made possible by universal population control and redistribution, and with uniform internalization of external costs, free trade and free capital mobility still increase the separation of ownership and control and the forced mobility of labor which are so inimical to community. Community economic life can be disrupted not only by your fellow citizen who, though living in another part of your country, might at least share some tenuous bonds of community with you, but by someone on the other side of the world with whom you have no community of language, history, culture, law, etc. These foreigners may be wonderful people—that is not the point. The point is that they are very far removed from the life of the community that is affected significantly by their decisions. Your life and your community can be disrupted by decisions and events over which you have no control, no vote, no voice.

Specialization and integration of a local community into the world economy does offer a quick fix to problems of local unemployment, and one must admit that carrying community self sufficiency to extremes can certainly be impoverishing. But short supply lines and relatively local control over the livelihood of the community remain obvious prudential measures which require some restraint on free trade if they are to be effective. Libertarian economists look at *Homo economicus* as a self-contained individual who is infinitely mobile and equally at home anywhere. But real people live in communities, and in communities of communities. Their very individual identity is constituted by their relations in community. To regard community as a disposable aggregate of individuals in temporary proximity only for as long as it serves the interests of mobile capital is bad enough when capital stays within the nation. But when capital moves internationally it becomes much worse.

When the capitalist class in the U.S. in effect tells the laboring class, "sorry, you have to compete with the poor of the world for jobs and wages—the fact that we are fellow citizens of the same country creates no obligations on my part"—then admittedly not much community remains, and it is not hard to understand why a U.S. worker would be indifferent to the nationality of his or her employer. Indeed, if local community is more respected by the foreign company than by the displaced American counterpart, then the interests of community could conceivably be furthered by foreign ownership in some specific cases. But this could not be counted as the rule, and serves only to show that the extent of pathological disregard for community in our own country has not yet been equaled by others. In any event the further undercutting of local and national communities (which are real) in the name of a cosmopolitan world "community" which does not exist is a poor trade, even if we call it free trade. The true road to international community is that of a federation of communities and communities of communities—not the destruction of local and national communities in the service of a single cosmopolitan world of footloose money managers who constitute, not a community, but merely an interdependent, mutually vulnerable, unstable coalition of short term interests.

D. Free trade and free capital mobility have interfered with macroeconomic stability by permitting huge international payments imbalances and capital transfers resulting in debts that are unrepayable in many cases and excessive in others. Efforts to service these debts can lead to unsustainable rates of exploitation of exportable resources; and to an eagerness to make new loans to get the foreign exchange with which to pay old loans, with a consequent disincentive to take a hard look at the real productivity of the project for which the new loan is being made. Efforts to pay back loans and still meet domestic obligations lead to government budget deficits and monetary creation with resulting inflation. Inflation, plus the need to export to pay off loans, leads to currency devaluations, giving rise to foreign exchange speculation, capital flight, and hot money movements, disrupting the macroeconomic stability that adjustment was supposed to foster.

To summarize so far: free trade sins against allocative efficiency by making it hard for nations to internalize external costs; it sins against distributive justice by widening the disparity between labor and capital in high wage countries; it sins against community by demanding more mobility and by further separating ownership and control; it sins against macroeconomic stability. Finally, it also sins against the criterion of sustainable scale in a more subtle manner that will now be considered.

E. It has already been mentioned in passing that part of the free trade dogma of adjustment thinking is based on the assumption that the whole world and all future generations can consume resources at the levels current in today's high-wage countries without inducing ecological collapse. So in this way free trade sins against the criterion of sustainable scale. But, in its physical dimensions, the economy really is an open subsystem of a materially closed, non-growing and finite ecosystem with a limited throughput of solar energy. The proper scale of the economic subsystem relative to the finite total system really is a very important question. Free trade has obscured the scale limit in the following way.

Sustainable development means living within environmental constraints of absorptive and regenerative capacities. These constraints are both global (greenhouse effect, ozone shield), and local (soil erosion, deforestation). Trade between nations or regions offers a way of loosening local constraints by importing environmental services (including waste absorption) from elsewhere. Within limits this can be quite reasonable and justifiable. But carried to extremes in the name of free trade it becomes destructive. It leads to a situation in which each country is trying to live beyond its own absorptive and regenerative capacities by importing these capacities from elsewhere. Of course they pay for these capacities and all is well as long as other countries have made the complementary decision—namely to keep their own scale well below their own national carrying capacity in order to export some of its services. In other words, the apparent escape from scale constraints enjoyed by some countries via trade depends on other countries' willingness and ability to adopt the very discipline of limiting scale that the importing country is seeking to avoid. What nations have actually made this complementary choice? All countries now aim to grow in scale, and it is merely the fact that some have not yet reached their limits that allows other nations to import carrying capacity. Free trade does not remove carrying capacity constraints—it just guarantees that nations will hit that constraint more or less simultaneously rather than sequentially. It converts differing local constraints into an aggregated global constraint. It converts a set of problems, some of which are manageable, into one big unmanageable problem. Evidence that this is not understood is provided by the countless occasions when someone who really should know better points to The Netherlands or Hong Kong as both an example to be emulated, and as evidence that all countries could become as densely populated as these two. How it would be possible for all countries to be net exporters of goods and net importers of carrying capacity is not explained.

Of course the drive to grow beyond carrying capacity has roots other and deeper than the free trade dogma. The point is that free trade makes it very hard to deal with these root causes at a national level, which is the only level at which effective social controls over the economy exist. The adjustment theorist will argue that free trade is just a natural extension of price adjustment across international boundaries, and that "right prices" must reflect *global* scarcities and preferences. But if the unit of community is the nation, the unit in which there are institutions and traditions of collective action, responsibility and mutual help, the unit in which government tries to carry out policy for the good of its citizens, then "right prices" should *not* reflect the preferences and scarcities of other nations. Right prices *should* differ between national communities. Such differences traditionally have provided the whole reason for international trade in goods—trade that can continue if balanced—i.e., if not accompanied by the free mobility of capital (and labor) that homogenizes preferences and scarcities globally, while reducing national economic policy to ineffectiveness unless agreed upon by all freely trading nations.

IV.

To summarize: it has been argued that the first two goals of adjustment (right prices and price level stability) are a necessary part of the sustainable development era. It has been shown that the third element of adjustment, free trade, must be abandoned because it is in conflict with: 1. the first two goals of adjustment that have been retained, and 2. goals that were downplayed by adjustment (just distribution) but critical for sustainable development, and 3. the goal that was totally ignored by adjustment, but is the principal goal of sustainable development, namely a scale of the economic subsystem that is within the carrying capacity of the ecosystem. It remains to try to spell out a bit more the positive vision of sustainable development.

As already indicated the basic vision underlying sustainable development is that of the economy as a physical subsystem of the ecosystem. A subsystem cannot grow beyond the scale of the total system of which it is a part. If the total system provides services that the subsystem cannot provide for itself, then the subsystem must avoid impinging on the parent system to an extent and in ways that impair its ability to provide those services. The scale of the economy must remain below the capacity of the ecosystem sustainably to supply services such as photosynthesis, pollination, purification of air and water, maintenance of climate, filtering of excessive ultraviolet radiation, recycling of wastes, etc. Adjustment in the service of growth has pushed us beyond a sustainable scale. To maintain the present scale of population and per capita consumption, we are consuming natural capital and counting it as income. The effort to overcome poverty by further growth in scale of throughput is self-defeating once we have reached the point where growth in scale increases environmental costs faster than it increases production benefits. Beyond this point, which we have in all likelihood already passed, further growth makes us poorer, not richer. The alternative is to stop growth in scale, and seek to overcome poverty by redistribution and qualitative improvement in efficiency of resource use, rather than further quantitative increase in the resource throughput. A policy of limiting throughput will automatically redirect energies toward increasing the efficiency with which it is used. If technology can easily and greatly increase efficiency then the transition could be relatively painless. If not then it will be more difficult. In either case it remains necessary. The basic policy is the same whether one is a technological optimist or pessimist.

In an effort to avoid facing these realities those wedded to the adjustment paradigm have come up with one more adjustment which they contradictorily call "sustainable *growth*".

Much confusion is generated by using the term sustainable growth as a synonym for sustainable development. Respect for the dictionary would lead us to reserve the word growth for quantitative increase in physical size by assimilation or accretion of materials. Development refers to qualitative change, realization of potentialities, transition to a fuller or better state. The two processes are distinct, sometimes linked, sometimes not. For example, a child grows and develops simultaneously; a snowball or cancer grows without developing; the planet earth develops without growing. Economies frequently grow and develop at the same time, but they can do either separately. But since the economy is a subsystem of a finite and nongrowing ecosystem, then as its growth leads it to incorporate an ever larger fraction of the total system into itself, then its behavior must more and more approximate the behavior of the total system, which is development without growth. It is precisely the recognition that growth in scale ultimately becomes impossible, and already costs more than it is worth, that gives rise to the urgency of the concept of sustainable development. Sustainable development is development without growth in the scale of the economy beyond some point that is within biospheric carrying capacity. Many believe that the present scale is beyond long term carrying capacity and that sustainable development will in its initial phase require a period of negative growth. Even if one is a technological optimist and believes that development in the productivity of the resource throughput can increase faster than the volume of the throughput needs to diminish, this is still very radical. The term sustainable growth aims to deny this radical transformation, and to suggest that growth is still the number one goal. Growth just needs to be a bit more environmentally friendly. "Sustainable *growth*" is just one more "adjustment" to the standard view. Sustainable *development* is an alternative to the standard growth ideology and is incompatible with it. Sustainable development, development without growth, does not imply the end of economics—if anything economics becomes even more important. But it is a subtle and complex economics of maintenance, qualitative improvement, sharing, frugality, and adaptation to natural limits. It is an economics of better, not bigger.

David Phillips

DOLPHINS AND GATT

Introduction

It was April, 1988 and the situation for dolphins was bleak. More than 100,000 were being killed every year—drowned and crushed in the machinery of the commercial tuna fishing fleets. The senseless slaughter was taking place because in the eastern tropical Pacific ocean, huge purse seine fleets from six nations found that they could catch more tuna and catch it faster by exploiting the fact that schools of dolphins and large yellowfin tuna swam together. By intentionally setting their mile-long nets on the dolphins they could catch the tuna that swam beneath. The tuna would supply the lucrative US markets for canned tuna. The dead dolphins were simply thrown overboard.

The furthest thing from our minds, as we filed a federal lawsuit alleging the failure of the US government to enforce the Marine Mammal Protection Act (MMPA), was that the tuna/dolphin issue would become the clearest sign yet of the collision course between GATT and environmental protection.

It shouldn't have been such a surprise. Wildlife has always played a crucial role as an environmental indicator. The miner's canary detected the unsafe gasses deep in the mines. Fish die-offs were an early signal that pollution of lakes and rivers had become so bad that human health was at risk. So, too, the dolphins now have become the warning light on what GATT has in store for health and the environment.

The following analysis describes the showdown at GATT over dolphin protection, and its future implications.

In 1984, the US Congress recognized that foreign tuna fleets from Mexico, Venezuela, Vanuatu, Ecuador, and Panama were causing the vast majority of dolphin deaths yet were not subject to the same dolphin protection requirements as the US tuna fleet. Foreign fleets carried fewer observers, were not required to use the same equipment and techniques, and had not implemented national or international regulatory programs. For these reasons, Congress inserted language in the MMPA known as the "comparability provisions" requiring that if foreign countries wished to export their tuna into the US markets, their national fleets would have to implement dolphin conservation programs and achieve a lower dolphin mortality rate comparable to that of the US tuna fleet.

From 1984 through 1988 the US Commerce Department failed to enforce these requirements even once, despite the Agency's own evidence that the dolphin kill rates on foreign tuna boats were four times higher than US rates.

In 1988, during the reauthorization of the MMPA, the Congress took away the Commerce Department's discretion and inserted specific language requiring that for nations wishing to export tuna to the US during the 1989 fishing season they could not exceed two times the US rate of dolphin kill. For 1990 and thereafter national fleets could not exceed a dolphin kill of 1.25 times the US rate.

The Congressional message behind these requirements was abundantly clear. Congressman Gerry Studds, at his hearing on October 4, 1989, described the intent of the embargo provisions:

> We do not have the power to regulate foreign fishing operations in foreign waters or on the high seas. But we *do* have the right to bar our markets to any nation that does not share our concern for the conservation of marine mammals. The amendments we approved last year require the Executive branch to exercise that right, to tell any nation that harvests tuna without taking dolphin-protection measures comparable to ours that they will no longer have access to America's supermarket shelves . . .

It was against this backdrop that Earth Island Institute brought suit in 1990. Our legal arguments were sound. In August, 1990 and again in October, 1990 the US Federal District Court ruled in our favor ordering the government to impose tuna import embargoes. The government appealed the rulings to the 9th Circuit Court of Appeals, and strenuously fought imposition of the embargoes. On February 22, 1991, however, the US Appeals court ruled unanimously in our favor that the tuna embargoes were required under law.

As a result of these actions tuna import embargoes were put in place against Mexico, Venezuela, Ecuador, Panama, and Vanuatu.

The tuna import embargo provisions of the MMPA were based on sound scientific rationales and were not applied discriminatorily. Requirements on foreign fleets were less stringent than those for the US fleet, so it was clearly not a protectionist measure. The countries had mechanisms at their disposal to meet the required rates, and in fact three of the nations (Panama, Ecuador, and Vanuatu) did so and were removed from the embargo. The sanctions had become a fundamental component of the international effort to accomplish the goals of the Marine Mammal Protection Act and address the largest killing of marine mammals in the world.

The import provisions were extremely effective. Coupled with other dolphin-protection provisions of the MMPA and the 1990 decision by the largest tuna companies to buy only dolphin-safe tuna, the dolphin kill levels began to drop dramatically. US dolphin mortality was reduced from 12,643 in 1989 to 5,100 in 1990 to 1,004 in 1991, more than a 90% reduction. Foreign dolphin mortality also decreased significantly. It seemed that dolphin killing might finally be ended, until GATT was brought into the act.

On January 25, 1991 the Mexican Government filed a challenge under GATT of the legality of the tuna import embargo provisions of the Marine Mammal Protection Act. They sought to overturn the embargoes and allow dolphin-unsafe tuna back on US supermarket shelves. Mexico claimed that how they caught tuna was nobody else's business.

A dispute resolution Panel at GATT was convened. Arguments took place in Geneva in May, 1991. All US and Mexico's legal submissions, oral arguments, as well as the interventions of other GATT Contracting Governments pertaining to this issue were kept entirely secret. Behind closed doors three unelected and largely unaccountable trade officials weighed the fate of the US dolphin protection law. Earth Island Institute tried to assist the US government in standing up for the dolphins, sending staff and a member of our legal team to Geneva. However, we ran right into GATT's wall of secrecy and were kept out.

The GATT Ruling

On August 16, 1991, US Trade Representative officials announced that the GATT Panel had struck down the tuna import restrictions under the MMPA as GATT illegal.

The GATT Panel decision was sweeping and calamitous in its findings. Rather than interpreting GATT's broad language to provide exceptions for trade restrictions based on legitimate environmental concerns, the Panel found that neither GATT Articles XX (b) or (g), which pertain to the conservation of exhaustible natural resources and the protection of human, plant, and animal health, applied in the case of the tuna/dolphin issue. They ruled that these provisions were precluded from use for protection of any resources outside of national geographic boundaries. The Panel's ruling was a clear indication that to GATT trade would supersede all efforts to protect resources of the global commons.

Further, the Panel ruled that the tuna import embargo was also GATT illegal because the "method of production" of a product could not be taken into account in determining equal treatment under GATT. The Panel found that the US must treat imports of dolphin-safe and dolphin-unsafe tuna equally. It was a shocking rebuke to international efforts to limit unsustainable and environmentally devastating harvesting processes.

Both of the GATT findings were quickly recognized as a wholesale assault on the environmental laws in the US, and around the world. Congressman Henry Waxman, Chairman of the House Subcommittee on Health and the Environment, held a hearing within a month of the Panel's report, and warned of the ruling's threat to efforts to protect the ozone layer and other health laws, stating:

> The GATT ruling vividly reminds us that trade agreements can involve far more than tariffs—that those agreements can undermine domestic laws designed to protect human health and the environment, whether here or abroad.

Implications of the Panel Ruling

The US, Mexico, and GATT faced a dilemma. If the tuna/dolphin Panel ruling was accepted by the full GATT Council, a demand would be made to the US to eliminate the embargo provisions of the Marine Mammal Protection Act. The US would also be subject to sanctions, reciprocal trade retaliation, and monetary damage awards if the embargoes remained in place. The US administration was well aware that such an overt action by GATT to seek the dismantling of US environmental protection laws would threaten Congressional support for both GATT and the pending North American Free Trade Agreement (NAFTA). Congress, and the public, were in no mood to jettison the dolphin protection laws.

The Mexican government, recognizing the threat the Panel ruling posed to the NAFTA agreement, began urging a delay. Privately, Mexican President Salinas indicated that he wished Mexico had never filed the tuna/dolphin challenge with GATT.

As for GATT, they had opened a large can of worms. Requiring the elimination of trade restrictions enacted for the protection of the global environment would mean the dismantling of a whole host of US and foreign environmental protection laws. Trade sanctions to ensure enforcement of the United Nations ban on the use of driftnets would be at risk. And that would be just the beginning. Under the logic of the Panel ruling, efforts to prevent imports of elephant ivory, whale and other endangered species products, and tropical hardwoods could be invalidated. Efforts to implement provisions of the Montreal Protocol on the ozone layer and the Convention on International Trade in Endangered Species (CITES) could be crippled. US and European Commission laws covering forest conservation, migratory birds, and fisheries would be severely undermined.

The ruling caused an uproar that continues to shake the foundations of GATT. The worst fears of a growing number of GATT watchers had been confirmed. Reacting to the furor caused by the ruling, the US and Mexico jointly blocked consideration of the Panel ruling by the GATT General Council. Normally Panel reports are adopted by GATT within 60 days. It has now been nearly two years without Council action.

What's Next:

The Panel ruling continues to cast a dark cloud over GATT. Some trade experts expect a second tuna/dolphin Panel to attempt to "green" the ruling, perhaps making more clear exemptions for multilateral treaties. However, without substantial overhaul, GATT will continue to pose a grave threat to environmental protection laws around the world.

Thus far, the US Congress—pressed on by a public that is extremely supportive of US action to protect the global environment—has not let the GATT Panel ruling on tuna/dolphin get in the way of its action. Recently, Congress passed legislation placing trade restrictions on the importation of wild birds. The law directs the Interior Secretary to ban or set quotas for all species of exotic bird from a country that has not enacted programs ensuring conservation. A new law was also enacted to impose heavy trade sanctions against countries violating the UN ban on driftnet fishing. Both laws defy the GATT Panel's view.

Arthur Dunkel, Director General of GATT, while suggesting that a new round of GATT negotiations is necessary to address the issue of trade and the environment, nonetheless stands behind GATT's insistence that trade restrictions to protect dolphins must go. Thus, the ominous glimpse provided by the tuna/dolphin case could be simply the first of many regarding the sacrifices GATT would have us make in the name of trade.

−12−

David Morris

FREE TRADE: THE GREAT DESTROYER

Free trade is the religion of our age. With its heaven as the planetary economy, free trade comes complete with comprehensive analytical and philosophical underpinnings. Higher mathematics are used to prove its basic theorems.

But in the final analysis, free trade is less an economic strategy than a moral doctrine. Although it pretends to be value-free, it is fundamentally value driven. It assumes that the highest good is to shop. It assumes that mobility and change are synonymous with progress. The transport of capital, materials, goods, and people takes precedence over the autonomy, the sovereignty and, indeed, the culture of our local communities. Rather than promoting and sustaining the social relationships that create a vibrant community, the free trade theology relies on a narrow definition of efficiency to guide our conduct.

The Postulates of Free Trade

For most of us, the tenets of free trade appear almost self-evident.

- Competition spurs innovation, raises productivity, and lowers prices.
- The division of labor allows specialization, which raises productivity and lowers prices.
- The bigger the production unit, the greater the division of labor and specialization, and thus the greater the benefits.

Today this adoration of bigness permeates all political persuasions. The Undersecretary of the Treasury proposes creating 5 to 10 giant U.S. banks. "If we are going to be competitive in a globalized financial services world, we are going to have to change our views on the size of American institutions," he declares. The vice-chairman of Citicorp warns us against "preserving the heartwarming idea that 14,000 banks are wonderful for our country." The *New York Times* editorializes against aiding struggling small farmers because "that would only retard the transition to efficient farm size." The liberal *Harper's* magazine agrees, "True, farms have gotten bigger, as has nearly every other type of economic enterprise. They have done so in order to take advantage of the economies of scale offered by modern production techniques." Democratic presidential adviser Lester Thurow criticizes anti-trust laws as an "old Democratic conception (that) is simply out of date." He argues that even IBM with $50 billion in sales is not big enough for the global marketplace. "Big companies do sometimes crush small companies," Thurow concedes, "but far better that small American companies be crushed by big American companies than that they be crushed by big foreign companies."

In These Times, which until recently called itself an independent socialist weekly, concluded "Japanese steel companies have been able to outcompete American steel companies partly by building larger plants."

- The infatuation with large scale systems leads logically to the next postulate of free trade: the need for global markets. As Adam Smith, the 18th century Scottish economist and father of free trade observed in his classic book *The Wealth of Nations*, "Specialization is limited by the extent of the market." Anything that sets up barriers to ever-wider markets reduces the possibility of specialization and thus raises costs. Which makes us less competitive.
- The last pillar of free trade is the "law of comparative advantage."

Comparative advantage comes in two forms: absolute and relative. The easiest to understand is absolute. Differences in climate and natural resources suggest that Guatemala should raise bananas and Minnesota should raise walleyed pike. Relative comparative advantage is a less intuitive, but ultimately a much more powerful concept. As the 19th century British economist David Ricardo, the architect of free trade economics, explained: "Two men can both make shoes and hats and one is superior to the other in both employments; but in making hats he can only exceed his competitor by one-fifth or 20 percent, and in making shoes he can exceed him by one-third or 33 percent. Will it not be for the interest of both that the superior man should employ himself exclusively in making shoes and the inferior man in making hats?"

Thus, even if one community can make every product more efficiently than another, it should specialize only in those items it produces most efficiently, in relative terms, and trade for the others. Each community, and ultimately each nation, should specialize in what it does best.

What are the implications of these tenets of free trade? That communities and nations abandon self-reliance and embrace dependence. That we abandon our capacity to produce many items and concentrate only on a few. That we import what we need and export what we produce.

Bigger is better. Competition is superior to cooperation. Material self-interest drives humanity. Dependence is better than independence. These are the pillars of free trade. In sum, we make a trade. We give up sovereignty over our affairs in return for a promise of more jobs, more goods, and a higher standard of living.

The economic arguments in favor of free trade are powerful. Yet for most of us it is not the soundness of its theory, but the widely promoted idea that free trade is an inevitable development of our market system which makes us believers. We believe that economies, like natural organisms, evolve from the simple to the complex, from the lower to the higher phyla.

From the Dark Ages, from city-states to nation-states to the planetary economy, and soon, to space manufacturing, history has systematically unfolded. Free trade supporters believe that trying to hold back economic evolution is like trying to hold back natural evolution. The suggestion that we choose another developmental path is viewed, at best, as an attempt to reverse history, and, at worst, as an unnatural and even sinful act.

This kind of historical determinism has its own corollaries. We not only move from simple to complex economies. We move from integrated economies to segregated ones, separating the producer from the consumer, the farmer from the kitchen, the power plant from the appliance, the dump site from the garbage can, the banker from the depositor and, inevitably, the government from the citizenry. In the process of development we separate authority and responsibility. Those who make the decisions are not those affected by the decisions.

Just as homo sapiens is nature's highest achievement, so the multi-national and supranational corporation becomes our most highly evolved economic animal. The planetary economy demands planetary institutions. The nation-state itself begins to disappear, both as an object of our affection and identification, and as a major actor in world affairs.

The planetary economy merges and submerges nations. Yoshitaka Sajima, vice-president of Mitsui and Company, USA, asserts, "the U. S. and Japan are not just trading with each other anymore—they've become part of each other." Former Republican Governor of Tennessee, Lamar Alexander, agreed when he declared the goal of his economic development strategy was "to get the Tennessee economy integrated with the Japanese economy."

In Europe, the Common Market has grown from six countries in the 1950s to 10 in the 1970s, to 12 today, and barriers between these nations are rapidly being abolished. Increasingly, there are neither Italian nor French nor German companies, only European supra-corporations. The U.S. and Canadian governments just signed a free trade agreement to merge our two countries economically. Northern Mexico is all but integrated into the U.S. economy.

Promotion of exports is now widely accepted as the foundation for a successful economic development program. Whether for a tiny country like Singapore or a huge country like the United States, we come to see exports as essential to a nation's economic health.

Globalism commands our attention and our resources. Our principal task, we are told, is to nurture, extend, and manage emerging global systems. Five nations now* patrol the Persian Gulf to protect our oil pipelines. Trade talks are on the top of everybody's agenda, from Gorbachev to Reagan. Political leaders strive to devise stable systems for global financial markets and exchange rates. The best and the brightest of this generation use their ingenuity to establish the global financial and regulatory rules that will enable the greatest possible uninterrupted flow of resources among nations.

This emphasis on globalism rearranges our loyalties and loosens our neighborly ties. "The new order eschews loyalty to workers, products, corporate structure, businesses, factories, communities, even the nation," the

* This paper was first written and published in 1988 in the *Clinton Street Quarterly*.

New York Times announces. Martin S. Davis, chairman of Gulf & Western, declares, "All such allegiances are viewed as expendable under the new rules. You can not be emotionally bound to any particular asset."

We are now all assets.

Jettisoning loyalties isn't easy. But that is the price we believe we must pay to receive the benefits of the global village. Every community must achieve the lowest possible production cost even when that means breaking whatever remains of their social contract and long standing traditions.

The revised version of the American dream is articulated by Walter Joelson, chief economist at General Electric: "Let's talk about the difference in living standards rather than wages. What in the Bible says we should have a better standard of living than others? We have to give back a bit of it." Stanley J. Mihelick, executive vice-president for production at Goodyear, is even more explicit, "Until we get real wage levels down much closer to those of the Brazils and Koreas, we cannot pass along productivity gains to wages and still be competitive."

Wage raises, environmental protection, national health insurance, and liability lawsuits—anything that raises the cost of production and makes us less competitive—threatens our economy. We must abandon the good life to sustain life itself. We are in a global struggle for survival. We are hooked on free trade.

The Doctrine Falters

At this very moment in history when the doctrines of free trade and globalism are so dominant, the absurdities of globalism are becoming ever more evident. Consider the case of the toothpick and the chopstick.

A few years ago I was eating at a Saint Paul restaurant. After lunch I picked up a toothpick wrapped in plastic. On the plastic was printed the word 'Japan'. Now Japan has little wood and no oil. Nevertheless it had become efficient enough in our global economy to bring little pieces of wood and barrels of oil to Japan, wrap the one in the other and send them to Minnesota. This toothpick may have travelled 50,000 miles. But never fear, we are now retaliating in kind. A Hibbing, Minnesota factory now produces a billion disposable chopsticks a year for sale in Japan.

In my mind's eye I see two ships passing one another in the northern Pacific. One carries little pieces of Minnesota wood bound for Japan; the other carries little pieces of Japanese wood bound for Minnesota. Such is the logic of free trade.

Nowhere is the absurdity of free trade more evident than in the grim plight of the Third World. Developing nations borrowed money to build an economic infrastructure in order to specialize in what they do best, and thereby expand their export capacity. To repay these debts, Third World countries must increase their exports.

One result of these decisions has been a dramatic shift from producing food for internal consumption to producing food for export. Take the case of Brazil. Brazilian per capita production of basic foodstuffs (rice, black beans, manioc, and potatoes) fell 13 percent from 1977 to 1984. Per capita output of exportable foodstuffs (soybeans, oranges, cotton, peanuts, and tobacco) jumped 15 percent. Today, although some 50 percent of Brazil suffers malnutrition, one leading Brazilian agronomist still calls export promotion "a matter of national survival." In the global village a nation survives by starving its people.

What about the purported benefits of free trade, such as higher standards of living?

It depends on whose standard of living you're talking about. Inequality between and in most cases, within, countries has increased. Two centuries of trade has exacerbated disparities in world living standards. According to Swiss economist Paul Bairoch, per capita GNP in 1750 was approximately the same in the developed countries as in the underdeveloped ones. In 1930 the ratio was about 4 to 1 in favor of the developed nations. Today it is 8 to 1.

Inequality is both a cause and an effect of globalism. Inequality within one country is a cause of globalism because it reduces the number of people with sufficient purchasing power. Consequently, a producer must sell to wealthy people in many countries to achieve the scale of production necessary to produce goods at a relatively low cost. Inequality is an effect of globalism because export industries employ few workers who earn disproportionately high wages, and because developed countries tend to take out more capital from Third World countries than they invest in them.

Free trade was supposed to improve our standard of living. Yet even in the United States, the most developed of all nations, we find that living standards have been declining over the last fifteen years. Most dramatically, according to several surveys, in 1988 we are working almost half a day longer for lower real wages than we were in 1970. We have less leisure time, less family, less community time. If the present trend continues we may have less leisure time in the 1990s than we had in the 1790s.

A New Way of Thinking

It is time to re-examine the validity of the doctrine of free trade and its corollary, the planetary economy. To do so we must begin by speaking of values. Human beings may be acquisitive and competitive, but we are also loving and cooperative. Several studies have found that the voluntary, unpaid economy may be as large and as productive as the paid economy. There is no question that we have converted more and more human relationships into commercial transactions, but there is a great deal of question as to whether this was a necessary or beneficial development.

We should not confuse change with progress. Bertrand Russell once described change as inevitable and progress as problematic. Change is scientific. Progress is ethical. We must decide what values we hold most dear, and then design an economic system that reinforces those values.

Reassessing Free Trade's Assumptions

Let me review the basic assumptions of free trade that I described at the beginning, only this time critically.

If price is to guide our buying, selling, and investing, then price should tell us something about efficiency. We might measure efficiency in terms of natural resources used in making, and also, by measuring the amount of waste produced in converting a raw material into a consumer or industrial product. Traditionally we have measured efficiency in human terms; that is, by measuring the amount of labor hours spent in making a product.

But price is no measure of efficiency. In fact, price is no reliable measure of anything. The prices of raw materials, labor, capital, transportation, and waste disposal are all heavily subsidized. But today wage rate inequities among comparably skilled workforces can be as great as 30 to 1. This disparity overwhelms even the most productive worker. An American worker might produce twice as much per hour as a Mexican worker, but is paid ten times as much.

In Taiwan, for example, strikes are illegal. In South Korea unions cannot be organized without government permission. For all intents and purposes South Africa uses slave labor. Many developing nations have no minimum wage, maximum hours, or environmental legislation. As economist Howard Wachtel notes, "Differences in product cost that are due to totalitarian political institutions or restrictions on economic rights reflect no natural or entrepreneurial advantage. Free trade has nothing to do with incomparable political economic institutions that protect individual rights in one country and deny them in another."

The price of goods in developed countries is also highly dependent on subsidies. For example, we decided early on that government should build the transportation systems of the country. The public, directly or indirectly, built our railroads, canals, ports, highways, and airports.

Heavy trucks do not pay taxes sufficient to cover the damage they do to roads. We provide water to California farmers at as little as five percent of the going market rate. We provide huge direct subsidies to corporate farmers. And we allow the costs of agricultural pollution to be picked up by the society as a whole. Having intervened in the production process in all these ways, we then discover it is cheaper to grow a tomato in California and ship it to Massachusetts than to grow it on the East Coast. We are told this is due to California's climatic advantages, but if we withdrew all our subsidies, it might very well be cheaper to raise produce near the point of sale.

Prices don't provide accurate signals between nations, nor do they provide accurate signals within nations. We tend to confuse price and cost. Price is what an individual pays; cost is what the community as a whole pays. Most of our economic programs result in an enormous disparity between the price of a product or service to an individual and the cost of that same product or service to the society as a whole.

When the utility company wanted to send electricity across someone's property, and that individual declined the honor, we gave the private utility governmental authority to seize the land needed. This is exactly what happened in western Minnesota in the late 1970s. We argued that since bigger power plants produced electricity more cheaply than smaller ones, it was therefore in the public interest to erect these power lines. If we had allowed landowners to refuse to sell, the price of electricity would be higher today, but it would reflect the cost of that power more accurately.

These days sky-high transmission towers carry as much as 745,000 volts of electricity. Recent scientific studies have found that children living near transmission lines have twice the incidence of cancer as children living elsewhere.

If this new medical evidence leads to a number of lawsuits on behalf of people living near power lines, then utilities may soon find it cheaper to dispense with transmission lines, and build power plants nearer the site of users. If this happens, then the price of electricity will better reflect its cost.

Another example: Because we consider the benefit of unrestricted air transportation to outweigh any damage to our health and sanity, we have eliminated the authority of communities to regulate flights and noise. As a consequence, we allow planes to awaken us or our children in the middle of the night. By one survey, some 4 million people in the United States suffer physical damage due to airport noise. If communities were given the authority to control noise levels by planes, as they already control noise levels from radios and motorcycles, the price of a plane ticket would increase significantly. Its price would be more in line with its actual cost to society.

It is often hard to quantify social costs, which doesn't mean they are insignificant. Remember urban renewal? In the 1950s and 1960s we levelled inner city neighborhoods to assemble sufficient land area to rebuild our downtowns. Skyscrapers and shopping malls arose, the property tax base expanded, and we considered it a job well done. Later sociologists, economists, and planners discovered that the seedy areas we destroyed were not fragmented, violence-prone slums, but more often were cohesive ethnic communities where generations had grown up and worked, where children went to school and played. If we were to put a dollar figure on the destruction of homes, the pain of broken lives, and the expense of relocation and re-creation of community life, we might find that the city as a whole actually lost money in the urban renewal process. If we had used a full cost accounting system, we might never have undertaken urban renewal.

Our refusal to understand and count the social costs of certain kinds of development has caused suffering in rural as well as urban areas. In 1944 Walter Goldschmidt, working under contract with the Department of Agriculture, compared the economic and social characteristics of two rural California communities that were alike in all respects, except one. Dinuba was surrounded by family farms; Arvin, by corporate farms. Goldschmidt found that Dinuba was more stable, had a higher standard of living, more small businesses, higher retail sales, better schools and other community facilities, and a higher degree of citizen participation in local affairs. The USDA invoked a clause in his contract forbidding him to discuss his finding. The study was not made public for almost 30 years. Meanwhile, the USDA continued to promote research that rapidly transformed the Dinubas of our country into Arvins. The farm crisis we now suffer is a consequence of this process.

How should we deal with the price versus cost dilemma as a society? In most cases we can protect our way of life from encroachment by the global economy, achieve important social and economic goals, and pay about the same price for our goods and services. In some cases we might have to pay more, but we should remember the higher prices may be offset by the decline in overall costs. Consider the proposed Save the Family Farm legislation drafted by farmers and introduced in Congress by Iowa Senator Tom Harkin. It proposes that farmers limit production of farm goods nationwide at the same time as the nation establishes a minimum price for farm goods that is sufficient to cover operating and capital costs and provides farm families with an adequate living. The law's sponsors estimate such a program would increase the retail cost of agricultural products by three to five percent, but this would be more than offset by dramatically reduced public tax expenditures spent on farm subsidies. And this doesn't take into consideration the benefits of a stable rural America. The loss of that stability entails the trauma of people leaving farms that have been in their families for generations, and the influx of jobless rural immigrants into already economically depressed urban areas, and the resulting increased expenditures for medical bills, food stamps, welfare.

Economists like to talk about "externalities." The costs of job dislocation, rising family violence, community breakdown, environmental damage, and cultural collapse are all considered "external." External to what, one might ask?

The theory of comparative advantage itself is fast losing its credibility. Time was when technology spread slowly. Three hundred years ago in northern Italy, stealing or disclosing the secrets of silk-spinning machinery was a crime punishable by death. At the beginning of the industrial revolution Britain protected its supremacy in textile manufacturing by banning both exports of machines and emigration of men who knew how to build and run them. A young British apprentice, Samuel Slater, brought the industrial revolution to the U.S. by memorizing the design of the spinning frame, and migrating here in 1789.

Today, technology transfer is simple. According to Dataquest, a market research firm, it takes only three weeks after a new U.S.-made product is introduced before it is copied, manufactured, and shipped back to the U.S. from Asia. So much for comparative advantage.

Nations and communities still differ on their inventive capacity and managerial and organizational efficiency. These, however, are the kinds of "products" that are most easily transferred via communications lines. For example, Japanese-run factories in the United States achieve productivity and quality levels approaching those in Japan. It is not the American worker, but the American manager who is uncompetitive. A better way of doing things should continue to be imported from abroad, but that need not mean abandoning the nation's own productive capacity. For example, Du Pont holds the patent for the plastic called PET that is used to make more than 5 billion bottles worldwide. However, Du Pont neither manufactures the bottles, nor the resin from which they are made, nor even the machines for making them. Instead it licenses the technology. Such licensing of patented knowledge and management techniques may well become the basis for much of world trade in the future.

We are able to import a better idea from the other side of the world. We should also pay for the privilege of using it. The costs to society of doing so are small, especially when compared to the high qualitative and quantitative costs to society of importing products and materials.

Which brings us to the issue of scale. There is no question that when I move production out of my basement and into a factory, the cost per item produced declines dramatically. But when the factory increases its output a hundredfold, production costs no longer decline proportionately. The vast majority of the cost decreases are captured at fairly modest production levels.

In agriculture, for example, the USDA studied the efficiency of farms and concluded, "Above about $40–50,000 in gross sales—the size that is at the bottom of the end of medium sized sales category—there are no greater efficiencies of scale." Another USDA report agreed, "Medium sized family farms are as efficient as the large farms."

Harvard Professor Joseph Bain's pioneering investigations in the 1950s found that plants far smaller than originally believed can be economically competitive. Further, it was found that the factory could be significantly reduced in size without requiring major price increases for its products. In other words, we might be able to produce shoes for a region rather than for the nation at about the same price per shoe. If we withdrew government subsidies to the transportation system, then locally produced and marketed shoes might actually be cheaper than those brought in from abroad.

Modern technology makes smaller production plants possible. For instance, traditional float glass plants produce 550-600 tons of glass daily, and cost $100 million to build. With only a $40–50 million investment, new mini-plants can produce about 250 tons per day making glass for a regional market at the same cost per ton as the large plants.

The advent of programmable machine tools may accelerate this tendency. Fifteen years ago industrial engineers developed machine tools that could be programmed to reproduce a variety of shapes so that now a typical Japanese machine tool can make almost 100 different parts from an individual block of material. What does this mean? Erich Bloch, director of the National Science Foundation, believes manufacturing "will be so flexible that it will be able to make the first copy of a product for little more than the cost of the thousandth." "So the ideal location for the factory of the future," says Patrick A. Toole, vice-president for manufacturing at IBM, "is in the market where its products are consumed."

In summary, when we analyze the foundations of the free trade doctrine in the light of present day realities, what do we find? Price is no longer a reliable indicator of comparative efficiency. Comparative advantage has lost much of its validity. Economies of scale are suspect. It now appears that we could miniaturize our economies with little economic penalty, and with the immeasurable benefit of preserving our local communities and cultures.

A Globe of Villages

Let me now explore the possibilities and strategies for a new kind of world economy, one whose metaphor would be a globe of villages, not a global village. It would be a planetary economy that emphasizes community and self-reliance though not self-sufficiency. As biologist Russell Anderson suggests, self-reliance is "the capacity for self-sufficiency, not self-sufficiency itself." Self-reliance would give us the capacity to survive if cut off from suppliers by natural or man-made intervention. It encourages us to maintain a diversity of skills within our societies, and to localize and regionalize productive assets. Self-reliance calls for a strategy that welcomes "foreign" capital, but not at the expense of local ownership. It promotes competition but also encourages cooperation. A self-reliant society promotes satisfaction rather than consumption.

I should emphasize here that I am not promoting national self-reliance. The United States has by far the largest domestic market in the world. We rank among the top nations in population, geographic size, and natural resources. The United States could easily be self-reliant and even self-sufficient. Aiming for national self-reliance, however, would provide no lessons for a world where most people live in small countries with relatively few natural resources. Thirty-four members of the United Nations have populations below one million, and another 31 have populations between one and five million.

The doctrine of local self-reliance, if applied only to the United States, could easily degenerate into what my British friends call "local selfish sufficiency." The challenge is to create an economy that allows us to produce most of what we need from our own local resources—natural, human and capital—within our more densely populated economies. To do so would be to develop the organizational forms and technologies compatible with the needs of much of the world. Consider for example that the country of El Salvador has about the same population density as the Twin Cities metropolitan area or that the municipal budget of New York City is greater than the gross national product of Chile. We will always be blessed with the advantages of a highly skilled work force, widespread technical capacity, and a peace that many countries can only envy. To develop a model for the world to emulate, we must concentrate on miniaturizing our own national economy.

The state of Minnesota may represent an excellent laboratory to test a new development path. Half our 4.5 million people live in an urban center, a demographic picture similar to many developing and smaller nations. If we could achieve a balanced, locally owned and largely internally-generated economy, we would provide a model for both the developed and developing world.

I also want to stress that I am not preaching parochialism. To the contrary. Localism is not isolationism. Progress comes from sharing the fruits of invention. Robert Green Ingersoll, the great orator of the last century, accurately described commerce as "the great civilizer. We exchange ideas when we exchange fabrics." But today we need not exchange ideas by exchanging fabrics. We can exchange ideas directly. We do not need a few traders travelling to distant shores to bring back new commercial developments. We have news networks, and many of us can travel to distant places ourselves.

It would be difficult to prove that the enormous expansion of global trade in the last century, or even in the last 20 years, has brought greater understanding between religions, cultures, races, and nations. Perhaps much of the information that moves around the world is useful to the global economy, but not to localities or small economies. The data does not flow from community to community, but among global corporations.

Although the sheer amount of information thrown at us is astounding, such data does not inform us. When is the last time you learned from the media of another culture that does things in a better way than our own does? In the United States, there is nothing more parochial than the global village. We hear of England when there is a sale at Harrod's, of Thailand when a hotel fire breaks out, of Ethiopia when famine strikes.

Think about what we know of Russia. We have grown up hating and fearing Russia. We have spent a trillion dollars since 1960 alone, largely to defend ourselves against Russia. On the other hand, what do we know about the Russian people, her history, her culture, her geography? No, the planetary economy has not brought us understanding.

A globe of villages could transfer information horizontally, from community to community, and in so doing, could pave the way for a new kind of economy. Electronic highways are quite distinct from concrete highways.

Already computers are one of the fastest growing segments of our economy, and one of the fastest growing sub-segments of that industry is software. Although the development and manufacture of computer chips requires relatively large organizations and production facilities, the creation and dissemination of software programs such as VisiCalc or Hypercard was accomplished by a very small group via telephone lines.

In a globe of villages production will be regionalized and planetary trade will increasingly consist of electronics, not materials; ideas, not products.

The Example of Garbage

How might we move toward a globe of villages? Consider how we might apply the principles of what I call "the new localism" to a most pressing local problem—garbage management.

The garbage issue affecting Minneapolis-St. Paul and other cities teaches us important lessons. Communities literally changed the rules governing waste disposal. We did not run out of space for dumps. Rather we closed down existing dumps and refused to build new ones. We made a political decision to internalize the costs of disposal, and in doing so we substantially raised the price of disposal. In fact, the cost of garbage disposal has risen faster and further than did the cost of oil in the 1970s.

Our local and national officials, however, approached the garbage problem with the analytical tools of the planetary economy. They relied almost exclusively on price with little regard to cost. They developed no values to guide their effort. They defined garbage as a disposal issue, not an economic development opportunity. They decided to embrace the solution that appeared to demand the least institutional or political change, to maintain and nurture a bureaucratic and regulatory system which itself is an outgrowth of the old way of thinking.

Above all our policy-makers embraced the fundamental import-export paradigm of the global village. They chose to dispose of up to 80 percent of our garbage by burning it, which will force us to continue and perhaps even expand our imports of raw materials. They chose a process that would result in the production of toxic incinerator ash. Since, however, their citizens had refused to site conventional garbage dumps, it was doubtful they would agree to site a hazardous waste dump. Thus, policy-makers chose a technology whose waste product had to be dumped in remote areas. By choosing combustion, we chose to continue the separation of the producer from the consumer. We chose to make ourselves even more dependent.

Now consider an approach to a garbage policy that embraces the concept of a globe of villages: one that strengthens community by reducing imports; one that captures the maximum value from local resources; one that emphasizes resource efficiency and expands the productive capacity of the community.

The Twin Cities disposes of some 2.5 million tons of human and solid waste a year. Technically, we can recycle 75–80 percent of our waste stream. What would that accomplish?

We would create many more jobs. Based on Canadian studies, six times as many jobs are created by recycling than by landfilling. If a similar ratio holds true for recycling versus incineration, the Twin Cities would create 6,000 additional jobs by choosing recycling over combustion. Most of these jobs would be suitable for unskilled and semi-skilled workers, that is, for the chronically unemployed, who represent a major problem in our inner cities.

Cities that recover materials avoid paying disposal costs. However, the real benefit to the local economy comes from converting scrap into useful products; processing aluminum into ingots, paper into pulp, and making ingots into bicycles and pulp back into paper. How far a community can go in this direction is a function of its size and density, industrial mix, and political will. The Twin Cities could go quite far.

Take the example of scrap tires, a small but troublesome waste item. Every American throws away the equivalent of one 20-pound tire a year. Tires have a nasty habit of resurfacing years later. Tire dumps have caught on fire and burned for months. The stagnant water in tires is a primary breeding ground for mosquitoes. In consideration of all these factors, Minnesota banned land disposal of tires two years ago.

Tires can be shredded and burned, but that captures only the direct energy value, maybe a penny a pound at today's oil prices. Tires shredded into even finer pieces can be added to road asphalt and be sold for a few pennies more. But the real benefit comes when the scrap is converted into a valuable final product. A Minnesota-based firm has developed a liquid polymer that can be added to pulverized tires which allows the scrap tire to compete with products made from virgin rubber and with plastics. This would allow the reprocessed rubber to be sold for up to fifty cents per pound.

For the Twin Cities the cost of tire disposal in 1985 was about $4 million. If all tires could be recovered, treated and sold for 50 cents a pound, the Twin Cities would avoid almost all of its disposal costs and create a new industry with $20 million in sales. That industry, and associated ones (one Ohio firm moved to Babbitt to be near its primary materials supplier) would create higher paying jobs. Moreover, they would add to the research and development foundation of the area. The tire process is patented and can be licensed for use by other communities who would gladly pay for the benefits it would bring. We would then begin trading knowledge generated in the process of discovering new ways to make us more self-reliant.

Tire recycling is just now taking off. But we already have an intriguing glimpse of our decentralized industrial future in the steel industry. Twenty years ago the only steel mill technology available used iron ore and huge amounts of energy. One to two million tons per year was and is still considered the minimum efficient plant scale using this technology.

But in the mid 1970s the mini-mill was invented. Today's mini-mills use far less energy and water per ton produced. They rely on scrap steel. And they have captured 20 percent of the market. With each technical advance the industry is able to compete with a greater variety of products manufactured by conventional mills.

The average mini-mill produces about 200,000 tons a year and competes with conventional mills ten times its size. In addition, as other materials like plastics and aluminum replace steel, our consumption of steel has remained stable even though seven years' worth of scrap steel is sitting in our driveways and our junkyards. We can now imagine an almost closed-loop future—mini-mills relying on local scrap piles to produce for regional customers. We are moving toward E. F. Schumacher's ideal: "local production from local resources for local use."

The Carbohydrate Economy

We might reduce by up to 80 percent the amount of raw materials we need to import, but we will always need some imports. Nevertheless, the materials of the future may still be locally available.

Which leads me to the story of chemurgy, a fascinating part of our history. Directly after World War I, midwestern farmers faced problems that seem familiar today. Demand fell, prices collapsed, and bankruptcies surged, while agricultural production continued to rise. A group of scientists, engineers and business leaders gathered to discuss a way out of this dilemma. They concluded that farmers needed to look beyond the human stomach as their sole market.

In 1936, 300 leaders gathered for the first meeting of the Farm Chemurgic Council. Their objective was to develop industrial uses for farm crops. Members included Henry Ford and George Washington Carver. By 1941 Henry Ford was ready to unveil his biological car. The body was made of a soybean-derived plastic, as were the seat covers and the steering wheel. The fuel was corn-derived ethanol. The tires were made from goldenrods. Ford firmly believed that after World War II, we would grow our cars.

After the war, however, the price of oil dropped. The Marshall Plan opened up export markets for American farmers. Federally supported programs in chemurgy all but disappeared. Carbohydrate science withered on the vine, so to speak, while hydrocarbon science took off.

In the 1980s chemicals and fuels made from plant matter are not competitive with those from fossil fuels. Yet the price difference narrows considerably when we take into account the overall cost of the alternatives. We are currently spending about $50 a barrel to defend our access to mid-East oil. At that price, fuels made from plant matter are competitive. Moreover, the pollution costs of burning fossil fuels have still not been internalized into their prices. We also know that 15 years from now the United States will have all but exhausted its domestic petroleum reserves.

Furthermore, we are spending $20 billion in subsidies to American farmers, primarily paying them not to grow. We could spend less money more wisely by creating new markets for materials made from farm products than by paying our farmers not to produce or to store their surplus.

Imagine a chemical and fuels industry based on cellulose, botanochemical plants replacing petrochemical plants. Botanochemical plants would probably be much smaller and more dispersed than petrochemical facilities. By one calculation Minnesota would need about half a dozen.

The key point here is that we can begin today to use the paradigm of a globe of villages to solve immediate social problems. We need not be discounted as utopians, selling a vision of a far off and unattainable perfect future.

A New Future

I conclude with the wisdom of John Maynard Keynes, the English economist, "I sympathize with those who would maximize economic entanglement among nations. Ideas, knowledge, science, hospitality, travel—these are the things which should by their nature be international. But let goods be homespun whenever it is reasonably and conveniently possible and, above all, let finance be primarily national."

When we abandon our ability to produce for ourselves, when we separate authority from responsibility, when those affected by our decisions are not those who make the decisions, when the cost and the benefit of production or development processes are not part of the same equation, when price and cost are no longer in harmony, we jeopardize our security and our future.

You may argue that free trade is not the cause of all our ills. Agreed. But free trade as it is preached today nurtures and reinforces many of our worst problems. It is an ideological package that promotes ruinous policies. And most tragically, as we move further down the road to giantism, globalism, and dependence we make it harder and harder to back up and take another path. If we lose our skills, our productive base, our culture, our traditions, our natural resources, if we erode the bonds of personal and familial responsibility, it becomes evermore difficult to recreate community. It is very, very hard to put Humpty Dumpty back together again.

Which means we must act now. The unimpeded mobility of capital, labor, goods and raw materials is not the highest social good. We need to challenge the postulates of free trade head on, to preach a different philosophy, to embrace a different strategy. There is another way. To make it the dominant way, we must change the rules, indeed, we must change our own behavior. And to do that requires not only that we challenge the emptiness of free trade, but that we promote a new idea: economics as if community matters.

– 13 –

Wendell Berry

A BAD BIG IDEA

After World War II, the United States and seventeen other nations entered into the General Agreement on Tariffs and Trade (also known as GATT) for the purpose of regulating international trade and resolving international trade disputes. Beginning in 1986, with the so-called Uruguay round of GATT negotiations, the Reagan and Bush administrations, working mostly in secret, undertook to make a set of changes in GATT that would have dire economic and ecological effects on the more than one hundred nations now subscribing to the agreement—and that would significantly reduce the freedom of their citizens as well. Whether or not the Clinton administration will continue the Reagan-Bush agitation for these changes remains to be seen.

The U.S. proposals on agriculture were drafted mostly by Daniel Amstutz, formerly a Cargill executive, and they are backed by other large supranational corporations. Made to order for the grain traders and agrochemical companies that operate in the "global economy," these proposals aim both to eliminate farm price supports and production controls and to attempt to force all member nations to conform to health and safety standards that would be set in Rome by Codex Alimentarius, a group of international scientific bureaucrats that is under the influence of the agribusiness corporations. Pressure for these revisions has come solely from these corporations and their allies. There certainly has been no popular movement in favor of them—not in any country—although there have been some popular movements in opposition.

When very important persons have plunder in mind, they characteristically invent ugly euphemisms for what they intend to do, and the promoters of these GATT revisions are no exception:

Tariffication refers to the recommended process by which all controls on imports of agricultural products will be replaced by tariffs, which will then be reduced or eliminated within five to ten years. This would have the effect of opening U.S. markets (and all others) to unlimited imports.

Harmonization refers to a process by which the standards of trade among the member nations would be brought into "harmony." This would mean lowering all those standards regulating food safety, toxic residues, inspections, packaging and labeling, and so on that are higher than the standards set by Codex Alimentarius.

And *fast track* refers to the capitulation by which our Congress has ceded to the president the authority to make an international trade agreement and to draft the enabling legislation, which then is not subject to congressional amendment and which must be accepted or rejected as a whole within ninety session days.

If the proposed revisions in the GATT are adopted, every farmer in every member nation will be thrown into competition with every other farmer. With restrictions lowered to international minimums and with farmers under increasing pressure to make up in volume for drastically reduced unit prices, this will become a competition in land exploitation. Such conservation practices as are now in use (and they are already inadequate) will of necessity be abandoned; land rape and the use of toxic chemicals will increase, as will the exploitation of people. American farmers, who must continue to buy their expensive labor-replacing machines, fuel, and chemicals on markets entirely controlled by the suppliers, will be forced to market their products in competition with the cheapest hand labor of the poor countries. And the poor countries, needing to feed their own people, will see the food vacuumed off their plates by lucrative export markets. The supranational corporations, meanwhile, will be able to slide about at will over the face of the globe to wherever products can be bought cheapest and sold highest.

It is easy to see who will have the freedom in this international "free market." The proposed GATT revisions, as one of their advocates has said, are "exactly what exporters need"—the assumption being, as usual, that what is good for exporters is good for everybody. But what is good for exporters is by no means necessarily good for producers, and in fact these proposed revisions expose a long-standing difference of interest between agribusiness marketers and farmers. We in the United States have seen how unrestrained competition among farmers, increasing surpluses and driving down prices, has directly served the purposes of the agribusiness corporations. The large agribusiness corporations have, in fact, remained hugely and consistently profitable right through an era of severe economic hardship in rural America. They are clearly in a position to take excellent advantage of "free-market" competition, for the proposed GATT revisions would permit them to practice the same exploitation without restraint in the world at large.

What these proposals actually propose is a revolution as audacious, far-reaching, and sudden as any the world has seen. Though they would deny to the people of some 108 nations any choice in the matter of protecting their land, their farmers, their food supply, or their health, these proposals were not drafted and, if adopted, would not be implemented by anybody elected by the people of any of the 108 nations. Their purpose is to bypass all local, state, and national governments in order to subordinate the interests of those governments and of the people they represent to the interests of a global "free market" run by a few supranational corporations. By this single device, if it should be implemented, these corporations would destroy the protections that have been won by generations of conservationists, labor organizers, consumer advocates—and, indeed, by democrats and lovers of freedom. This is an unabashed attempt to replace government with economics and to destroy any sort of local (let alone personal) self-determination. The intended effect would be to centralize control of all prices and standards in the international food economy and to place this control in the hands of the corporations that are best able to profit from it. The revised GATT would thus be a license issued to a privileged few for an all-out economic assault on the lands and peoples of the world. It would establish a "free" global economy that would be a tighter enclosure than most Americans, at least, have so far experienced.

The issue here really is not whether international trade shall be free but whether or not it makes sense for a country—or, for that matter, a region—to destroy its own capacity to produce its own food. How can a government, entrusted with the safety and health of its people, conscientiously barter away in the name of an economic idea that people's ability to feed itself? And if people lose their ability to feed themselves, how can they be said to be free?

The supporters of these GATT revisions assume that there is no longer any possibility of escape from the global economy and, furthermore, that there is no need for such an escape. They assume that all nations are therefore already properly subservient to the global economy and that the highest purpose of national governments is to serve as attorneys for the supranational corporations. They assume also (like far too many farmers and consumers) that there is no possibility of a food economy that is not decided on "at the top" in some center of power.

But in so assuming, these people unwittingly have provided the rest of us with our best occasion so far to understand and to talk about the need for sound and reasonably self-sufficient local food economies. They have forced us to realize that politics and economics are in fact as inseparable as are economics and ecology. They have made it clear that if we want to be free, we will have to free ourselves somehow from the purposes of these great supranational concentrations of greed, wealth, and power. They have forced us to realize that a General Agreement on Tariffs and Trade may be able to set the standards for governments but that it cannot set the standards for individuals and local communities—unless those individuals and communities allow it to do so. They have, in other words, made certain truths self-evident.

The proposed GATT revisions offend against democracy and freedom, against people's natural concern for bodily and ecological health, and against the very possibility of a sustainable food supply. Apart from the corporate ambition to gather the wealth and power of the world into fewer and fewer hands, these revisions make no sense, for they ignore or reduce to fantasy all the realities with which they are concerned: ecological, agricultural, economic, political, and cultural. Their great evil originates in their underlying assumption that all the world may safely be subjected to the desires and controls of a centralizing power. For this is what "harmonization" really envisions: not the necessary small local harmonies that actually can be made among neighbors and between people and their land but rather the "harmony" that might exist between exploiter and exploited after all protest is silenced and all restraints abandoned. The would-be exploiters of the world would like to assume—it would be so easy for them if they could assume—that the world is everywhere uniform and comfortable to their desires.

The world, on the contrary, is made up of an immense diversity of countries, climates, topographies, regions, ecosystems, soils, and human cultures—so many as to be endlessly frustrating to centralizing ambition, and this perhaps explains the attempt to impose a legal uniformity on it. However, anybody who is interested in real harmony, in economic and ecological justice, will see immediately that such justice requires not international uniformity but international generosity toward local diversity.

And anybody interested in solving, rather than profiting from, the problems of food production and distribution will see that in the long run the safest food supply is a local food supply, not a supply that is dependent on a global economy. Nations and regions within nations must be left free—and should be encouraged—to develop the local food economies that best suit local needs and local conditions.

–14–

Mark Ritchie

AGRICULTURAL TRADE
LIBERALIZATION

Implications for Sustainable Agriculture

Two competing visions have emerged concerning the future of agriculture. One approach, often referred to as sustainable agriculture, calls for social and economic initiatives to protect the environment and family farms. This approach emphasizes the uses of public policy to preserve our soil, water and biodiversity, and to promote economically secure family farms and rural communities.

Sustainable agriculture emphasizes farming practices which are less chemical and energy-intensive, and marketing practices which place a high priority on reducing the time, distance, and resources used to move food between production and consumption. Another goal is to maximize food freshness, quality and nutrition by minimizing processing, packaging, transportation and preservatives.[1]

A competing vision, often referred to as the free market, free trade, or de-regulation approach, pursues "economic efficiency" aimed at delivering crops and livestock to agri-processing and industrial buyers at the lowest possible price. Almost all social, environmental and health costs are "externalized" under this approach, ultimately to be paid for by today's taxpayers or by future generations. Based on neo-classical economic theories dating back hundreds of years, proponents of this approach argue that any government intervention in the day to day activities of business diminishes economic efficiency. Free market and free trade policies are heavily promoted by the agribusiness corporations involved in the trading and processing of farm commodities who want to pay as low a price as possible and those supplying farm inputs who want to sell a maximum amount of chemicals, fertilizers, etc.[2]

Supporters of this free market approach often gather under the rallying cry of "get the government out of agriculture." They seek to scale back or eliminate farm programs such as price supports, supply management, and land-use provisions designed for environmental protection. In world trade, they support the opening of state and national borders to unlimited and deregulated imports and exports.

Debate between these two conflicting views has become the central argument over modern agriculture policy. Agricultural trade negotiations taking place under the auspices of both the North American Free Trade Agreement (NAFTA) and the General Agreement on Tariffs and Trade (GATT) have pushed this controversy into the headlines of the world's leading newspapers.

Early History

Debates over agricultural trade and the environment go back to the beginning of recorded history. For example, a book entitled *Grain Through the Ages*, published by Quaker Oats Company, describes this debate in the first and second century B.C. in the Roman Empire. It states:

> One reason for the decline of grain farming in Italy was the importation of grain into Rome from the rich grain lands of Sicily and Egypt. In Sicily these grain lands had been appropriated by rich men and scheming politicians who farmed them with slave labor. As a result the markets of Rome were flooded with cheap grain. Grain became so cheap that the farmers who still owned small pieces of land could not get enough money for the grain they raised to support their families and pay their taxes. They were forced to turn their farms over to rich landowners. On the land of Italy slave gangs working under the overseers took the place of the old Roman farmers, the very backbone of the state.
>
> The farmers, after their land had been lost, went into the city walls, leaving the scythe and the plough. They worked now and then at a small wage. They ate mostly bread made of wheat which was distributed to them by any politician who wanted their votes at an election. They lived in great lodging houses three or four stories high.

The land itself became poor. . . . The use of slaves meant that the land was badly worked because usually the slaves did as little as they possibly could unless they were under the eye of the overseer.

This example from ancient Italy highlights many of the concerns we still face today. The importing of grain into Italy from Sicily and Egypt, where it was produced at lower costs due to slavery, drove down market prices, eventually pushing small farmers off their land. They moved into the cities, where they lived off welfare manipulated by politicians. Their small farms were consolidated into huge estates, operated by absentee owners and slaves. In the end, the land itself was destroyed by this economic process.

Although these inter-relationships between agricultural trade and the environment were noted as far back as early Roman history, the ideological debate over "free trade" is relatively recent, dating back to the 18th and 19th century. Perhaps the defining moment of this debate was in 1846, when the free trade advocates in the British parliament voted to repeal their so-called Corn Laws. These laws regulated imports of wheat in order to protect British farmers from sudden drops in prices. In calling for the repeal of the Corn Laws, free trade theorist Richard Cobden was quite aware of the environmental implications of his free trade proposals. In one of his most famous speeches before Parliament he proudly explained that free trade would lead to a dramatic intensification of British agriculture, including "draining, extending the length of fields, knocking down of hedgerows, clearing away trees which now shield the corn." He went on to extol the virtues and benefits of forcing the farmers to "grub up hedges, grub up thorns, drain, and ditch."

Many, if not most, of Cobden's free trade colleagues understood that free trade proposals would put enormous economic pressure on British farmers, just as the cheap imports from slave estates had done to the farmers in Italy, and that in their struggle to survive British farmers would intensify their methods of production, including the draining of wetlands, cutting hedgerows and deforestation.

Modern History

The modern "free trade vs. sustainable agriculture" debate sharpened in the early 1980s. During those years, President Reagan, with the help of the Republican-controlled Senate, implemented the most free-market oriented US farm bill since the 1920s. Much of this policy was contained in the 1981 and 1985 Farm Bills.

There are two central economic elements in every farm bill. First, Congress sets minimum prices that must be paid to farmers by domestic and foreign buyers. This is accomplished through a government administered price-support mechanism called the Commodity Credit Corporation nonrecourse loan program. This minimum price, often called the "loan rate," has been set at roughly one-half to two-thirds the average cost of production for wheat, corn, and other major crops during most of the 1980s.

Second, Congress sets a "target" price for farmers. This target price, while above the minimum price, is still below the average cost of production. Farmers receive government payments, called deficiency payments, to bridge the gap between the loan rate and the target price. Although these payments are often called "farm subsidies," they primarily benefit domestic and overseas buyers by holding prices at very low levels. For many farmers, especially younger ones who are still buying their land and machinery, their total income, including the government payments, is not enough to cover all costs, leading them first to "cost cutting" in all aspects of their operations, including environmental protection and natural resource conservation measures. Many have been ultimately forced into bankruptcy and foreclosure.

Reagan aggressively pursued what he called "market-oriented" policies, including the dramatic lowering of farm prices. There were at least four major effects of these policies. First, a huge number of farmers were forced out of business. It is worth noting that while record numbers of farmers went into bankruptcy, food processors earned record profits.

Second, government costs soared. Low prices meant huge deficiency payment costs. At the same time, the broader rural economic crisis caused by farm bankruptcies forced the government to bail out thousands of rural businesses, banks, and ultimately the entire Farm Credit System.

Third, many farmers reacted to falling farm prices by further intensifying their production methods. They hoped to make up in higher volume for the lower prices, but the increased use of chemicals and fertilizers only added to environmental and public health problems. To make matters worse, this intensification created enormous surpluses, forcing the Reagan administration in 1983 to impose one of the largest, most expensive, and most environmentally damaging land set-aside programs in U.S. farm history, called the Payment in Kind (PIK) program.

Fourth, the total value of U.S. farm exports declined sharply. A number of farm policy analysts had warned that inelasticity in world food markets would mean that demand for food would remain relatively constant despite sharp drops in prices. Lower farm prices, they argued, would reduce the total value of US farm exports, especially in the grains sector. But agribusiness economists convinced Congress that lower prices would "drive other exporting countries out of the world market." Former Senator Boschwitz, a ranking Republican on the Agriculture Committee, stated this as an explicit goal in a 1985 letter to *Time Magazine*. "If we do not act to discourage these countries now, our worldwide competitive position will continue to slide and be much more difficult to regain. This should be one of our foremost goals of our agricultural policy and the Farm Bill." Economists promised huge growth in export volume, enough to offset losses due to low prices.

Contrary to the computer projections made by the agribusiness economists, the value of US farm exports fell. Although the volume of exports rose, lower prices meant that their value fell from the late 1970s level of $40 billion per year to less than $30 billion by 1985. In constant dollars, farm exports in 1990 reached only half the 1981 level, even though the number of bushels shipped was higher. This low price/high volume policy required a significant increase in our imports of oil, fertilizer, tires and machinery imports, all of which became more costly over the same period, ultimately increasing our trade deficit. Reagan's free trade farm policies made the US trade deficit significantly worse.

What happened to the optimistic computer projections? The flaw in the agribusiness logic was that other countries cannot simply stop producing or exporting farm products just because the U.S. corporations want them to or because our government sets the world prices at extremely low levels. Many countries desperately need the earnings they receive from farm exports to pay their foreign debts and cannot simply quit. The United States controls the lion's share of many of the world's farm-commodity markets, up to 70 percent in some crops. When the US dropped its prices, other countries simply lowered their prices to match. Other major exporting countries, such as Brazil, Thailand and Argentina, could not stop exporting no matter how low the price, as their debt servicing obligations make them dependent on food exports for hard currency earnings. Some of these countries, facing lower prices, tried to boost the volume of their exports in hopes of making up for the lower prices. Economic behavior in the real world stubbornly refuses to conform to academic theories.

Political Reaction to Free Market Policies

Political reaction to Reagan's free market policies in the US was sharp. Farmers and small-town residents blocked foreclosure auctions and occupied government offices and banks. In 1984 and 1986, voters threw out numerous incumbent Senators and Representatives, including Republican Senators in the farm states of Iowa, North Dakota, South Dakota, Georgia, and Illinois. Rural America demanded an end to the destruction of their farms, families, livelihoods and communities.

The protests came not only from farmers and small town residents. Consumer and environmental groups also began to express concern over the safety of food and the ecological impact of chemical and energy-intensive production methods being encouraged by free market policies. The National Toxics Campaign, for example, launched a nationwide effort to change federal farm policies in ways that would reduce the use of chemical and energy-intensive methods of production.[3] They advocated farm programs which would set farm prices at levels equal to the full cost of production, including all environmental costs, while limiting production to the amount needed to balance supply with demand. A number of family farm groups and rural citizens' organizations also advocated this approach, often called quantitative supply management, seeing it as a way to restore economic vitality to rural America.

Agrichemical companies became concerned about many of these new proposals, fearing that they could lead to ever stricter pesticide regulations. Laws were being passed that greatly increased companies' financial liability for harm to workers, farmers and communities that happened during the production, storage or application of their products. To avoid these regulations and liabilities, many chemical companies began to move the production of the most dangerous products overseas. Corporate farm operators also moved their most chemical and labor-intensive farming, such as cotton, fruit and vegetables, overseas for the same reasons—to avoid regulation and liability.

Reacting to this sharp increase in overseas production of US food supplies, a number of states and the federal government imposed increasingly stricter pesticide residue regulations on imported foods. By 1989, as much as 40 percent of imported food items inspected by the Food and Drug Administration were rejected for reasons of unsafe chemical residues, contaminate levels or other violations of US standards according to the House Committee on Energy and Commerce.[4] Nonetheless, due to budget cuts, the FDA now inspects only 2% of all the imports. This has prompted a number of states, including California, Minnesota and Wisconsin, to implement additional food safety regulations at the state level in response to intense consumer lobbying.

The problems created by these "free-market" policies generated a rebellion in both the countryside and in the cities. Corporate agribusiness and the agrichemical companies who had benefitted the most from Reagan's free trade approach began to fear that a political backlash might result in its dismantling, especially if a Democrat were elected to the White House.

Countering the Backlash

Agribusiness began to explore ways to counter the backlash. Food companies and exporters wanted to ensure that farm prices would not be raised back up to cost-of-production levels. They wanted to ensure that it would continue to be easy to import cheap food from abroad. Agrichemical companies wanted to block any new local, state or federal pesticide regulations and they opposed quantitative supply management programs designed to reduce production by setting aside land which would reduce the use of fertilizers and other yield-enhancing chemicals.

One of the most creative strategies designed by agribusiness to counter the backlash was the decision to move policymaking on these issues out of the hands of state legislatures and Congress and into the arena of international trade negotiations. Using this strategy, social or environmental regulations in the form of farm policy reforms or food safety standards could be termed "trade barriers" and then dismantled under the guise of "liberalizing trade." New rules for international trade could even roll back pesticide and other environmental regulations, while prohibiting restrictions on imported foods.

In US trade policy, the executive branch has the opportunity to overrule

Congress and preempt local and state governments. Trade negotiations, for example, are conducted in secret by the White House. It is extremely difficult, even for most members of Congress, to get information about what is being negotiated until it is too late to analyze implications or to affect the outcome. Further, special rules govern the approval of trade agreements. Under the "fast track" approval process, Congress cannot amend in any way the proposed agreement. Time for debate is very limited. Congress can only rubberstamp the final text, either yes or no.[5]

US-Canada Free Trade Negotiations

Bi-national talks between the US and Canada, concluded in 1989, were the first of the modern trade talks to be used extensively to promote the free trade agenda of agribusiness. The final agreement opened the US-Canada border to greatly increased shipments by multinational food companies in both directions. These talks were used to weaken or repeal food safety and farm security laws historically opposed by agribusinesses on both sides of the border.[6]

Canada, for example, had to loosen its stricter regulations on pesticides and food irradiation. And there have been moves to weaken the Canadian Wheat Board and to drastically alter the system of supply management used to protect Canadian family farmers in the poultry, egg and dairy business. All of these policies or programs were seen as a "bad example" by agribusiness, who feared that US consumers and farmers would begin to demand similar programs in the same way that many US citizens now are demanding Canadian-style health insurance.

In addition to setting back efforts to achieve a more sustainable agricultural system, the US-Canada agreement was a setback for environmental protection in general. It virtually eliminated Canadian government spending to support ecological efforts such as wetlands protection and forest replanting. These types of government subsidies were labeled "trade distorting" and essentially banned. In fact, only two types of government subsidies are allowed under the US-Canada deal: to help expand oil and gas exploration and to subsidize companies and factories producing military weapons.[7] These are now the only "legal" government-sponsored developments allowed in Canada.

Another free trade measure imposed by the US-Canada agreement guarantees long-term, low-cost access to Canadian oil, gas and uranium resources, encouraging continued dependency on non-renewable fuels. The US also got access to Canadian water, which will likely stimulate, rather than restrict, reckless exploitation of the US's dwindling water supplies by encouraging practices such as the irrigation of fragile deserts and the mining of our groundwater in semi-arid areas.

Among the wide range of environmental protection measures that have been challenged as unfair trade barriers under this free trade deal are US laws banning asbestos, Canadian rules to protect ocean fishery stocks from depletion, state-level laws in the US to encourage small-scale factories through tax incentives, and requirements that newsprint must contain recycled paper. In each case, the challenging country believed the social or environmental policy of the other country placed the domestic industry at a competitive disadvantage.

An important lesson that can be learned from the US-Canada Free Trade Agreement is that there were negative effects for family farmers and the environment on both sides of the border. Deregulated trade is not an equation that benefits either one country's interest or the other's, determined by which side's negotiators were more clever. To the contrary, both countries' negotiators pursued the interests of their respective transnational corporations instead of the interest of the general public. The US-Canadian deal is a good example of how family farmers, consumers and the environment on both sides of the border can lose out under "free trade."

Expanding the US-Canada Free Trade Deal to Mexico

Unfortunately, agribusiness and agrichemical companies still are not satisfied. They believe that the US-Canada agreement did not go far enough. Almost before the ink was dry on the final agreement, the very same corporations began to aggressively pursue the next step in their global deregulation strategy, extending the US-Canada Free Trade Agreement to Mexico. They see this as the next step in their plan for a single Western Hemispheric free trade zone, an "Enterprise of the Americas Initiative."[8]

There are two main threats to sustainable agriculture in the North American Free Trade Agreement (NAFTA) negotiations. The first is the stated objective of increasing the "scale of production."[9] A number of specific provisions in the text will lead to both increased corporate concentration in the processing sector and the further expansion of large scale "factory farms" in all three countries.[10]

The second threat is the stated goal of eliminating each government's ability to regulate the importing and exporting of goods. If local, state, and national governments can no longer regulate the flow of goods across their borders, as a result of the NAFTA talks, farmers, consumers, workers and the environment will suffer.

Destroying Mexican Family Farmers

One of the major demands of the multinational grain companies based in the US is unlimited access for their exports of corn and other grains to Mexico. At present, almost 3 million Mexican peasants grow corn and sell this crop at price levels set high enough by the government to ensure that they have enough cash income to survive. This system requires that the Mexican government very carefully regulate imports to ensure that this price level is not undermined.

Economists in both Mexico and the US predict that, if the grain companies are successful in their efforts to force open the Mexican corn market, the price that will be paid to Mexican peasants will fall dramatically, forcing one million or more families off their land. Most of these families have worked at some time in the United States, so it is assumed that many will head North in search of either farmworker jobs in the countryside or service sector work in the major cities. Others will head to Mexico's urban areas, such as Mexico City and Guadalajara, already dangerously polluted.

Destroying Family Farms in the US

The United States, too, has used import regulations to sustain a domestic agricultural sector. For example, Congress has established strict controls on the level of beef imports allowed into this country in the Meat Import Act of 1979. But fast-food hamburger retailers pushed the Bush Administration hard to make sure that any NAFTA agreement will abolish or weaken these controls, allowing them to import more hamburger meat. Since beef can be produced most cheaply on cleared rainforest land in southern Mexico, a sharp increase in US beef imports from this region would cause an acceleration in the destruction of the rainforest. A further worry is that Mexico would be used to trans-ship beef grown on destroyed rainforest regions in Central and South America, a practice that has already begun.[11]

Unlimited beef imports would also lower the income of family-sized cattle producers in the US. These producers have to sell at prices low enough to compete with rainforest beef. If the NAFTA is accepted as currently proposed, they would be forced to sell less, since an increasing share of the US beef supply would be imported. With more beef coming from overseas, there would also be a smaller market for US-grown hay, corn and other feedstuffs. Replacing US beef with rainforest-fed beef not only devastates US beef farmers, but also those who produce feedgrains fed to US cattle.

If beef imports are not regulated, there will be serious environmental problems created in the United States, in addition to those affecting Mexico's rainforests. Currently, many US beef cattle graze on the hillsides and meadows of the Upper Midwest. The state of Minnesota, for example, has generally poor soil in the northern region, with the exception of the Red River Valley. It is often hilly with thin topsoil, and quite fragile. The only agriculture production suited for this land, and indeed needed to maintain this land, is beef and dairy cattle raising. If beef from the rainforest land comes across the border from Mexico and drives down US beef prices, Minnesota's diversified, small, family beef operations will be put out of business. Their fragile land would most likely be put into row crops, soybeans or corn, in hopes of getting enough income to at least pay taxes and expenses. On these hillsides, it only takes one or two growing seasons before these crops would cause the topsoil to wash away at a non-sustainable rate, ultimately destroying the productivity of the land.

Beyond the two objectives stated in the draft NAFTA text—increasing the size of farms and deregulating imports and exports—there are other specific measures that would interfere with efforts to achieve economic and ecological sustainability of agriculture in all three countries.

Eliminating Winter Produce in the US

US fruit and vegetable production is seriously threatened by free trade. US producers currently operate under substantial regulations concerning chemicals and worker rights. They pay higher taxes and extend more worker benefits than producers in Mexico. Even if US and Mexican produce growers had the same pesticide regulations on paper, since the Food and Drug Administration inspects only 2 percent of the food coming across the border, there is little chance that violators of food safety regulations would be caught. Consumer confidence would be damaged by a few isolated incidents of poisoning like the Chilean grape incident a few years ago.

The entire winter-produce industry could be threatened. If farmers in Florida, Texas and California are to take the enormous risks inherent in wintertime crop production, they must be confident of steady markets, profitable enough in good years to cover the occasional crop failures due to weather, disease, and pests. Unlimited imports would make markets and profits unpredictable. These risks would be unacceptably high. Eventually, our domestic winter fruit and vegetable production could disappear. The consequent dependence on imported fruits and vegetables could have dire effects on US food safety and security, especially in light of the Chilean grape scare.

Furthermore, importing fruits, vegetables, and other food items which can be efficiently grown here in the United States unnecessarily increases our trade deficit. The more items we import that can be grown or produced by farmers or workers in the United States, the greater our overall deficit.

Edward Angstead, president of the Growers and Shippers Association of Central California, reported that total production costs for frozen broccoli in Mexico are less than pre-harvest costs in California. The biggest difference is the cost of labor. Angstead estimates the cost of farm labor in Mexico at $3 per day, compared to $5–15 per hour in California. Pillsbury Company's Green Giant division is in the midst of moving a frozen-food packing factory from Watsonville, California to Mexico in anticipation of a NAFTA. They believe that this agreement will allow them to bring products formerly produced in Watsonville back into the US without tariffs and with few food safety controls. Low wages, weaker environmental laws and the lack of workplace safety regulations makes the short-term economic advantage obvious.[12]

The loss of Watsonville's Green Giant factory means that the farmers in the area who grew crops for the plant lost their market, farmworkers who picked those crops lost their jobs, and the workers in the cannery also lost jobs. The impacts on the surrounding town are devastating.

Similarly, there is a shift taking place in the textile and apparel industry, with factories closing and moving to Mexico, reducing markets for US produced cotton. The closing of textile mills has secondary impact, too. They often are a source of off-farm employment for many farm families, providing additional income to supplement low farm prices. As such they serve as the economic backbone of many small towns; their loss will further destroy rural communities. The same is happening in the US meatpacking industry, already hit by plummeting wages. Beef and pork slaughter is moving to Mexico for lower wages, weaker occupational-health regulations and less strict environmental standards. Cargill Corporation, for example, has already relocated part of its meatpacking operations to Mexico in anticipation of the North American Free Trade Agreement. Over time, cattle and hog production will move closer to these meatpacking facilities, since livestock cannot be shipped over long distances without serious loss. Again, workers, their communities, and the environment will suffer.

Making Organic Farming Unsustainable

Free trade between the US and Mexico may deliver a "double-whammy" to organic farmers on both sides of the border. First, the general lowering of prices on commercially grown fruits and vegetables will make it hard to charge the prices needed to cover organic growers' additional costs.

Second, expansion of fruit and vegetable production in Mexico will increase the overall use of chemicals, futher disrupting and interfering with natural pest-control patterns. Organic farmers cannot apply pesticides to control pests driven to their fields by their neighbors' spray. Since they are dependent on natural predators for their own biological pest management, any increase in chemical spraying on neighboring farms will negatively impact their efforts to use biological pest management.

Internationally recognized organic farming advocate Colin Hines, in the July 1991 edition of *The Living Earth* journal, summarized his concerns as follows: "Round the corner lurks a gleaming new engine for accelerating free trade, which if unleashed will make the idea that there is any future for organic agriculture the mere stuff of dreams."

Reducing Consumer Confidence

Increased food trade between the US, Mexico and Canada will likely have a negative impact on consumer confidence in the safety and quality of food. Food processors will need to genetically alter, over-process and over-package their products in order to survive long trips and periods of storage. Quality, taste and nutritional value will be diminished. In the absence of uniform food-safety laws or country-of-origin labeling regulations, consumers cannot be sure about their food. Efforts to "harmonize" such regulations in the proposed US-Mexico trade negotiations are likely to be simply an underhanded attempt to weaken them.

For example, some Mexican milk now comes from cows treated with Bovine Growth Hormone (BGH), a milk-production drug banned in Minnesota and Wisconsin in response to consumer and dairy farmer demands. US consumers have expressed their grave concerns about this product's potential human health effects, especially when they found out that experimental milk from BGH test-herds here in the US was being mixed with commercial milk. Over a dozen surveys have shown that consumers will buy less milk and fewer dairy products if the products might contain BGH.[13] US dairy farmers face the potential loss of markets and lower prices if Mexican milk containing BGH is allowed into the country. BGH-milk will seriously undermine consumer confidence in a pure and wholesome product.

This erosion of consumer confidence has already occurred as a result of the US-Canada Free Trade Agreement, which sharply reduced the inspection of meat products coming across the border. Public testimony about the serious problems posed by the lack of proper regulations by US government inspectors set off a storm of negative publicity and press coverage which increased consumer fears about the safety of meat.

Higher Energy Consumption Adds to Global Warming

Three elements of the US-Mexico-Canada free trade proposal will lead to increased petroleum use, adding more CO_2 to the atmosphere and therefore increasing global warming. First, food products will be transported over longer distances. The average US chicken already travels 2,000 miles before it is consumed. Second, more energy will be required to process and package foods for long-distance shipping and long-term storage. Third, farmers will intensify their production methods to boost yields in response to lower prices, leading to higher doses of petrochemical fertilizer and pesticide, and increased use of petroleum-fueled machinery.

The US, Mexican and Canadian governments have begun laying plans for accommodating the sharp increase in truck and rail shipping that they believe will take place under any free trade agreement. Some of their plans could significantly raise the costs of farming. At a meeting of transportation ministers from all three countries, for example, US Secretary of Transportation Samuel Skinner praised Mexico's recent encouragement of private ownership of formerly public roads. Calling tollroads "the way of the future," Skinner predicted that they would become more common in the US, too, substantially raising the cost of transporting food products, an added burden for the farmers.

Threats to Genetic Diversity

In an overview of environmental dangers posed by NAFTA, the National Wildlife Federation (NWF) highlighted the dangers to biological resource conservation and genetic diversity.[14] Modern agricultural production depends on the continued evolution of crop varieties that not only yield high output but also resist diseases, pests and drought. NWF warns that free trade could threaten the survival of diverse genetic resource pools, leaving society without the genetic raw materials needed to protect our food security.

Another look at the potential impacts on biological resources can be found in a publication called "Rise of the Global Exchange Economy and the Loss of Biological Diversity" written by University of California professor of agricultural and resource economics, Dr. Richard Norgaard. In this piece, Dr. Norgaard argues that "During the past century, world agriculture has been transformed from a patchwork quilt of nearly independent regions to a global exchange economy. This change in social organization also contributes to the loss of diversity."

Creating Conflicts Between Farmers and Consumers

Allowing imported products to escape domestic standards can create antagonism and division between US farmers and consumers. If US farmers cannot use DDT or Alar while imports with residues of these chemicals are allowed, their competitiveness, and thus survival, will be threatened, forcing them to support a weakening of domestic standards. At a time when serious cooperation is needed to solve major environmental problems, the NAFTA talks appear to be creating new and unnecessary conflict between farmers, environmentalists, and consumers.

GATT: Obstructing Sustainable Agriculture on a Global Scale

By far the greatest single threat to the possibility of sustainable agriculture comes from the current global free trade negotiations taking place under the auspices of the General Agreement on Tariffs and Trade (GATT). This worldwide agreement, which includes more than 100 countries, establishes rules for the conduct of international trade. First drafted in 1947, there is currently an effort to re-write these rules as part of the Uruguay Round, named after the country where these talks were launched in 1986. Agribusiness companies joined with other business interests, such as financial services, drug and chemical companies, and computer manufacturers to push the Reagan Administration to take the lead in what could be called the "global deregulation round."

Although there are more than a dozen major areas under negotiation at GATT, all of which have serious implications for the environment, the U.S. government's proposals for the global deregulation of agricultural trade are perhaps the most far-reaching.

In October 1989, the Bush Administration presented to all GATT member nations their final version of the kind of comprehensive agricultural proposal they wanted to impose on other GATT members.[15]

Noted farm columnist Jonathan Harsch described the strategy of the Reagan White House for using GATT to lock in policies favoring agribusiness in the following way: "Good Republicans acknowledge that what they are doing now in the GATT talks should make it virtually impossible for anyone, even Jim Hightower, to reverse the direction of US farm policy."[16]

If accepted, this proposal would alter the rules governing world trade in food, natural fibers, fish and forestry products and would seriously limit the right of GATT member nations to implement a wide range of natural resource protection laws at local, provincial and national levels.[17]

Destroying US Agricultural Programs

One of the main objectives of the Bush Administration's plan was to force a sharp reduction in, or the elimination of, domestic farm supports around the world in order to force down world market prices. Grain traders and agrochemical firms have long worked to eliminate farm programs because they are "impediments" to their ability to maximize profits. They convinced President Bush to use GATT as a way of attacking them.

These policies would harm small and medium-sized family farmers and have major environmental consequences:

- *There would be a large increase in the amount of land under cultivation.*

    Current farm policy in the US, Europe and elsewhere has allowed many farmers to leave unproductive more than 100 million acres over the past few years, both to control production and to protect the environment. If farm programs are phased out under the US proposal, much of this now idle land would go back into production.
- *Farm and pasture land would be managed much more intensively through the use of more chemicals and fertilizers.*

    According to the Fertilizer Institute, the reduction of farm prices "will provide incentives to farmers to improve their productive efficiency." In other words, price cuts will force farmers to buy more chemicals in the hope of boosting production enough to make up for falling prices.
- *Falling farm prices would leave small and medium-sized family farmers with less income.*

    Most family farmers would end up with less income, making it financially difficult or impossible for them to take the risks necessary to make the conversion to more sustainable practices vital to soil and water conservation.
- *Conservation-oriented farm programs could be eliminated.*

    A number of farm programs are combined or linked with conservation efforts, such as wetlands and wildlife habitat protection schemes. Operation of these would become difficult or impossible without subsidies.
- *Families farming the land could be replaced by absentee landlords and corporations.*

    It is likely that a large number of farm families and peasants around the world will be forced out of business, even if they intensify production to their maximum ability. Some of these producers will be replaced by absentee or corporate owners who have the capital necessary to increase fertilizer and chemical use enough to survive.
- *Diversified livestock producers would be replaced by large-scale feedlots and confinement operations.*

    The reduction in feed prices would put large livestock producers at an enormous competitive advantage over smaller, diversified family operations who grow their own feed. Not only would this squeeze out smaller producers, it would also add to environmental problems caused by manure run-off from these huge operations. The concentration of livestock into large units brings additional problems with diseases too, leading to an increased reliance on antibiotics and the use of nuclear irradiation to control threats to human health. Large-scale producers are major advocates of the legalization of growth hormones and stimulants.

- *Small producers who have survived by growing specialty crops will be pushed out by large producers entering their markets.*

Some large-scale producers would shift their production into new, specialty crops, now grown mostly by smaller, more environmentally-sound farms. This could result in a collapse of market prices for these specialty crops, driving the smaller producers out of business.

- *Conversion of farmland into industrial and commercial uses.*

The displacement of family farmers could lead to an acceleration in the conversion of farmland into factories, roads, shopping malls, landfills, and other commercial developments.

Import Controls on Raw Materials

One of the most important features of the Bush Administration's GATT proposal, like their plans for NAFTA, was the demand that nations would no longer be able to limit the volume of agricultural or other raw material imports. Existing import quotas would be subjected to a process called "tariffication," in which import controls are converted into import taxes, called tariffs, and then phased down or out within 5–10 years. This would be a disaster for sustainable agriculture in both the poor countries of the South and in the North.

Many poor countries now use import controls, often in the form of quotas, to protect their local agriculture and fisheries from being wiped out by cheap imports from industrialized countries like Australia, Canada, the US or Europe. If these countries are prohibited from imposing import quotas, their own local farmers will be forced to use ever more intensive and environmentally damaging methods of production in an attempt to survive. Those farmers who are not able to intensify will eventually be pushed off their land, leading to the consolidation of smallholdings into huge corporate-style farms. This is exactly what has been occurring in the US with the support and encouragement of the Department of Agriculture for the last 40 years.

Prohibiting import controls in the North would also have social and environmental consequences. For example, environmental organizations which are calling for a ban on the import of tropical hardwoods are concerned that the US proposal to eliminate quantitative import controls is an attempt to ensure that GATT rules will prevent a tropical timber ban from ever being adopted in the US or elsewhere.

As noted earlier, fast-food hamburger restaurants in the United States are attempting to use both the NAFTA and the GATT talks to overturn provisions of the Meat Import Act, which now limits the amount of beef allowed into this country. If successful, there will be a sharp rise in beef imports, much of which will be produced on pastures cleared from rainforests in Central and South America.

Similarly, confectionery and soft drink companies like Coca-Cola, Pepsi, and Mars are pushing to open US borders to unlimited imports of sugar. Contrary to the claims by these corporations that ending sugar import controls would help poor people in the Third World, the majority of the sugar imported into the US comes from huge plantations which are often on land that was formerly used by small farmers to grow food for their families. The sugar workers are often treated little better than slaves. More sugar imports will only lead to more and more land being seized from peasants, thereby creating more hunger, poverty and environmental destruction.

Export Controls on Natural Resources

Article XI of the already existing GATT treaty gives all countries the right to impose export controls on food and other critical resources in times of shortage. This is designed to prevent corporations from exporting desperately-needed food in order to sell it for a higher price somewhere else. The Bush Administration proposed that this provision of GATT be abolished to ensure that US corporations, no matter where they are operating in the world, would have unrestricted access to all the raw materials they need or want.

Ironically, many citizens in the United States, especially in the Pacific northwest states, have come out in strong opposition to this proposal. Legislatures in both states have passed outright bans on the exports of raw logs, both for ecological reasons and to protect jobs in local sawmills. Japanese importing corporations, who have come to be dependent on raw log exports from this region, have bitterly objected, claiming that this violates the US "free trade" position at GATT. The Bush Administration sided with the Japanese corporations on this issue, and they attempted to use the GATT talks to give them the power to preempt and overturn these state laws. This did not go unnoticed. The governors of the states most affected, Washington, Oregon, and Idaho, even went so far as to issue a joint statement condemning the Bush Administration's attempts to usurp their power to limit raw log exports to protect the environment and jobs.

Weakening Consumer Health and Environmental Safety Standards

Few issues have caused as much conflict in this round of agricultural trade talks as the wide differences between each nation's food safety and environmental standards. Corporations are lobbying for new GATT rules which could both limit the right of nations to set stricter standards and allow federal governments to preempt state pesticide and food safety legislation. This plan, called "harmonization" by the Bush Administration, limits the right of nations to impose consumer protection regulations on imported foods through the following procedures:

- Nations who attempt to set higher food safety standards than those recognized by GATT would be subject to challenge by other countries on the grounds that these higher standards would exclude their products from being imported. Countries with the higher standards would have to defend these standards or be subject to retaliation or have to pay compensation to the objecting countries.
- "Scientific evidence" would be the only consideration in human health and environmental regulations applied to imports. No social, economic, religious or cultural concerns could be used to set import standards, no matter how important.
- The Rome-based UN agency Codex Alimentarius, made up of government officials plus executives from chemical and food companies, would set the standards acceptable to GATT.

If "harmonization" is prescribed by GATT, then national government attempts to enforce domestic standards stricter than those recommended by Codex on pesticide residues on imported food (or other food safety concerns) could result in GATT-sanctioned trade retaliation or in demands for compensation to exporting countries. For example, a food item imported into the United States is banned under current legislation if it is found to have DDT residues above extremely low "background" levels. However, since Codex has set Maximum Residue Levels (MRLs) for DDT many times higher than the US, disputes may arise between nations exporting foods with Codex-permitted DDT residues and the US. The exporting nation could take this issue to a GATT dispute panel, who would compare US limits to Codex. The stricter US standards could be ruled "illegal." If the US Congress refuses to revise the statute to meet GATT specifications, trade retaliation could result.

This option has been referred to by some as "greenmail," where countries demand financial "compensation" in return for promising not to export goods with pesticide residues above domestic tolerance levels. If Codex standards become a "ceiling" or upper limit on the regulations that can be enforced on imported goods, farmers in countries with stricter standards will find themselves competing with imported foods produced under much less strict environmental regulations. When this situation begins to threaten their economic survival, they may feel compelled to lobby for lower standards to create a "level playing field," causing a serious conflict of interest between farmers and environmentalists. Not only could this conflict result in an expensive and time-consuming battle, it may also destroy the alliances that have been built in recent years among farmers, consumers and environmentalists. In the end, "harmonization" may result in the lowering of safety standards on both imported and domestically produced foods.

Undermining Local, State and National Authority

Many public health advocates around the world feared that the Bush Administration was trying to use GATT-enforced "harmonization" as an instrument to overturn or weaken various pesticide regulations and food safety laws in the United States and elsewhere. Indeed, Codex is presided over by a White House appointee from the US Department of Agriculture. In an interview, Republican National Chair (and former U.S. Trade Representative and Agriculture Secretary) Clayton Yeutter expressed his belief that George Bush should use GATT to do just this:

> If the rest of the world can agree on what the standard ought to be on a given product, maybe the US or EC will have to admit they are wrong when their standards differ.[18]

Under legislation being considered by the US Congress, dangerous pesticides banned in the US could no longer be shipped abroad—where they are presently used on crops which are then exported back to the United States, creating the so-called "circle of poison". Since Codex does not ban a number of chemicals prohibited in the US, it could be against GATT rules for Congress to prohibit their export, or the re-import of foods with residues of these banned products. John Wessel, director of the US Food and Drug Administration's Contaminants Policy Staff and spokesperson for the Bush Administration on this issue, strongly condemned congressional attempts to pass "circle of poison" legislation, arguing that the proposed laws would:

> . . . have the potential of bringing international food trade to a halt. If there is a need for providing a level playing field for farmers, then it should be the responsibility of the Codex Committee on Pesticide Residues rather than an individual country.[19]

"Harmonization" is also clearly designed to restrict the ability of local and regional governments to set environmental and consumer protection standards. For example, the citizens of California have voted to prohibit the use of any carcinogenic pesticides on food grown or sold in the state. But, under "harmonization" this law could not be enforced on foods imported from overseas without the possibility of trade retaliation. Clayton Yeutter has stated publicly that one of his main goals at GATT was to overturn state and local food safety regulations that have been passed in recent years.

Clayton Yeutter was close to achieving his goal even without a successful conclusion of the current Uruguay Round. Using the dispute settlement process, the Bush Administration got the GATT bureaucracy to make two important rulings with long-term and very negative implications for protecting the safety of our food and the security of our environment. The first was a case brought by Mexico against the US Marine Mammal Protection Act (MMPA). In this instance, GATT ruled that the US must repeal the MMPA because it was illegal under their interpretation of GATT rules. The second was a GATT panel ruling which requires national governments to use all powers authorized under their constitution to force state and local governments to comply with GATT rules. For example, if a state has a pesticide regulation more strict than international standards, like California's Proposition 65, which requires the labeling of foods treated with carcinogens, Congress is obligated under GATT to preempt these state laws in order to enforce the weaker global standards.

Yeutter also saw ways to use "harmonization" to lower standards in other countries. Government and food industry officials in the US have been very active in support of "harmonization," partially because they believe it can be used to lower the standards they must meet when they export their produce. A good example is the proposed EC ban on the genetically-engineered cattle growth hormone, bovine somatotropin (BST). In a letter to Europe's Agriculture Commissioner, Ray MacSharry, then Agriculture Secretary Yeutter objected to this proposed ban, using GATT as his main justification. Yeutter stated his belief that a moratorium on the use of BST could both disrupt the GATT talks and encourage consumer demands for similar regulations in the US.

Yeutter argued that an EC ban on BST would "contravene our mutual objective of achieving international harmonization in this sensitive area of food safety. It would also add fuel to the fires of those who wish to have public policy decisions made on the basis of emotion and political pressure."[20]

In the same speech he went on to say, "arguments about synthetic hormone's impact on production also should not be used as a basis for FDA consideration. I don't want government agencies deciding on the basis of alleged economic ground what should or should not enter the American market. Let's let the marketplace provide that determination."[21]

Preventing the Adoption of the "Fourth Criteria"

Over the last 100 years, three criteria for evaluating new chemical additives to food have evolved: safety, quality and efficacy. A number of consumer and environmental organizations are working to establish social and economic values as the "fourth criteria." Many chemical, pharmaceutical and food companies fear that if this "fourth criterion" becomes generally accepted it will lead to tougher laws and regulations.

Recent examples of the "fourth criteria" in practice are the bans on the commercial use of BST, passed by a number of US states including Wisconsin and Minnesota, because the use of this drug could bankrupt thousands of dairy farmers. Under the GATT harmonization proposal, these laws could not be applied to imported goods without running the risk of retaliatory action. In an official GATT report, the US representative argued that:

> The basis for authorizing products should be a thorough scientific appraisal against the three traditional criteria of safety, quality and efficacy. The EC was now considering whether . . . BST should also be reviewed on the basis of social and economic implications. According to the United States, such a political criterion could set a very dangerous precedent. . . .[22]

Undermining Our Democracy

One of the most important public concerns is whether GATT will be used to undermine the democratic institutions of the US. Lynn Greenwalt, vice-president for international affairs at the National Wildlife Federation, summarized this concern at a May 1990 press conference on GATT and the environment:

> We have come together today to note, and perhaps prevent, the passing of an era. An era when local communities had a say in how their natural resources were used. An era when the state and federal governments could take steps to stop the destruction of our environment. These basic rights may be sacrificed by US negotiators in the name of free trade.

During the same month, the US professional journal, *Nutrition Week*, expressed its fears about the same issues:

> The role of science in the regulatory process is advisory. Health and safety rules are decided by the elected representative of the people—that is by those who are accountable to the citizens of the Republic. Rules and regulations are developed with the advice of scientists, subject to comment and review by those affected by the proposed rule or regulation and approved by an individual appointed by the President—the chief executive officer. The executive branch is accountable to the Congress, and the actions of the executive are subject to judicial review.
>
> The US trade proposal would change all of that. A scientific court would be accountable only to those individuals or interests that appoint the members of the court. The decisions of the scientific court would not be reviewable. The function of the court, although scientific in appearance, would

be framed always in economic goals and objectives. Science would no longer be an advisor, but would determine what is best for the economic future of the people of the world. [23]

Many non-governmental organizations in the US have had bad experiences with faulty or dishonest science, ranging from the thalidomide scandal to promises of "risk-free" nuclear power. The prospect of seeing democracy undermined by a global "science court" is truly alarming.

Intense Lobbying

Correctly anticipating a tough fight against their GATT proposals, officials in the Bush Administration worked hard to reverse the mounting opposition. To farm groups, they promised that GATT is the best way to overturn domestic pesticide and food safety laws and that it will be possible to use GATT dispute panels to open foreign markets. A report from the California World Trade Commission, *International Standards and Agricultural Trade*, summarizes the arguments:

- Uniform national standards are essential to successful negotiations and implementation of current GATT talks to harmonize health and safety rules.
- California, in its zeal to lead the world in regulating chemical use, may become so out of step with the competition that it will put its $17 billion agriculture industry out of business.
- The Uruguay Round talks on harmonizing plant and animal health restrictions are becoming increasingly important to California as food safety and environmental concerns grow. [24]

A former member of Yeutter's GATT team in Geneva, C. Ford Runge, now works for the largely agribusiness-funded Center for International Food and Agricultural Policy. He has devoted considerable time trying to convince farm groups that GATT can be used to "keep stricter environmental standards from adversely affecting their cost of production." According to Runge: "Farmers will have to turn to international organizations to help them confront the issues of environmental standards." [25]

In addition to seeking the support of farm groups, Administration officials met with representatives of environmental and consumer organizations, arguing that free trade, as an ideological position, should have their support. Although a few corporate-sponsored environmental groups, such as Resources for the Future, did support the US GATT proposal, an overwhelming majority came out strongly against.[26]

Pressure from GATT and Codex Staffs

Although it is expected that the staff members of international agencies should remain strictly neutral in these negotiations, in reality they play a powerful role in determining the direction and parameters of the discussions. In this regard, both Codex and GATT staff have expressed very strong support for "harmonization" on a number of occasions.

A meeting of senior GATT staff with a delegation of consumer, environmental, church, farm and trade union representatives from the US, Europe and Japan was summarized by *Nutrition Week*:

> New terms being hammered out here (Geneva) to guide world trade during the . . . 1990s will eliminate or weaken health and safety rules and regulations for food, drugs and the environment . . . The immediate target is the Delaney clause of the Food, Drug and Cosmetic Act that prohibits in the US the use of food additives that cause cancer in humans or test animals. The Delaney clause is the only food safety law that sets a zero tolerance for chemicals and other substances used as food additives. . . . "World Trade cannot survive with a zero tolerance," said Jean Marc Luc, [former] Director of the GATT Agricultural Division.[27]

In a speech to the 1989 session of the Codex Commission, its chairman expressed his delight over this "international harmonization project":

> The current developments underway within the Uruguay Round of Multilateral Trade Negotiations offer the exciting prospect of the Codex standards being used as the basis for the harmonization of national regulations as a long-term objective under GATT.[28]

Moves to Protect Environmental Legislation

A number of GATT member nations recognize the need for GATT to better balance free trade with environmental protection. For example, the European Community's GATT proposal states:

Countries which have achieved a high health status will find it difficult to systematically relinquish their national standards in favour of lower, albeit "international" standards. It will, therefore, be necessary to provide for countries to apply more stringent standards, where appropriate.[29]

Various resolutions proposed in the US Congress have addressed the need for a special process within GATT to begin incorporating ecological concerns. In early 1990, Congressman James Scheuer (D-NY) introduced a resolution that called on Congress to reject any final GATT agreement that did not adequately address environmental protection. Included in this resolution was the threat that Congress will not approve the GATT agreement without the following safeguard position.

Agreement among contracting parties to initiate special consultations (which shall include non-governmental organizations and parliamentarians from member countries as full participants) to discuss environmental issues . . . which consultations must address, among other relevant issues:

A. the steps that can be taken to ensure that the implementation of GATT does not undermine national environmental protection measures and health and safety standards, and the promotion of sustainable development;

B. means by which GATT can be used to enhance environmental protection and the promotion of sustainable development; and,

C. mechanisms by which public access to information regarding, and public participation in, the GATT process can be encouraged.[30]

After the publication of GATT's final draft in December of 1991, congressional leaders began to take a more aggressive stance towards these negotiations. Congressman Henry Waxman (D-CA), chair of the House of Representative's health and environment committee, and Majority Leader Richard Gephardt (D-MO) introduced House Concurrent Resolution 246 to warn President Bush of their intention to block any GATT or NAFTA agreement that "jeopardizes United States health, safety, labor, or environmental laws (including the Federal Food, Drug, and Cosmetic Act and the Clean Air Act)." Passing by a unanimous vote in the fall of 1992, this resolution demonstrates the strength of the opposition in the Congress to the Bush Administration's free trade agenda. This opposition was also reflected in the November 1992 congressional elections, where a large number of new members were elected who campaigned on a specifically anti-NAFTA platform.

Recognizing this strong opposition, then Governor Bill Clinton outlined the nature of the flaws in the Bush Administration's NAFTA text and promised in his campaign that he would never submit the agreement to Congress unless supplemental agreements addressing key farm, labor, and environmental issues were included. Since the election, the Clinton Administration has attempted, thus far unsuccessfully, to convince Congress and the public that these supplemental agreements will in fact correct these flaws. Meanwhile, public and congressional opposition has grown as more of the precise details and likely effects of the Bush NAFTA have become known.

Towards Sustainable Trade

On both the world scale and among the three nations of North America, there is much that needs to be reformed in both commercial and political relations. The current debates surrounding both the GATT and the NAFTA are unique opportunities to begin addressing these concerns. Obviously, in order to have a chance to promote a positive outcome it is necessary to defeat the concept of global deregulation and the "new world order" tentatively promoted by the Bush Administration. However, advocates for sustainable development in general, and sustainable agriculture specifically, must go beyond mere opposition. We must forge our own positive vision for economic, political, and trading relations among nations.

There are real problems in the current trading regimes that need to be addressed as part of these talks. Varying food-safety standards need to be addressed. A positive "trade and development agreement" would set minimum standards or "floors" for regulations, rather than the "ceilings" proposed by the Bush Administration. Any comprehensive development treaty must explicitly outlaw export "dumping," the exporting of goods by corporations at prices below the cost of production. US and European grain-trading corporations regularly dump grain and dairy products at half the cost of production. This practice, which is destroying food self-sufficiency in poor countries and ruining family farmers everywhere, must be stopped.

Advocates of sustainable agriculture, across America and around the world, are beginning to look carefully at a wide range of trade-related policy issues. They can see the urgent need to ban food product dumping in order to protect small farmers in both the North and the South. They can see the need to ensure that the full costs of production, including environmental costs, are considered in the setting of farm prices. If these things are not done, we will almost certainly wake up one day to find that global food stocks are no longer sufficient to handle the emergencies which will inevitably occur.

As a consensus evolves, we must accelerate our organizing in order to turn these ideas into policies. Agriculture groups from the US must work with their colleagues from around the world with the goal of establishing a common set of basic demands and solutions. This common agenda must then be promoted aggressively to all governments and to the public at large.

During the last decade there have been two breakthroughs in our understanding of the interrelationships between economy and ecology. The first is the inseparable connection between the environmental balance of the natural world and the modern industrial economy. Agriculture is at the center of this connection. Our relationship to the land—how we treat it and who shares in its fruits—are central issues in our quest for a sustainable future. Close coordination between economic policy and environmental policy is a fundamental requirement for sustainability, both ecological and financial.

The second breakthrough is the acknowledgement that most ecological issues are global, respecting no boundaries. International cooperation and coordination in addressing ecological dangers is becoming an absolute necessity for human survival. It is not enough to build a sustainable agriculture system in one state or region. Indeed it is not possible. We need global agricultural policies that support, enhance, and enable the development of ecologically and economically sustainable agriculture in each and every region of the planet. This means that we must have both regional and global trade agreements that go beyond outdated theories of free trade to embrace the policies necessary for a sustainable future, for sustainable development, for sustainable progress.

The controversy and debate created by the current trade negotiations must be translated into momentum for establishing new and more just relations among all nations. Nothing less can be accepted if we are serious about the survival of the planet.

Conclusion

Over half the inhabitants of our fragile planet are farmers, producing food, fiber and, increasingly, the fuel needed for themselves and for city dwellers.

Agriculture is the primary occupation on Earth. Agriculture is also the number one influence on our planet's ecology. DDT sprayed in Mexico shows up in Canadian fish. Destroying rainforests to produce hamburger eliminates habitat for thousands of endangered species. More than 80% of the water in many desert regions, including California and Saudi Arabia, is used for agriculture.

World market forces since WWII have turned much of agriculture upside-down—from life giving to life threatening. By consciously driving down crop prices, agribusiness has driven 30 million U. S. farmers off the land since 1940, forcing the 5 million who are left to become increasingly dependent on poisonous chemicals and giant machinery. Overcrowded cities, polluted water supplies, and overburdened tax systems are just a few of the many serious by-products of this massive dislocation.

We must forge entirely new policies in order to re-generate a sustainable, family-based system, including "carrots" to accelerate the transition back to sustainability and "sticks" making the most deadly practices illegal or uneconomic. Most important, we will need to pay fair prices to our farmers, enough to cover the full environmental costs of production. But this will be a miniscule cost compared to the benefits of sustainable, family farm agriculture such as increased employment, de-urbanization, protecting water and air quality, more nutritious food, conservation of natural resources and wildlife and greater food security for all nations, both rich and poor. Less chemical-intensive, more sustainable farming will also mean far less health risk for consumers and for everyone who handles these chemicals, especially the farmers.

Such dramatic shifts in policy, however, require that we change the underlying assumptions that shape our nation's trade policies, especially the idea that the Earth and its natural resources can be used and abused endlessly.

For several thousand years, a similar assumption was made about human beings: that they could be used and abused endlessly through slavery. At the end of the 19th century, after a hundred years of intense political organizing, slavery was finally outlawed in most countries.

Now, we face a task much like that of these 19th century abolitionists. We must lay to rest the idea that the Earth's resources can be enslaved. Yes, there will be economic consequences, as there were with the abolition of slavery, but these cannot justify delay. The very survival of future generations depends upon our success today at achieving a sustainable agriculture, one that balances the economic and ecological relationships between people and the land.

NOTES

1. For additional views on sustainable agriculture see: Jackson, W., W. Berry and B. Coleman, eds. "Meeting the Expectations of the Land," San Francisco: North Point Press, 1984 and Benson, J.M., and H. Yogtmann, eds. "Towards a Sustainable Agriculture," Oberwill, Switzerland: Verlag Wirz AG, 1978.
2. For additional views on free trade from the perspective of corporate agribusiness see: Runge, C. Ford, H. von Witzke, S. Thompson, "Liberal Agricultural Trade as a Public Good: Free Trade Versus Free Riding Under GATT," Center for International Food and Agriculture Policy, University of Minnesota, June 1987.
3. O'Connor, J. T., "Shadow on the Land," National Toxics Campaign, Cambridge, Massachusetts, 1988.
4. "Hard to Swallow: FDA Enforcement Program for Imported Food," Staff Report by the Subcommittee on Oversight and Investigations of the Committee on Energy and Commerce, U.S. House of Representatives, July 1989.
5. For comprehensive look at fast track see "The Consumer and Environmental Case Against Fast Track," L. Wallach and T. Hilliard, Public Citizen's Congress Watch, Washington, DC, 1991.
6. For more information see "Take Back the Nation," M. Barlow and B. Campbell, Key Porter Books, Toronto, and Review of European Community and International Environmental Law, "Environmental Impact of Canada-US Free Trade Agreement," M. Ritchie, March 1992.
7. Coop, J. "Free Trade and the Militarization of the Canadian Economy," Lawyers for Social Responsibility, Toronto, August 1988.
8. For more information on the Enterprise of the Americas Initiative see statement by Stephen Hellinger of the Development Group for Alternative Policies before House Subcommittee on Western Hemisphere Affairs, February 27, 1991.
9. North American Free Trade Agreement, Draft Text Article 501, May 1992.
10. For a complete analysis of the NAFTA Draft Text see "North American Free Trade Agreement Draft Text: Preliminary Briefing Notes," Action Canada Network, Canadian Center for Policy Alternatives and Common Frontiers, Toronto, April 1992.
11. For more information see Natural Resources Defense Council Issue Paper,

"GATT, Tropical Timber Trade, and the Decline of the World's Tropical Forests," November 1990.

12. For more information about the Watsonville situation see *The Nation*, Nov. 5, 1990, p. 514.

13. "Consumer Reactions to the Use of BST in Dairy Cows," National Dairy Promotion and Research Board, April 1990.

14. National Wildlife Federation Study, "Environmental Concerns Related to a United States-Mexico-Canada Free Trade Agreement," November 1990.

15. U.S. Trade Representative's Office, "Submission of the United States on Comprehensive Long-term Agricultural Reform," October 1989.

16. Harsch, J., "Washington Farm Scene," *Wisconsin State Farmer*, May 13, 1988.

17. For a complete review of all ecological concerns related to GATT, *see* Shrybman, S., "International Trade and the Environment", *The Ecologist*, Vol. 20, No. 1, January/February, 1990; Ritchie, M., *Environmental Implications of GATT*, Institute for Agriculture and Trade Policy, 1990.

18. "Washington," *Farm Journal*, May, 1989, p. 10.

19. *Food Chemical News*, April 2, 1990, pp. 7–9.

20. Clayton Yeutter, US Secretary of Agriculture, letter to Ray MacSharry, EC Agriculture Commissioner, July 8, 1989.

21. Van Beek, L., "Yeutter Asks for International BGH Policy," *Wisconsin Agri-News*, October, 1989.

22. *News of the Uruguay Round*, GATT Secretariat, Geneva, April 1990.

23. Leonard, R., "Science, Economics Role to be Redefined in the 1990s," *Nutrition Week*, May 3, 1990, p. 4.

24. *International Standards and Agricultural Trade: A California Perspective*, California State World Trade Commission, Sacramento, CA, April 3, 1990.

25. Taylor, R., "Relationship between environment, trade policy important to region's future," *Minnesota Wheat*, January 1990.

26. For example, see *Agriculture in the Uruguay Round of the GATT*, Resources for the Future, Washington, DC, August 1988. Environmental and consumer organizations opposing significant elements of the GATT final draft included the Sierra Club, National Toxics Campaign, Greenpeace, Friends of the Earth, Natural Resources Defense Council, Public Citizen, Community Nutrition Institute, Consumer Federation of America, Earth Island Institute, and the National Consumers League.

27. Leonard, R., "New World Trade Rules to Replace Health, Safety Standards," *Nutrition Week*, March 1, 1990, p. 1.

28. Report on the 18th Session of Codex Alimentarius Commission, July 1989.

29. Submission of the European Communities on Sanitary and Phytosanitary Regulations and Measures, 1989, p. 2.

30. House Resolution 336, May 24, 1990.

William Greider

THE GLOBAL MARKETPLACE:
A CLOSET DICTATOR

With the end of the Cold War burdens, Americans were understandably inclined to turn inward and attend to the many neglected priorities at home. But American democracy is now imprisoned by new circumstances—the dynamics of the global economy—and this has produced a daunting paradox: Restoring the domestic political order will require a new version of internationalism.

The rise of transnational enterprises and production systems, the easy mobility of capital investment and jobs from one country to another, has obvious benefits as a modernizing influence on the world. It searches out lower costs and cheaper prices. But its exploitative effects on both rich and poor nations remain unchecked.

As a political system, the global economy is running downhill—a system that searches the world for the lowest common denominator in terms of national standards for wages, taxes and corporate obligations to health, the environment and stable communities. Left unchallenged, the global system will continue to undermine America's widely shared prosperity, but it also subverts the nation's ability to set its own political standards, the laws that uphold the shared values of society.

The economic consequences of globalized production have already been experienced by the millions of U.S. industrial workers who, during the last two decades, were displaced when their high-wage jobs were transferred to cheaper labor in foreign countries. This transformation, more than anything else, is what has led to the declining real wages in the United

States and the weakening manufacturing base. The deleterious impact on American wages is likely to continue for at least another generation.

But the economic effects are inseparable from the political consequences. The global competition for cost advantage effectively weakens the sovereignty of every nation by promoting a fierce contest among countries for lower public standards. If one nation's environmental laws are too strict or its taxes seem too burdensome, the factory will be closed and the jobs moved elsewhere—to some other nation whose standards are lax, whose government is more compliant.

For ordinary Americans, traditionally independent and insular, the challenge requires them to think anew their place in the world. The only plausible way that citizens can defend themselves and their nation against the forces of globalization is to link their own interests cooperatively with the interests of other peoples in other nations—that is, with the foreigners who are competitors for the jobs and production but who are also victimized by the system. Americans will have to create new democratic alliances across national borders with the less prosperous people caught in the same dilemma. Together, they have to impose new political standards on multinational enterprises and on their own governments.

The challenge, in other words, involves taking the meaning of democracy to a higher plane—a plateau of political consciousness the world has never before reached. This awesome task does not begin by examining Americans' own complaints about the global system. It begins by grasping what happens to the people at the other end—the foreigners who inherit the American jobs.

On the outskirts of Ciudad Juarez, across the river from El Paso, Texas, the sere hillsides are a vast spectacle of human congestion. A canopy of crude huts and cabins, made from industrial scraps, is spread across the landscape, jammed together like a junkyard for abandoned shipping crates. The houses are not much more than large boxes, with walls of cardboard and floors made from factory pallets or Styrofoam packing cases. The tarpaper roofs are held in place by loose bricks; an old blanket or sheet of blue plastic is wrapped around the outhouse in the yard. Very few homes have running water and many lack electricity. Streets are unpaved and gullied. There are no sewer systems. For mile after mile, these dwellings are visible across the countryside—dusty, treeless subdivisions of industrial poverty.

The *colonias* of Ciudad Juarez are like a demented caricature of suburban life in America, because the people who live in Lucio Blanco or Zarogoza or the other squatter villages actually work for some of America's premier companies—General Electric, Ford, GM, GTE Sylvania, RCA, Westinghouse, Honeywell and many others. They are paid as little as fifty-five cents an hour. No one can live on such wages, not even in Mexico. With the noblesse oblige of the feudal padrone, some U.S. companies dole out occasional *despensa* for their struggling employees—rations of flour, beans, rice, oil, sugar, salt—in lieu of a living wage.

In addition to the cheap labor, the U.S. companies who have moved production facilities to the Mexican border's *maquiladora* zone enjoy the privilege of paying no property taxes on their factories. As a result, Ciudad Juarez has been overwhelmed by a burgeoning population and is unable to keep up with the need for new roads, water and sewer lines and housing. The migrants who came from the Mexican interior in search of "American" jobs become resourceful squatters, scavenging materials to build shelters on the fast-developing hillsides. In time, some of these disappointed workers decide to slip across the border in the hope of becoming real Americans.

"A family cannot depend on the *maquila* wage," explained Professor Gueramina Valdes-Villalva of the Colegio de la Frontera Norte in Juarez, an experienced critic who aided workers at the Center for Working Women. "If you evaluate what these wages translate into in purchasing power, you see a steady deterioration in what those wages provide. They can't buy housing because there is a housing shortage. When they go into the squatter situation, they can't invest in public services. We have a shortage of water, sewers, electricity, streets. The city is pressed heavily by the two sectors who do not pay taxes—the *maquiladora* companies and the minimum-wage workers.

"The saddest thing about it is, not only does the city become unbearably unlivable, but then the city becomes unproductive too. As the city deteriorates, it becomes more expensive for companies to locate here. For the first time last year, we had negative growth in Juarez. Some of the employers are leaving. We can see the companies looking at their other options. Eastern Europe has become very attractive to them."[1]

If Americans wish to visualize the abstraction called the global economy, they need only drive across the U.S. border into Mexico and see the

human consequences for themselves, from Matamoros and Juarez to Nogales and Tijuana. A vast industrial belt of thirteen hundred plants has
grown up along the border during the last twenty years, encouraged by
special duty-free provisions but fueled primarily by low wages and the neglect of corporate social obligations.

By moving jobs to Mexico, companies not only escape higher industrial
wages, but also U.S. laws and taxes, the legal standards for business conduct on health and safety and social commitments that were established
through many years of political reform in America. Mexico has such laws
but it dare not enforce them too energetically, for fear of driving the companies elsewhere.

The *maquiladora* factories, notwithstanding their handsome stucco fa-
cades and landscaped parking lots, are the modern equivalent of the
"sweatshops" that once scandalized American cities. The employers are
driven by the same economic incentives and the Mexican workers in Ciudad Juarez are just as defenseless. The Juarez slums reminded me of the
squalid "coal camps" I saw years before in the mountains of Eastern Kentucky. Those still-lingering "pockets of poverty" were first created in the
late nineteenth century by the coal and steel industries and they employed
the very same industrial practices—low wages, neglect of public investment, dangerous working conditions, degradation of the surrounding environment, the use of child labor.

The well-being of Americans is intertwined with this new exploitation, not simply for moral reasons or because most of the Mexican plants
are owned by American companies, but because this is the other end of the
transmission belt eroding the structure of work and incomes in the United
States. Jobs that paid ten dollars or eleven dollars an hour in Ohio or Illinois
will cost companies less than a tenth of that in Ciudad Juarez. The assembly work turns out TV sets, seatbelt harnesses, electrical switches and
transformers, computer keyboards, disposable surgical garments, lug-
gage locks, battery packs and a long list of other products.

Juarez, of course, is but a snapshot of the much larger reality around the
world. Corporate apologists often point out that if the American jobs did
not migrate to Mexico, they would go somewhere else—Singapore or Brazil, Thailand or now perhaps Eastern Europe—where the consequences
would be less easily observed by Americans. This is true. The easy mobility
of capital is the core element in the modern global economy. It is made pos-

sible by invention, brilliant planning and the new technologies that connect corporate managers with far-flung factories and markets and allow them to relocate production almost anywhere in the world.

To confront the effects of the global system, Americans must educate themselves about the world—to understand not only their own losses but also what is happening to others. Ciudad Juarez (or any other border city) is an excellent place to start, mainly because it starkly refutes so many of the common assumptions surrounding globalization. Aside from profit, the justifying and widely accepted rationale for global dispersion of production is the benefit to the poor, struggling masses. Their economies, it is said, will move up to a higher stage of development and incomes will rise accordingly. The auto workers in Ohio will lose, certainly, but the new auto workers in Juarez will become middle-class consumers who can afford to buy other products made in America. Thus, in time, everyone is supposed to benefit.

On the streets of Juarez, the workers tell a different story: Their incomes are not rising, not in terms of purchasing power. They have been falling drastically for years. These workers cannot buy American cars or computers. They can barely buy the basic necessities of life.

Fernando Rosales had just quit his job at Chrysler, where he assembled safety harnesses, because it paid the peso equivalent of only $4.20 a day. While he builds a squatter house in Lucio Blanco, Rosales searches for work as an auto mechanic, away from the *maquila* plants.

"I came here six years ago, thinking I would better myself, but I won't be able to do that," Rosales said. "It's been very difficult. The only benefits I had were transportation—they sent a bus for us—and one meal a day. Maybe for the government, it's okay. But for the people it really is shameful that American companies pay such low wages."

"The wages are very low, that's just the way it is," said Daniel Fortino Maltos, twenty-one years old and married with a baby. He works for General Electric at a plant making capacitors, as does his wife. "Young people generally leave after a few months or a year because the salary is so low, they can't make it," he explained.

Outside Productos Electricos Internacionales, another GE plant, a group of teenage workers on their lunch break described the same conditions. "The turnover is roughly every three months," said Fernando Rubio. "They just bring new ones in. There is such a big demand for workers, people can leave and go elsewhere." General Electric operated eight plants in Juarez, more than any other company.

Many of the workers blame the Mexican government for their condition, not the American employers. An older woman, Laura Chavez, who just quit her job at Delmex, a General Motors plant, expected to find another easily because of the extraordinarily high turnover in the *maquila* factories. "Look, it's not enough," she said. "If you're going to be living off that salary, it's not enough. I don't blame the companies. I blame the Mexican government because the wages are whatever the government requires."

In Mexico, the federal government does periodically raise the legal minimum-wage level but, for the last decade, the increases have lagged further and further behind the rising cost of living—thus providing cheaper and cheaper labor for the American employers.

Indeed, the *maquiladora* industry boasts of this attraction in the glossy publication it distributes to prospective companies. In 1981, the industry association reported, the labor cost for a *maquila* worker was $1.12 an hour. By the end of 1989, the real cost had fallen to 56 cents an hour.[2]

What these workers have surmised is correct: Their own government is exploiting them too. Mired in debt to American banks since the early 1980s, Mexico has been desperate to raise more foreign-currency income to keep up with its foreign-debt payments. Aside from oil, the *maquiladora* industry provides the country with its largest influx of U.S. dollars, and the Mexican government has attracted more U.S. enterprise by steadily depressing the wages of the workers. If it had not, Mexico might have lost the jobs to its principal low-wage competitors (Singapore or Taiwan or South Korea) and lost the precious foreign-currency income it needed to pay its bankers.

Wages for workers are, thus, falling on both ends of this global transmission belt. The people who lost their premium manufacturing jobs in the United States are compelled to settle for lower incomes. But so are the Mexican peasants who inherited the jobs. On both sides of the border, workers are caught in a vicious competition with one another that richly benefits the employers.

The wage depression in Mexico is an extreme case, but not at all unique in the world. In many of the other countries attracting global production, similar exchanges occur that victimize workers and their communities and often benefit the country's established oligopoly of wealth and political power. The CEO of an American clothing company was asked if his company's imported goods from China might, in fact, have been manufactured with slave labor. "Everybody is a slave laborer," he replied. "The wage is so cheap."[3]

Instead of an experienced workforce, the *maquiladora* zone has created a bewildering stream of young people tumbling randomly from one job to another.

"We have begun to see more fourteen-year-olds in the plants—children fourteen to sixteen years old," Valdes-Villalva said. "The *maquila* workers are very young on the whole, we're talking sixteen to twenty-one years old. Usually, the companies are careful to see that the youngest girls and boys get permission slips from their parents.

"Workers do not age in this industry—they leave. Because of the intensive work it entails, there's constant burnout. If they've been there three or four years, workers lose efficiency. They begin to have problems with eyesight. They begin to have allergies and kidney problems. They are less productive."

The workers themselves matter-of-factly describe the reality of children who have left school for these jobs. "Quite a lot say they are sixteen but I know they are probably thirteen or fourteen or fifteen years old," said Sylvia Facoln at the GE plant. "I know of people who are less than fourteen years old and I myself brought one of them to work here. It's very common in all the *maquilas*."

The scandal of major American corporations employing adolescent children to do the industrial work that once belonged to American adults has been documented in many settings, yet it provokes no political response in either Washington or Mexico City. The *Arizona Republic* of Phoenix ran a prize-winning series on the *maquiladora* across from Nogales, Arizona, where, among other things, the reporter found thirteen-year-old Miriam Borquez working the night shift for General Electric (the same company that cares deeply about educating disadvantaged minorities at home).

The girl quit school to take the job, she explained, because her family needed the money. They were living in a nine-by-sixteen tin hut. The *Arizona Republic*'s conservative editorial page lamented: "Has greed so consumed some businessmen that human lives in Mexico are less valuable than the next saxophone shipped to the U.S. from Sonora?"[4]

Maquiladora officials always protest their innocence in this matter.

Mexican labor laws permit them to hire fourteen-year-olds if their parents grant permission. These laws are faithfully observed, the officials explain, but companies cannot always verify the true age of young job applicants and children sometimes forge permission slips from parents or use someone else's documents. This is sometimes true, according to Ignacio Escandon, an El Paso businessman familiar with the Juarez labor market, but the excuse hardly relieves the corporations of their moral burden. "The companies don't ask many questions," Escandon said. "The demand for labor is constant."

There is a general lack of political scrutiny. Beyond anecdotes, no one knows the real dimensions of the exploitation. The use of child labor is one of the many aspects of the Mexican *maquiladora* that has never been authoritatively investigated, since neither government has much interest in exposing the truth.

Environmental damage from the *maquiladora* plants, likewise, has never been squarely examined by federal authorities though gross violations have been cited in numerous reports and accusations from private citizens and some state agencies. The National Toxics Campaign described the U.S.-Mexican border as already so polluted with dangerous chemicals that it may become "a two-thousand-mile Love Canal."

For years, Professor Valdes-Villalva and her associates have tried to track down what the companies do with the toxic chemicals that are brought into the Mexican plants. Mexican law requires that imported hazardous materials must be shipped back to the United States, but the researchers could only find customs documents covering less than 5 percent of the volume. They suspect—but can't prove—that the bulk is trucked to illegal dumps in the interior, future Superfund sites waiting to be discovered by Mexican authorities.

The health consequences that frightened American citizens when they first encountered the casual disposal of toxic wastes in their own communities now worry Mexican citizens too. Like the Americans before them, the concerned Mexicans are confronted by official denial and a lack of reliable information to confirm or refute their fears.

"What most concerns me is the health within the plants," Valdes-Villalva said. "This is where we are lacking. We have no money for research, but we hear these complaints from workers. We find high levels of lead in blood samples. We have situations in which we find a tremendous amount of manic-depressives, which does not follow the usual amount in the population. So what I'm beginning to think is that this is a central nervous system disorder, physical not psychological. It could be solvents. It's heavily concentrated in the electronics industry. There's also a tremendous number of Down's syndrome children. Other disorders you find in high incidence are cleft palates and other deformities."

Like the American citizens who have formed thousands of grassroots political organizations to combat industrial pollution, Mexican citizens who summon the courage to protest are utterly on their own—aligned against both industry and government, without the resources to challenge the official explanations or the political influence to force the government to act. But, of course, the Mexican citizens are in a much weaker position to undertake such political struggles. Their communities are impoverished. Their national economy depends crucially on these factories. Their own democratic institutions are weak and underdeveloped or corrupted.

The situation seems overwhelming, but not entirely hopeless. Along the border and elsewhere, some people of both nationalities are beginning to grasp the fact that citizens of neither nation can hope to change their own conditions without the support of the other. Mexicans cannot hope to stand up to General Motors or GE from the *colonias* of Ciudad Juarez. Nor can Americans expect to defend their own jobs or their own social standards without addressing the hopes and prospects and afflictions of their impoverished neighbors.

Genuine reform will require a new and unprecedented form of cross-border politics in which citizens develop continuing dialogues across national boundaries and learn to speak for their common values. Only by acting together can they hope to end the exploitation, not just in Mexico but elsewhere across the global production system. This kind of sophisticated internationalism has not been characteristic among Americans, to put it mildly.

That is the daunting nature of the global political dilemma. People like Valdes-Villalva have already seen it clearly and so do some Americans. A Coalition for Justice in the *Maquiladoras* was formed in 1991 by more than sixty American environmental, religious, community and labor organizations, including the AFL-CIO, in order to speak out against the injustices and confront the multinational corporations with demands for civilized conduct. Leaders from the Mexican *maquiladora* communities are being brought to the United States to spread the word to Americans on the true nature of the global economic system.[5]

"Moral behavior knows no borders," Sister Susan Mika, president of the coalition, declared. "What would be wrong in the United States is wrong in Mexico too."

Valdes-Villalva described the new democratic imperative:

"In order for workers to protect themselves, they have to see that they are tied to workers worldwide," she said. "It is the transnational economy that is undermining labor. A new union has to emerge that crosses national borders and makes a closer relationship among workers—a new kind of union that cooperates worldwide. Companies can make agreements among themselves about markets and production. The only competition in the global economy is between the workers."

Wolfgang Sachs, the German social critic, offered a mordant metaphor to describe the antidemocratic qualities of the global economy. The global marketplace, he said, has become the world's new "closet dictator."

"The fear of falling behind in international competition has become the predominant organizing principle of politics, North and South, East and West," Sachs wrote. "Both enterprises and entire states see themselves trapped in a situation of relentless competition, where each participant is dependent on the decisions of all other players. What falls by the wayside in this hurly-burly is the possibility for self-determination."[6]

For Americans, this is a new experience, profoundly at odds with national history and democratic legacy. We are now, suddenly, a nation whose citizens can no longer decide their own destiny. The implications offend the optimism and self-reliance of the American character, eclipsing our typical disregard for the rest of the world. Citizens of most foreign nations—smaller, less powerful and more dependent on others—have had considerable practical experience with the limitations and frustrations of global interdependency. Americans have not. They are just beginning to discover what global economics means for their own politics.

ACORN, the grassroots citizens' organization, discovered, for instance, that the prospect for financing low-income housing—a major priority for its members—had been seriously damaged by a new banking regulation that assigns an extremely high risk rating to bank lending for multifamily housing projects. "This will be a disaster for poor people unless Congress intervenes immediately," Jane Uebelhoer of ACORN testified. "This is outright government red-lining and it will be the end of low-income home ownership in Detroit, in Chicago, in New York and elsewhere."[7]

But the new credit regulation did not flow out of any legislation enacted by Congress and the president. It was a small detail in an international agreement forged among the central bankers from a dozen industrial countries, including the United States. The central bankers met periodically in Basel, Switzerland, for several years as the Committee on Banking Regulations and Supervisory Practices, trying to reconcile the different banking laws of competing nations and create a "level playing field" that would standardize the capital requirements for banks.

America's representative (and the leading promoter of the agreement) was the Federal Reserve, the nonelected central bank that enjoys formal insulation from political accountability. While America's most important multinational banks were consulted beforehand, no consumer representatives were included in the Federal Reserve's deliberations nor were any of the groups that speak for low-income home buyers.[8]

"When we talk to the federal regulators," Chris Lewis, an ACORN lobbyist, complained, "they say to us: 'Oh, that's an international treaty, we can't possibly do anything about that.' So now we have housing policy determined by central bankers with no accountability whatsoever."

American politics, in other words, is moving offshore. The nature of the global economy pushes every important political debate in that direction—further and further away from the citizens. As companies become multinational, able to coordinate production from many places and unify markets across national boundaries, they are taking the governing issues with them. From arcane regulatory provisions to large questions of national priorities, the corporations, not governments, become the connecting strand in offshore politics, since they are the only organizations active in every place and coping with all the world's many differences.

Arguments that were once decided, up or down, in the public forums of democratic debate are now floating off into the murk of international diplomacy and deal making. They are to be decided in settings where neither American citizens nor their elected representatives can be heard, where no institutional rules exist to guarantee democratic access and accountability.

Environmental activists discovered, for instance, that U. S. proposals for the current round of international trade negotiations would effectively vitiate domestic laws on food safety by assigning the question of standards to an obscure UN-sponsored commission in Rome. If the nation (or a state government) enacts laws on pesticides or food additives that exceed the health standards set by the Codex Alimentarius Commission in Rome, then other nations can declare that the environmental standards are artificial "trade barriers" designed to block foreign products and, therefore, subject to penalties or retaliation.

The goal proclaimed by trade negotiators is to "harmonize" environmental laws across the boundaries of individual nations to encourage freer trade. But that objective, inevitably, means lowering U. S. standards. Indeed, that is the objective for major components of American agribusiness, including the multinational chemical manufacturers who are enthusiastic supporters of what is blandly called "harmonization."

The Codex is an obscure agency utterly unknown to ordinary citizens, but the multinational companies that help devise its standards are well aware of its significance. At a recent session of the commission, the American delegation included executives from three major chemical companies—Du Pont, Monsanto and Hercules—serving alongside U. S. government officials. Among other things, the Codex standard permits DDT residues on fruit and vegetables that are thirty-three to fifty times higher than U. S. law allows.[9]

As environmentalists and some allied farm groups have argued, the current round of GATT negotiations is actually aimed at fostering a new generation of deregulation for business—without the inconvenience of domestic political debate.

"The U. S. proposals (for GATT) represent a radical attempt to preempt the authority of its own citizens and the citizenry of other countries to regulate commerce in the pursuit of environmental and social ends," David Morris of the Institute for Local Self-Reliance in St. Paul, Minnesota, declared. "It is an attempt to impose a laissez-faire philosophy on a worldwide basis, to allow the global corporations unfettered ability to transfer capital, goods, services and raw materials across national boundaries."

Other citizen groups and interests, from sugar growers to insurance companies to state governments, have also discovered that global politics is encroaching on their domains. Japan protests that state-set limits on

U. S. timber harvesting constitute a GATT violation. European trade officials complain that the state of Maine's new law on throwaway bottles is an artificial trade barrier that the federal government should preempt in accordance with the international trade agreement.

The centrifugal diversity of the American federalist system, in which states can legislate and experiment independent of the national government, is thus headed for collision with the leveling, homogenizing force of the global marketplace. One or the other will have to yield power and prerogatives.[10]

American democracy is ill equipped to cope with offshore politics, both in its institutional arrangements and in its customary responses to foreign affairs. Treaty making and diplomacy belong traditionally to the presidency, even though the U. S. Senate must ratify the results, and there is a time-honored tendency to defer to the chief executive in negotiating foreign relations so that the nation may speak with one voice.

The overall political effect of globalization is to further enhance the power of the presidency—just as the Cold War did—at the expense of representative forums, public debate and accountability. Once an issue has become part of high-level diplomatic exchanges, all of the details naturally become murkier, since negotiators do not wish to talk too freely about their negotiating strategies. The discussions often literally move offshore and behind closed doors—more irregular deal making that will have the force of law.

When international deals are being struck, it matters enormously who is doing the bargaining and who is in the room offering expert advice. The so-called G7, for instance, meets regularly to "coordinate" economic policies among the major industrial nations (including fiscal policy, a realm the Constitution assigns to Congress). Yet there is no visible procedure—much less legislated agenda—by which the Treasury secretary or the Federal Reserve chairman is empowered to make international economic policy for the nation. Those two officers, by their nature, represent a very narrow spectrum of American interests—mainly banks and the financial system—and they cannot be expected to reflect the full, rich diversity of American perspectives on economic issues. Bankers are well represented, but who speaks for the home builders or the auto industry or machine tools or the farmers?

Substantial institutional reforms are needed, obviously, to prevent global politics from gradually eclipsing the substance of democratic debate and action. At the very least, that would mean democratizing reforms to ventilate the U.S. negotiating routines in a systematic way so that everyone can follow the action. It might also require refusal to participate in any international forum or agency that lacks democratic access to the information and decision making. If the chemical companies can lobby the Codex in Rome for weaker health standards, then surely any other American citizen should be able to sit at the table too. When central bankers meet in Basel to decide U.S. housing policy, then housing advocates should also be in the room.

The first, overriding imperative, however, is to defend the nation's power to govern its own affairs. If democracy is to retain any meaning, Americans will need to draw a hard line in defense of their own national sovereignty. This is not just about protecting American jobs, but also about protecting the very core of self-government—laws that are fashioned in open debate by representatives who are directly accountable to the people. Among other things, this challenge requires Congress to confront the presidency and restrain it—to refuse to grant the chief executive the power to bargain away American laws in the name of free trade or competitiveness or any other slogan.

Offshore politics threatens the ability of free people to decide the terms of their own social relations; it allows the closet dictator to decide things according to the narrow interest of "efficiency." The "harmonizing" process begins with the regulatory laws that business interests consider meddlesome and too expensive, but the attack will lead eventually to the nation's largest social guarantees, welfare or Social Security or health, since those programs also add to the cost of production and thus interfere with the free-flowing commerce among boundaryless companies.

Who will decide what is equitable and just for American society? A closed meeting of finance ministers in Geneva? An obscure group of experts in Rome coached by corporate lobbyists? Such questions have already penetrated the fabric of self-government. Americans, in addition to their other democratic burdens, need to get educated on the answers.

The concept of the "boundaryless company" has now become commonplace among executives of major multinational corporations. They are American companies—sort of but not really, only now and then when it suits them. IBM, the flagship of American industrial enterprise, is composed of 40 percent foreign employees. Whirlpool is mostly not Americans. GE puts its logo on microwaves made by Samsung in South Korea.[11] Chrysler buys cars from Mitsubishi and sells them as its own. America's most important banks operate legally authorized "foreign facilities" right in Manhattan for the benefit of depositors who wish to keep their money "offshore."

The question of what is foreign and what is American has become wildly scrambled by global commerce. The multinational enterprises, unlike Americans generally, are already securing alliances in this fierce world of global competition—networks of joint ventures, coproduction and shared ownership with their ostensible rivals in the world, including state-owned enterprises in foreign nations. Every U.S. auto company has become partners one way or another with its competitors, the Japanese car companies. Producers of electronic equipment, computers, even aircraft have melded their American citizenship in similar arrangements.

Multinational executives work to enhance the company, not the country. The president of NCR Corporation told *The New York Times*: "I was asked the other day about United States competitiveness and I replied that I don't think about it at all." A vice-president of Colgate-Palmolive observed: "The United States does not have an automatic call on our resources. There is no mindset that puts this country first." And the head of GE Taiwan, where so many U.S. industrial jobs have migrated, explained: "The U.S. trade deficit is not the most important thing in my life . . . running an effective business is."[12]

John Reed, CEO of Citibank, America's largest troubled bank, has said he is actively scouting options for moving the corporation headquarters to a foreign country in order to escape U.S. banking laws. "The United States is the wrong country for an international bank to be based," Reed declared. Meanwhile, his bank's deposits are protected by the U.S. taxpayers and his lobbyists in Washington actively promote a multi-billion-dollar government bailout to save large commercial banks like Citibank from insolvency.[13]

These men are merely expressing the prevailing values of the "stateless corporation," as *Business Week* called it. This creature operates most successfully when it discards sentimental attachments like patriotism and analyzes global opportunities with a cold, clear eye. Some of these same corporations, it is true, wave the flag vigorously when bidding for defense contracts or beseeching the U.S. government for tax subsidies, but their exuberant Americanism dissipates rapidly when the subject is wages or the burden of supporting public institutions.

Their weak national loyalty has profound implications for the nation's politics because these men, on the whole, are also influential voices in shaping the outlines (and often the close details) of national economic policy— not just for trade policy, but for taxation and government spending priorities. Politicians in both parties (especially the Republican party) defer to their worldly experience. Most economists and political commentators have embraced their argument that America's future prosperity will be best served by a laissez-faire regime in which governments get out of the way and let the marketplace develop its global structure.

But here is the blunt question: Can these people really be trusted to speak for the rest of us? How can they faithfully define America's best interest when their own business strategies are designed to escape the bounds of national loyalty? The impressive fact about ordinary Americans is that, despite years of education and propaganda, they still cling stubbornly to their skepticism about the global economy. With the usual condescension, elite commentators dismiss the popular expressions of concern as uninformed and nativist, the misplaced fears of people ill equipped to grasp the larger dimensions of economics.

Ordinary citizens generally form their economic opinions and perceptions, not from distant abstractions or even from the endless tides of propaganda, but from their own commonsense values and their own firsthand experiences. Common sense tells people that it cannot be good for America's long-term prosperity to lose millions of high-wage manufacturing jobs. Even if this hasn't affected their own employment, it means that middle-class families are losing the wherewithal to be viable consumers, and sooner or later, that has to hurt the overall economy.

The majority of Americans are not wrong in their unsophisticated skepticism. The new reality of global competition generates a vicious economic trap for worldwide prosperity: a permanent condition of overcapacity in production that ensures destructive economic consequences. Simply put, the world's existing structure of manufacturing facilities, constantly being expanded on cheap labor and new technologies, can now turn out far more goods than the world's consumers can afford to buy. That is, more cars, computers, aircraft, appliances, steel and so forth are made than the marketplace can possibly absorb.

The auto industry is an uncomplicated example: Auto factories worldwide have the capacity to produce 45 million cars annually for a market that, in the best years, will buy no more than 35 million cars. "We have too many cars chasing too few drivers," a Chrysler executive remarked. The economic consequences are obvious: Somebody has to close his auto factory and stop producing. This marketplace imbalance in supply and demand is the larger reality that underlies the fierce competition for advantage among companies and among nations—the awesome force driving everyone toward the lowest common denominator.

Whose factory must be closed to bring the worldwide supply into balance with the worldwide demand? Whose workers will be laid off? The older, less modern factories are closed first, of course, but also the plants that pay the highest wages and the ones where government provides less generous tax subsidies to the employer. American workers in steel and autos and other industries have had a lot of experience watching this process at work—seeing factories they knew were viable and productive suddenly declared obsolete. But so will workers in the less abundant nations. This process closed Ohio factories and someday it will close Mexico's. So long as global productive capacity exceeds global demand by such extravagant margins, somebody somewhere in the world has to keep closing factories, old and new.

The companies have no choice. They must keep moving their production, keep seeking the lowest possible costs and most favorable political conditions, in order to defend their market shares. Eventually, as economist Jeff Faux has written, South Korea will be losing jobs to cheap labor in Thailand and even China may someday lose factories to Bangladesh. The popular notion among struggling nations that they can someday become the next South Korea—as the reward for a generation or so of the degradation of their workers—is fatally at odds with the logic of permanent overcapacity. The Mexican *maquiladora* cities thought they were going to become the next South Korea, but instead they may be the next Detroit.[14]

In fundamental economic terms, the globalization process produces three interlocking economic consequences that together are deleterious to everyone's well-being. First, it destroys capital on a large scale by rendering productive investments useless to the marketplace. That is the meaning of closing viable factories that can no longer meet the price competition: The invested capital is lost, the idle factories are written off as tax losses. Modernizing production with new technologies always produces this destruction, of course, but the global dispersion of production lives on it—like a game of checkers in which advantage goes to the player who made the last jump.

Second, the overcapacity permanently depresses wage levels worldwide, since no workers anywhere can organize and bargain very successfully against the threat of a closed factory, whether they are well-paid Americans or impoverished peasants working somewhere in the Third World.

Finally, these two effects—the instability of capital investment and the depression of wages—combine to guarantee that global demand can never catch up with global supply. New consumers for the world's output, to be sure, emerge with new development, but other existing consumers are lost, as their jobs are lost or their wages decline in real terms. So long as the process is allowed to run its course, the flight will continue downhill—too many factories making too many goods for a marketplace where too many families lack the wherewithal to buy them.

It does not require great political imagination to see that the world system is heading toward a further dispersion of governing power so the closet dictator of the marketplace can command things more efficiently, from everywhere and nowhere. The historic paradox is breathtaking: At the very moment when western democracies and capitalism have triumphed over the communist alternative, their own systems of self-government are being gradually unraveled by the market system.

To cope with this complicated new world, every government naturally seeks to centralize its command of policy and thus become more hierarchical, less democratic. Societies like Japan have a natural advantage because they already practice a feudal form of state-administered capitalism, dominated by a one-party monopoly in politics, managed through government-assisted cartels and insulated from popular resistance. Some elites in the United States, though they do not say so directly, would like to emulate the efficiency of the Japanese political structure—equipping the chief executive with even more authority and putting citizens at even greater distance from government.

For many years, a wishful presumption has existed that, in time, the hegemony of global corporations would lead the way to the construction of a new international political order—world institutions that have the representative capacity to govern equitably across national borders. That prospect is not at hand in our time.

On the contrary, what is emerging for now is a power system that more nearly resembles a kind of global feudalism—a system in which the private economic enterprises function like rival dukes and barons, warring for territories across the world and oblivious to local interests, since none of the local centers are strong enough to govern them. Like feudal lords, the stateless corporations will make alliances with one another or launch raids against one another's stake. They will play weakening national governments off against each other and select obscure offshore meeting places to decide the terms of law governing their competition. National armies, including especially America's, will exist mainly to keep the contest free of interference.

In that event, the vast throngs of citizens are reduced to a political position resembling that of the serfs or small landholders who followed church or nobility in the feudal system. They will be utterly dependent on the fortunes of the corporate regimes, the dukes and barons flying their national flag. But citizens will have nothing much to say about the governing of these global institutions, for those questions will have moved beyond their own government. If national laws are rendered impotent, then so are a nation's citizens.

A different vision of the future requires great political imagination—a new democratic sensibility in which people in many places manage simultaneously to overcome their sense of helplessness. A single nation is not helpless before these forces, despite what conventional wisdom teaches, and the United States especially is not helpless. Citizens have enormous potential leverage over the global economy if they decide to use it through their own national governing system. A corporation's behavior abroad is not separable from its home country because it enjoys so many special benefits at home.

In the United States, a multinational corporation that wishes to be treated as an American citizen for the purposes of the law and government benefits can be made to play by America's rules, just as Japan's are, or else surrender all the tax subsidies, government contracts and other considerations, including national defense, that American taxpayers provide.

Why should Americans, for instance, provide research and development tax subsidies for corporations that intend to export their new production and to violate common standards of decency by exploiting the weak? Why should American military forces be deployed to protect companies that do not reciprocate the national loyalty?

These are among the many contradictions created by the global system that only nationalism can reconcile. American law cannot police the world and need not try, but it can police what is American. To take the starkest example, no U.S. company should be treated as a lawful entity, entitled to all the usual privileges, if its production is found to exploit child labor in other countries. The same approach applies across the range of corporate behavior, from environmental degradation to ignoring tax laws.

The American political system also has enormous leverage over the behavior of foreign-owned multinational enterprises—access to the largest, richest marketplace in the world. Because of that asset, the United States could lead the way to new international standards of conduct by first asserting its own values unilaterally. If trade depends upon price advantages derived mainly from poverty wages for children or defenseless workers prohibited from organizing their own unions or factories that cause great environmental destruction, this trade cannot truly be called free.

The purpose of asserting America's political power through its own marketplace would be to create the incentive for a new international system of global standards, one which all the trading nations would negotiate and accept. For a start, the United States ought to reject any new trade agreements that do not include a meaningful social contract—rules that establish baseline standards for health, labor law, working conditions, the environment, wages. The U.S. government might also prohibit the familiar tax-dodging practices of companies that exploit communities as the price for new jobs. Indeed, companies ought to post community bonds when they relocate—guaranteeing that they will not run away from their obligations to develop roads and schools and the other public investments.[15]

Fundamentally, it is not just the exploited workers in the United States who need a higher minimum-wage law. The world economy needs a global minimum-wage law—one that establishes a rising floor under the most impoverished workers in industrial employment. A global minimum-wage law would recognize, of course, the wide gaps that exist between rich and poor, but it could establish flexible ratios aimed at gradually reducing the differences and prohibiting raw exploitation like that in the *maquiladora* zone in Mexico. No one imagines that world incomes will be equalized, not in our time certainly. But, as nations move toward equilibrium, they ought to be governed by a global economic system that pushes the bottom up rather than pulling the top down.

The democratic imperative is nothing less than that: to refashion the global economy so that it runs uphill for everyone, so that it enhances democracy rather than crippling it, so that the economic returns are distributed widely among all classes instead of narrowly at the top.

NOTES

1. Professor Gueramina Valdes-Villalva, whom I interviewed in July 1990, worked for many years to aid the exploited *maquiladora* workers and to challenge the practices of the companies. She died in a plane crash in Texas on February 13, 1991. My guides and translators in Ciudad Juarez were two Americans, Sister Maribeth Larkin, an organizer with EPISO, the IAF organization in El Paso, and Ignacio Escandon, a businessman who is active in EPISO.

2. The statistics on falling labor costs are from *Twin Plant News: The Magazine of the Maquiladora Industry*, May 1990.

3. The "slave labor" remark was quoted by Lane Kirkland, president of the AFL-CIO, speech to the American International Club of Geneva, June 24, 1991.

4. The *Arizona Republic* and reporters Jerry Kammer and Sandy Tolan of Desert West News Service won the Robert F. Kennedy journalism award for their series on the Nogales industries, published in April 1989. *The Wall Street Journal* published a harrowing account of a twelve-year-old working in a Mexican shoe factory and described child labor as general throughout the country—exploiting five to ten million underage workers. See Matt Moffett, "Working Children: Underage Laborers Fill Mexican Factories," *Wall Street Journal*, April 8, 1991.

5. Formation of the Coalition for Justice in the *Maquiladoras* was reported in the newsletter of the Federation for Industrial Retention and Renewal, Spring 1991. Coalition members include FIRR, the National Toxics Campaign, the Interfaith Center for Corporate Responsibility, the AFL-CIO and a variety of others.

Some major labor unions such as the food and commercial workers' are beginning to develop their own strategies for cross-border politics with similar unions in Europe, Asia and Latin America, having discovered that they are up against the same companies and similar labor practices, regardless of their own nation.

6. Wolfgang Sachs, of the Essen Institute for Advanced Studies, wrote in *New Perspectives Quarterly*, Spring 1990.

7. Jane Uebelhoer of ACORN testified before the Senate Banking Committee, April 4, 1990.

8. The international agreement signed by the Federal Reserve and other central banks created a system of risk-based capital ratios for banking—capital requirements geared to the level of risk in each bank's portfolio. Housing suffered because the Federal Reserve assigned a 100 percent risk ratio for multi-family projects—a rating identical to the most speculative business loans—which would raise the cost of such lending for banks. The central bank, in effect, had promulgated a credit-allocation policy that would discourage investment in low-income housing—when the nation faced an obvious shortage. Federal regulators claimed that they were bound by international agreement, but the fact is that other nations' central banks were prepared to assign a more favorable risk rating to housing than was the Federal Reserve.

9. Details on Codex standards and the influence of American chemical companies are from Eric Christensen, "Food Fight: How GATT Undermines Food Safety Regulations," *Multinational Monitor*, November 1990. The GATT negotiations reached an impasse in early 1991 on other economic issues but presumably will resume.

10. Examples of GATT objections to U.S. state laws were recounted by Bruce Stokes, "State Rules and World Business," *National Journal*, October 27, 1990.

11. Details on IBM, Whirlpool and GE microwaves are from Robert B. Reich, *The Work of Nations: Preparing Ourselves for 21st Century Capitalism*, Alfred A. Knopf, 1991.

12. The three corporate executives from NCR, Colgate-Palmolive and GE were quoted by David Morris, "Trading Our Future."

13. John Reed's efforts to relocate Citicorp in a foreign country were described as his "pet project" by *The Wall Street Journal*, August 9, 1991. Lloyd Cutler, whose Washington law firm represents Citibank, has proposed a vast recapitalization of commercial banks by the Federal Reserve.

14. The contours of the global process were described by the Economic Policy Institute's director, Jeff Faux, "Labor in the New Global Economy," *Dissent*, Summer 1990.

15. Lane Kirkland, president of the AFL-CIO, spoke for this idea in terms of labor rights: "A trade policy that encourages or tolerates the spectacle of corporations roaming the world in search of the cheapest and most repressed labor is more

perversely protectionist than any tariff or quota, and serves in the last analysis to restrict and undermine markets and lower standards the world over. In the interest of basic fairness and the continued elevation of the human condition, the denial of workers' rights should be clearly defined internationally as the un-fair trading practice it is, through the incorporation of a social clause in the General Agreement on Tariffs and Trade." Speech to American International Club of Geneva, June 24, 1991.

LETTER FROM U.S. ENVIRONMENTAL AND CONSUMER GROUPS

The December 20, 1991 GATT Uruguay Round "Final Act" Text Must Be Rejected

January 8, 1992

Dear Representative:

On Dec. 20, GATT Director General Arthur Dunkel published the final text of the Uruguay Round of GATT. The Administration must return to Geneva with their response to it on January 13, 1992. We have analyzed the text. It is far worse from an environmental and consumer standpoint than earlier problematic GATT drafts. We consider the GATT "Final Act" text to be unacceptable.

As America's leading environmental, consumer and animal protection groups, we urge you to join us in rejecting the proposed GATT text, and in sending the message to the White House that no GATT Agreement is better than a bad GATT Agreement.

The GATT text threatens existing U.S. environmental and consumer laws, undermines national sovereignty to create such laws in the future, and attacks the American federal system of government by mandating preemption of state environmental and consumer laws. The GATT text also codifies the worst elements of the recent GATT tuna-dolphin panel decision. Further, the text includes expanded dispute resolution powers, and even establishes a new powerful global commerce agency which strengthens GATT's power without addressing GATT's fundamental problems. Finally, on-going GATT negotiations separate from the "Final Act" in market access and tariffs are likely to result in limitations on nations' ability to protect or sustainably manage national and international natural resources.

To avoid confronting these and other issues in a finalized GATT, or in the subsequent Congressional implementing legislation, U.S. environmental and consumer groups worked for the past three years with the Administration and Congress to create alternative GATT proposals in areas key to environmental and consumer protection. During these discussions, the President pledged not to promote trade agreements which would undermine environmental and consumer protections. If the President endorses this text in Geneva, we believe the President has broken his promise.

Specifically the GATT TEXT:

"Harmonizes" Environmental and Consumer Laws Downward by Subjecting Strong U.S. Laws to Challenge and Elimination as Trade Barriers

Any U.S. environmental or consumer standard that is stronger than named international standards is presumed to be a trade barrier. The text exposes such laws to challenge from other GATT nations, promoting the downwards "harmonization" of strong U.S. environmental and consumer standards.

The text names the Codex Alimentarius Commission as GATT's standard setter for food. Many Codex standards are less stringent than ours. For example, under Codex the U.S. would be required to accept imported food containing residues of DDT and other chemicals banned here.

Codifies the Ruling in the GATT Tuna-Dolphin Case

Despite Congressional urging, the Final Act does nothing to limit the damage of the August 1991 GATT tuna-dolphin ruling which declared key provisions of the U.S. Marine Mammal Protection Act (MMPA) of 1972 to be illegal barriers to trade. In the fall, 64 Senators and nearly 100 Representatives sent letters to the President opposing the panel ruling, refusing to weaken the MMPA and demanding changes to the GATT to make it compatible with environmental protections.

Instead, the GATT text codifies several of the worst aspects of the panel ruling. For instance, the text prohibits nations from enforcing environmental or health laws that reach beyond their borders. U.S. laws such as the Endangered Species Act and the African Elephant Conservation Act which use trade measures to protect species and the environment outside the U.S. could be decreed GATT-illegal under the text, and targeted for elimination.

Additionally, U.S. laws and international treaties protecting the "global commons"—the air, seas and species inhabiting them—which use the threat of trade sanctions for enforcement could also be decreed GATT-illegal under the text. Examples of such laws include the Clean Air Act, which uses trade sanctions to enforce the Montreal Protocol for ozone layer protection, and laws to protect whales, fish and birds such as the Pelly Amendment to the Fisherman's Protective Act.

Mandates "Affirmative" Action to Preempt State and Local Environmental and Consumer Laws

The GATT text requires signatory countries to take "positive measures" to bring their subfederal governments into compliance with GATT rules. For the U.S., this rule would mandate sweeping preemption of state and local standards. GATT's strong preemption rule would ensure that state governments could never be "ahead" of federal policy, thus effectively stopping progressive states that have cut the path for federal environmental and consumer policy for decades. California's "Proposition 65" is an example of a strong state environmental law that could be abolished.

Procedures Stacked Against Environmental and Consumer Protections

The GATT text delegates to unaccountable trade officials future decision-making power over issues such as food safety and U.S. natural resource conservation. It requires all rule-setting and dispute resolution to occur in secrecy, and without any citizen participation or government accountability. Further, the GATT text places the burden of proof on nations defending environmental and consumer laws from GATT challenge. Thus, if a U.S. environmental law were challenged, the U.S. would be required to prove our law is *not* an unfair trade barrier in a secret panel hearing.

Strong New Enforcement of Anti-consumer, Anti-environment Rules

New dispute resolution provisions include the automatic adoption of GATT dispute panel decisions 60 days after publication, unless there is consensus among the 108 GATT nations *to reject*, or an appeal is filed. All appeals must be decided within 90 days, and are automatically adopted unless there is consensus against within 30 days of publication. The GATT panel tuna-dolphin ruling, which the U.S. has temporarily blocked using current GATT rules, would have been adopted months ago under this rule. Congress would now be under strong international pressure to eliminate the popularly supported law (MMPA) in order to avoid U.S. liability for countervailing trade sanctions.

New Global Commerce Agency Administers the GATT Rules

The Final Act text creates a new global commerce agency called the Multilateral Trading Organization (MTO) with "legal personality," like the United Nations.

The creation of a new multilateral trading agency is not problematic per se. However, the MTO proposed in the "Final Act" text is charged with enhanced administration and enforcement of GATT rules. As explained above, those GATT rules are so problematic from the consumer and environmental standpoint that we believe strengthening GATT authority at this time is ill advised. The idea of an MTO based on GATT rules was rejected by over 800 non-governmental groups from the North and South meeting December 1991 in Paris on the upcoming UNCED meeting in Brazil.

Further, the MTO proposal contained in the GATT text requires nations to cede substantial sovereignty over local, state, and national issues. (The MTO "shall enjoy in the territories of each of the Members such legal capacity, privileges and immunities as may be necessary for the exercise of its functions.")

Because the MTO proposal is part of the GATT "Final Act" text, Congress would vote on it as part of the Uruguay Round implementing legislation under the fast track Congressional rule which allows no amendments and limited debate.

On-going Negotiations Will Limit National Sovereignty to Sustainable-manage Natural Resources

One important element of the Uruguay Round's negative impact on the environment is not codified in the "Final Act" text. GATT negotiations separate from the "Final Act" are still underway on tariffs and market access issues. A goal of those negotiations is the expansion of trade in tropical timber, fisheries, minerals and forestry products. The likely outcome of those negotiations will be limitations on Congress' ability to protect or sustainable-manage national and international natural resources.

For instance, Congress and several states have passed laws to limit logging by banning the export of raw logs taken from old growth forests. Several tropical nations have similar laws to protect their rain forests. Such export bans would be GATT-illegal under the rules now being negotiated. Japan, the world's largest raw log importer, has threatened to use the new GATT rules to eliminate the U.S. forestry laws to which it has long objected.

Conclusion

The GATT Final Act undermines environmental and consumer protection in the U.S. and across the world. It prevents nations from acting as global health and environmental leaders, eliminates the voices of those who must bear the environmental and health burdens of expanded economic activity, and provides no mechanism for popular sovereignty over the outcomes of the international decision-making process. While we recognize the importance of promoting sustainable international trade, we must reject the proposed GATT text.

We urge you to address the fundamental lack of environmental and consumer values and democratic process of the GATT Final Act by communicating your opposition to the text to the Administration, and by becoming a cosponsor of the Waxman/Gephardt resolution (H. Con. Res. 246) which announces Congress' intention to reject any trade agreement which undermines U.S. environmental, consumer or labor standards.

Sincerely yours,

ASPCA
American Cetacean Society
Animal Welfare Institute
Arizona Toxics Information
Border Ecology Project
Center for Science in the Public Interest
Citizen Action
Committee for Humane Legislation
Community Nutrition Institute
Clean Water Action Project
Consumer Federation of America
Defenders of Wildlife
Earth Island Institute
Environmental Investigative Agency
Friends of the Earth
Government Accountability Project
Greenpeace USA
Humane Society of the U.S.
Marine Mammal Fund
National Coalition Against the Misuse of Pesticides
National Consumers League
National Toxics Campaign
Public Citizen
Public Voice for Food & Health Policy
Rainforest Action Network
Sierra Club
Society for Animal Protective Legislation
Texas Center for Policy Studies

APPENDIX

CITIZENS TRADE CAMPAIGN

POLICY STATEMENT ON NAFTA

One of the most diverse coalitions to emerge in recent political history, the "Citizens Trade Campaign" is a broad-based coalition of environmental, labor, consumer, farm, religious, and other citizens' groups promoting a "citizens' agenda" in U.S. trade policy.

Coalition members are united in the position that the North American Free Trade Agreement (NAFTA) negotiated by former President Bush is fundamentally flawed, and therefore, unacceptable. It will encourage companies to move operations and factories to areas of cheap labor and lax environmental and worker safety regulation. It will result in a lower standard of living, disruption of our communities, and irreparable harm to our environment. NAFTA undermines the gains we have achieved over the years in food safety, labor standards and environmental protection. NAFTA harms not only residents of the United States, but also those of Canada and Mexico, by putting the demands of trade ahead of the needs of people.

NAFTA needs a dramatic re-casting by the Clinton Administration if it is to promote and protect the environment, workers, consumer health and safety, agricultural and rural communities, as well as reflect democratic decision-making.

Our common goal is to educate the public on the impact of the North American Free Trade Agreement. We believe that what North America needs is a fair trade agreement in which the following elements are necessary and essential pre-requisites:

- There must be trade-linked enforcement of worker rights and workplace standards. These rights and standards must include the right to organize and bargain collectively; workplace health and safety standards; meaningful minimum wage structures; a prohibition on child labor and forced labor; and the guarantee of non-discrimination in employment.

- There must be trade-linked enforcement of environmental, agricultural, health and safety laws and regulations.

- Companies must demonstrate that they have complied with the host country's labor, environmental, agricultural, health and safety laws and regulations before being allowed to gain NAFTA trade benefits. No runaway plants should receive NAFTA benefits.

- There must be adequate, guaranteed, and constant funding to address the anticipated environmental, health, and safety ramifications of NAFTA and to clean up the existing environmental degradation as a result of free trade policies, based on the "polluter pays" principle.

- There must be tougher rules of origin to ensure that any benefits derived from the agreement will accrue to workers and producers located in the United States, Mexico, and Canada, as well as meaningful safeguards to protect U.S. workers and agricultural producers against import surges. All goods must also be marked with their country of origin. Effective rules of origin must be enacted so that member nations do not become conduits for goods from non-participating nations.

- There must be the continuation of preferential procurement rights, including federal, state, and local "Buy American" laws and regulations and such other procurement laws and regulations designed to further environmental and social objectives.

- There must be specific guarantees that national, state and local governments may adopt and maintain environmental, agricultural, natural resources, public health, consumer product safety, food safety, transportation safety, and labor laws, that establish more stringent standards than international standards, without being subject to challenge as non-tariff barriers to trade.

- There must be specific guarantees that national, state and local governments may condition market access on the meeting of process and production standards relating to environmental and consumer health and safety protection, agriculture, human rights, labor rights, and worker and consumer safety.

- There must be specific guarantees that national, state and local governments may adopt and maintain natural resources, energy, and agricultural policies which prescribe conditions of trade in order to promote resource conservation and sustainable development.

- There must be adequate, guaranteed, and constant funding for such needed programs as food safety inspection and customs service; infrastructure in Mexico and along the borders; job creation; and trade adjustment assistance and training for workers harmed by U.S. international trade policy.

- There must be strict limitations on the "temporary entry" of persons to provide services and the prohibition of entry to affect a labor dispute. Any temporary entrant must, at minimum, be paid and work under conditions prevailing in the host country.

- There must be publicly accessible and open dispute resolution mechanisms to provide the broadest possible access and participation by the citizenry of all three nations, including workers, consumers, environmentalists, and human rights advocates.

- There must be broad designation of the superiority of international environmental, health, and safety agreements and international labor and human rights agreements over any conflicting terms of NAFTA, without any conditions such as least trade restrictivity.

- There must be specific guarantees that exceptions to NAFTA's intellectual property, services, and investment sections will be allowed to further such national and local social and environmental priorities as lowering pharmaceutical prices, making actionable lowering of environmental standards to attract investment and ensuring banks and other financial institutions are regulated to ensure their financial stability and contribution to the communities in which they are based.

For more information please contact Citizens Trade Campaign · 600 Maryland Ave., SW · Suite 202W · Washington, DC 20024

The Citizens Trade Campaign is a coalition of environmental, consumer, labor, family farm, religious and civic organizations promoting environmental and social justice in trade policy

CONTRIBUTORS

MARGARET ATWOOD, a writer of international prominence, is a former president of the Writers' Union of Canada.

WENDELL BERRY, essayist, poet, and novelist, lives and farms with his wife and family in Kentucky.

EDMUND G. (JERRY) BROWN, former governor of California, is the director of We The People.

JORGE G. CASTAÑEDA is visiting professor of public and international affairs at Princeton University.

HERMAN E. DALY is an economist in the Environment Department of the World Bank.

WILLIAM GREIDER covers politics for *Rolling Stone* and is author of *Secrets of the Temple* and *Who Will Tell the People*.

CARLOS HEREDIA is a member of the Mexican Action Network on Free Trade.

MARTIN KHOR, Research Director of the Consumers' Association of Penang (Malaysia), is Vice-President of the Third World Network, the Asia Pacific People's Network, and Friends of the Earth, Malaysia.

THEA LEE is an economist at the Economic Policy Institute in Washington, D.C.

JERRY MANDER, senior fellow at the Public Media Center, is author of *Four Arguments for the Elimination of Television* and *In the Absence of the Sacred*.

DAVID MORRIS works with the Institute for Local Self Reliance in St. Paul, Minnesota.

RALPH NADER, the noted consumer advocate, has for the past 25 years sponsored, edited, and written numerous books on subjects of public concern.

DAVID PHILLIPS, Executive Director of Earth Island Institute, is a biologist concentrating on endangered species protection.

MARK RITCHIE is president of the Institute for Agriculture and Trade Policy in Minneapolis.

VANDANA SHIVA, Director of the Research Foundation for Science, Technology and Natural Resource Policy in Dehradun, India, is author of *Staying Alive: Women, Ecology and Development*.

LORI WALLACH is Director of the Trade Program at Public Citizen in Washington, D.C.